IN-LINE SKATE
NEW ENGLAND

The Complete Guide
to the 101 Best Tours

IN-LINE SKATE
NEW ENGLAND

The Complete Guide
to the 101 Best Tours

Cynthia Lewis, Thomas Lewis,
and Carolyn Bradley

The Countryman Press
Woodstock, Vermont

If you find that any significant changes have occurred on the routes described in this guide, please let the authors and publisher know so that corrections may be made in future editions. Other comments and suggestions are also welcome. Address all correspondence to:

Editor
In-Line Skate New England
The Countryman Press
PO Box 748
Woodstock, VT 05091

Please be advised that there are hazards inherent to this sport. Although the authors have been careful to point out potentially dangerous situations, such as traffic intersections, railroad crossings, and steep descents, neither they, nor the publisher, can take responsibility for any accident or injury that might occur along the routes described in this guide.

Library of Congress Cataloging-in-Publication Data

Lewis, Cynthia Copeland.
    In-line skate New England : the complete guide to the 101 best tours / Cynthia and Tom Lewis and Carolyn Bradley.
         p.   cm.
    ISBN 0-88150-393-2 (alk. paper)
    1. In-line skating—New England—Guidebooks. 2. New England—Guidebooks.
    I. Lewis, Thomas J. (Thomas Joseph). II. Bradley, Carolyn. III. Title.
GV859.73.L48   1997
796.21'0974—dc21   96-39388
                                                                                  CIP

Text design by Sally Sherman
Cover design by Susan Wheeler
Cover photo by Steve Hooper
Maps by Paul Woodward, © 1997 The Countryman Press
Interior photographs by Steve Hooper and the authors

Published by The Countryman Press, PO Box 748, Woodstock, VT 05091

Distributed by W.W. Norton & Company, Inc., 500 Fifth Avenue, New York, NY 10110

Printed in the United States of America

10 9 8 7 6 5 4 3 2 1

ACKNOWLEDGMENTS

We are grateful to everyone who helped us in the process of gathering information and writing this book, especially Technica, Inc., for supplying our super skates and protective equipment; Peter Cornwall, president of the Danbury Railway Museum, Inc., for providing us with photographs; John Longmaid, Mount Desert Island, Maine; Kelly Duffy of Sport & Leisure in Lenox, Massachusetts; David Bradley of Hanover, New Hampshire; Joe Franz of Team Hyper, Boot and Blade Skate Shop in Burlington, Vermont; Luis Pires; Matt O'Brien of Eric Flaim's Motion Sports in Providence, Rhode Island; Ellen Bulger of New Haven, Connecticut; the Krause family of Keene, NH; Eleanor Ferrara and Lucy Bradley for many hours of Bradley babysitting; Melissa DeMott and Janelle Stettler for Lewis babysitting duty; Brian Bradley, for unending support and patience; Christina and Julianna Bradley for making their mother laugh; and Anya, Alexandra, and Aaron Lewis for cheerfully embracing their parents' latest project.

Contents

Introduction 13

Part One •••• CONNECTICUT

1 • Cove Island Park 30
2 • Sherwood Island State Park 31
3 • Seaside Park 32
4 • Chatfield Hollow State Park 34
5 • Hammonasset Beach State Park 36
6 • East Shore Park 38
7 • Mount Algo and the Housatonic River 39
8 • Mudge Pond 40
9 • Salmon Kill Road 43
10 • Cornwall Village 45
11 • Mohawk Mountain Ski Area 46
12 • Mohawk State Forest and Mountain 48
13 • Woodridge Lake 49
14 • American Legion and Peoples State Forests 53
15 • Farmington Valley Greenway 54
16 • Farmington Canal Linear Park 56
17 • Captain John Bissell Bridge 58
18 • Charter Oak Greenway 60

Part Two •••• RHODE ISLAND

19 • Misquamicut State Beach 64
20 • East Shore Road 66
21 • Scituate Reservoir 67
22 • Goddard Memorial State Park 69
23 • East Bay Bike Path 72

PART THREE •••• MASSACHUSETTS

24 • Monument Valley Road 78
25 • Housatonic River 79
26 • Swamp Road 81
27 • Stockbridge Golf Course 84
28 • Spring Street 86
29 • Old Stockbridge Road 88
30 • Northampton Bikeway 90

31 • Norwottuck Rail Trail 92
32 • Historic Deerfield 94
33 • Dover (Intermediate Loop) 97
34 • Dover (Advanced Loop) 99
35 • Dover (Expert Loop). 101
36 • Moose Hill 103
37 • Minuteman Bikeway 105
38 • Myles Standish State Forest 108
39 • Powder Point 110
40 • Wompatuck State Park 112
41 • Marblehead Neck 113
42 • Scusset Beach 116
43 • Shining Sea Trail. 117
44 • Davis Beach 119
45 • Cape Cod Rail Trail, Dennis. 120
46 • Cape Cod Rail Trail, Brewster 122
47 • Nickerson State Park. 124
48 • Cape Cod Rail Trail, Wellfleet 126
49 • Head of the Meadow. 128
50 • Race Point. 130

Part Four •••• VERMONT

51 • Town Common. 136
52 • West River 137
53 • Mount Snow. 139
54 • River Road, Putney. 141
55 • Townshend Dam. 143
56 • Jamaica State Park 144
57 • Ball Mountain Dam 146
58 • Stratton Sun Bowl 148
59 • Main Street, Grafton. 150
60 • Old Connecticut River Road 152
61 • Pomfret Road 153
62 • Quechee Golf Course 156
63 • Upper Valley 158
64 • State Capital 160
65 • Mad River. 162
66 • Waitsfield Covered Bridge. 163
67 • Stowe Recreation Path 165
68 • Moscow Road. 168
69 • South Burlington Bike Path 169

70 • Burlington Bikeway 171
71 • South Hero 173
72 • Adams Landing 175

Part Five •••• *NEW HAMPSHIRE*

73 • Connecticut River 180
74 • Surry Mountain Dam 183
75 • River Road, Hanover 184
76 • Franconia 186
77 • Albany Covered Bridge 188
78 • Cathedral Ledge 191

Part Six •••• *MAINE*

79 • Goose Rocks Beach 196
80 • Biddeford Pool 198
81 • Popham Beach 200
82 • South Portland Greenway 203
83 • Falmouth 204
84 • Christina's World 206
85 • Owls Head 209
86 • Chickawaukie Pond 211
87 • Camden 213
88 • Youngstown Road 216
89 • Saturday Cove 217
90 • Verona Island 219
91 • Newbury Neck 221
92 • Bass Harbor Point, Mount Desert Island 223
93 • Pretty Marsh, Mount Desert Island 225
94 • Seal Cove, Mount Desert Island 227
95 • Southwest Harbor, Mount Desert Island 229
96 • Fernald Cove, Mount Desert Island 231
97 • Beech Mountain, Mount Desert Island 233
98 • Northeast Harbor, Mount Desert Island 235
99 • Ingraham Point, Mount Desert Island 237
100 • Schooner Head, Mount Desert Island 239
101 • Lamoine Beach 240

Resources 243
All About Us 245

101 Best Skate Tours in New England

Connecticut

NO.	ROUTE	LOCATION	RATING	DIST. IN MI.	PATH	ROAD	AUTO TRAFFIC
1	Cove Island Park	Stamford	Beginner	0.9	X		None
2	Sherwood Is. St. Pk.	Westport	Intermed.	1.5	X		None
3	Seaside Park	Bridgeport	Beginner	2.4/3.0	X	X	Light
4	Chatfield Hollow State Park	Madison & Killingworth	Intermed.	3.0	X	X	Light–mod.
5	Hammonasset Beach State Park	Madison	Beginner	3.7	X		None–light
6	East Shore Park	New Haven	Beginner	2.0+	X		None
7	Mount Algo & the Housatonic River	Kent	Intermed.	5.2		X	Very light
8	Mudge Pond	Sharon	Int./Adv.	5.4/12.8		X	Very light
9	Salmon Kill Road	Salisbury & Lime Rock	Intermed.	7.4		X	Light
10	Cornwall Village	Cornwall	Intermed.	5.0		X	Very light
11	Mohawk Mtn. Ski Area	Cornwall	Intermed.	4.8		X	Very light
12	Mohawk State Forest & Mtn.	Cornwall	Expert	5.4		X	Very light
13	Woodridge Lake	Goshen	Intermed.	7.6		X	Very light
14	American Legion/ Peoples St. Forests	Riverton	Int./Adv.	7.4/8.6		X	Light
15	Farmington Valley Greenway	Simsbury	Beginner	4.2	X		None
16	Farmington Canal Linear Park	Cheshire & Hamden	Beginner	3.0/8.0	X		None
17	Captain John Bissell Bridge	Windsor & S. Windsor	Beginner	4.0	X	X	Light
18	Charter Oak Grnwy.	Manchester	Intermed.	11.4	X	X	None–light

Rhode Island

NO.	ROUTE	LOCATION	RATING	DIST. IN MI.	PATH	ROAD	AUTO TRAFFIC
19	Misquamicut State Beach	Westerly	Intermed.	6.0		X	Light–heavy
20	East Shore Road	Jamestown	Intermed.	7.8		X	Light
21	Scituate Reservoir	Scituate	Advanced	12.0		X	Light
22	Goddard Mem. St. Pk.	East Greenwich	Beginner	3.6		X	Light
23	East Bay Bike Path	Bristol	Beg./Int.	27.4	X		None

10 ••••

101 Best Skate Tours in New England

Massachusetts

NO.	ROUTE	LOCATION	RATING	DIST. IN MI.	PATH	ROAD	AUTO TRAFFIC
24	Monument Valley Rd.	Great Barrington	Advanced	9.0		X	Light
25	Housatonic River	Housatonic	Intermed.	4.6/5.4		X	Light
26	Swamp Road	West Stockbridge	Intermed.	10.0		X	Light
27	Stockbridge Golf Course	Stockbridge	Advanced	3.0		X	Light
28	Spring Street	Lee	Intermed.	4.8		X	Light
29	Old Stockbridge Rd.	Lenox & Stockbridge	Intermed.	4.2		X	Light
30	Northampton Bkwy.	Northampton	Beginner	5.2	X		None
31	Norwottuck Rail Trail	Northampton	Beginner	17.0	X		None
32	Historic Deerfield	Deerfield	Intermed.	4.4/10.0		X	Light
33	Dover (Int. Loop)	Dover	Intermed.	2.5		X	Light
34	Dover (Adv. Loop)	Dover	Advanced	7.6		X	Light
35	Dover (Exp. Loop)	Dover	Expert	9.8		X	Moderate
36	Moose Hill	Sharon	Expert	9.5		X	Light–mod.
37	Minuteman Bkwy.	Bedford	Beg./Int.	17.8	X		None
38	Myles Standish State Forest	Plymouth	Intermed.	7.1		X	Very light–light
39	Powder Point	Duxbury	Intermed.	3.3		X	Light–heavy
40	Wompatuck St. Pk.	Hingham	Beginner	6.6	X	X	Very light
41	Marblehead Neck	Marblehead	Intermed.	4.1		X	Light
42	Scusset Beach	Sagamore	Intermed.	3.6/7.2		X	Light–very light
43	Shining Sea Trail	Falmouth	Beginner	5.2/6.6	X		None–light
44	Davis Beach	West Dennis	Beginner	2.2		X	Light
45	Cape Cod Rail Trail, Dennis	Dennis & Harwich	Beginner	9.6	X		None
46	Cape Cod Rail Trail, Brewster	Brewster	Beginner	10.8	X		None
47	Nickerson State Park	Brewster	Expert	6.2	X		None
48	Cape Cod Rail Trail, Wellfleet	Wellfleet	Beg./Int.	10.2/11	X		None
49	Head of the Meadow	Truro	Beginner	3.8	X		None
50	Race Point	Provincetown	Intermed.	8.1		X	Light

101 Best Skate Tours in New England

Vermont

NO.	ROUTE	LOCATION	RATING	DIST. IN MI.	PATH	ROAD	AUTO TRAFFIC
51	Town Common	Whitingham	Int./Adv.	4.0+		X	Light
52	West River	Brattleboro	Intermed.	17.0		X	Moderate
53	Mount Snow	West Dover	Advanced	5.2		X	Light
54	River Road, Putney	Putney	Advanced	7.6		X	Light
55	Townshend Dam	Townshend	Beginner	1.0		X	Light
56	Jamaica State Park	Jamaica	Beginner	2.3		X	Light
57	Ball Mountain Dam	Jamaica	Intermed.	3.4		X	Light
58	Stratton Sun Bowl	Stratton	Adv./Exp.	4.4/5.2		X	Light
59	Main Street	Grafton	Beg./Int.	3.0/6.4		X	Light
60	Old Connecticut River Road	Springfield	Beginner	3.4		X	Light
61	Pomfret Road	South Pomfret	Advanced	9.4		X	Light
62	Quechee Golf Course	Quechee	Intermed.	5.0		X	Light
63	Upper Valley	Norwich & E. Thetford	Advanced	18.0		X	Light
64	State Capital	Montpelier	Intermed.	3.6		X	Light
65	Mad River	Moretown	Advanced	7.4+		X	Light
66	Covered Bridge	Waitsfield	Int./Adv.	2.2/5.4		X	Light
67	Stowe Rec. Path	Stowe	Intermed.	10.6	X		None
68	Moscow Road	Stowe	Intermed.	6.6		X	Light
69	South Burlington Bike Path	South Burlington	Beg./Int.	3.4/6.0	X		None
70	Burlington Bikeway	Burlington	Beginner	14.2	X	X	None–light
71	South Hero	South Hero	Beginner	6.2		X	Light
72	Adams Landing	Grand Isle	Beginner	4.0		X	Light

New Hampshire

NO.	ROUTE	LOCATION	RATING	DIST. IN MI.	PATH	ROAD	AUTO TRAFFIC
73	Connecticut River	Westmoreland	Int./Adv.	6.0/13.8		X	Light
74	Surry Mtn. Dam	Surry	Adv./Int.	6.0/1.0		X	Light
75	River Road, Hanover	Hanover	Intermed.	4.0		X	Light
76	Franconia	Franconia	Int./Adv.	12.8/22.8		X	Light–mod.
77	Covered Bridge	Albany	Intermed.	14.0		X	Very light
78	Cathedral Ledge	Conway	Int./Adv.	14.4/23.4		X	Light–mod.

101 Best Skate Tours in New England

Maine

NO.	ROUTE	LOCATION	RATING	DIST. IN MI.	PATH	ROAD	AUTO TRAFFIC
79	Goose Rocks Beach	Goose Rocks	Intermed.	3.5		X	Light–mod.
80	Biddeford Pool	Biddeford	Advanced	10.4/13.9		X	Moderate–heavy
81	Popham Beach	Bath	Advanced	14.0		X	Light–mod.
82	S. Portland Grnwy.	South Portland	Beginner	4.6	X		None
83	Falmouth	Falmouth	Intermed.	5.5		X	Light–mod.
84	Christina's World	Cushing	Adv./Int.	16.7/12.9		X	Light–very light
85	Owls Head	Rockland	Adv./Int.	14.6/9.6		X	Moderate
86	Chickawaukie Pond	Rockport	Intermed.	12.8		X	Moderate
87	Camden	Camden	Intermed.	6.4		X	Light
88	Youngstown Rd.	Lincolnville	Advanced	5.6		X	Light
89	Saturday Cove	Northport	Advanced	9.6		X	Very light
90	Verona Island	Bucksport	Intermed.	9.1/17.2		X	Very light
91	Newbury Neck	Surry	Adv./Int.	16.6/7.2		X	Light–very light
92	Bass Harbor Point, Mt. Desert Island	Bass Harbor	Intermed.	8.0		X	Very light–moderate
93	Pretty Marsh, Mt. Desert Island	Pretty Marsh	Advanced	13.2		X	Light
94	Seal Cove, Mt. Desert Island	Seal Cove	Intermed.	9.4		X	Light–mod.
95	Southwest Harbor, Mt. Desert Island	Manset	Intermed.	4.4		X	Light–mod.
96	Fernald Cove, Mt. Desert Island	Somesville	Advanced	10.2		X	Light–mod.
97	Beech Mountain, Mt. Desert Island	Somesville	Expert	5.8		X	Very light
98	Northeast Harbor, Mt. Desert Island	Northeast Harbor	Intermed.	6.6		X	Light
99	Ingraham Point, Mt. Desert Island	Seal Harbor	Advanced	4.0		X	Very light
100	Schooner Head, Mt. Desert Island	Bar Harbor	Intermed.	5.0		X	Light
101	Lamoine Beach	Lamoine	Intermed.	10.4		X	Very light

Whatever you do, don't call it "rollerblading!" It's in-line skating, and it's the fastest-growing sport in the country. Rollerblade® Inc. might have led the charge but, technically, Rollerblade didn't invent the sport. An 18th-century Dutchman earned that honor after nailing wooden spools to his shoes in an attempt to simulate ice skating. He didn't get too far. Nor did Joseph Merlin with his metal-wheeled boots in 1760 (unfortunately, they did not allow stopping or turning). And Robert John Tyers's 1823 "rolito" was regarded as an amusing contraption with absolutely no practical value.

Hockey players Scott and Brennan Olson fared better. In 1980, the brothers from Minneapolis found a discarded skate in a heap of equipment in a sporting goods store. They redesigned it for cross-training with a hockey boot, polyurethane wheels, and a rubber heel brake. They began selling the skates out of their home and Rollerblade, Inc., was born. Other skate manufacturers hastily jumped on the in-line wagon. Seventeen years later, equipment sales have topped $1 billion, and 25 million people are skating—more than the numbers that play baseball, football, or soccer!

Part of skating's popularity stems from the fact that it's one of the best overall workouts available. Not only can in-line skating tone your muscles, but it can strengthen your heart as well. According to a study commissioned by Rollerblade®, recreational skaters who maintain moderate speeds receive the same aerobic benefits as do runners. (The researchers also found skating to be superior aerobically to stair-stepping exercise.) And, unlike running, skating combines low-impact motion with high-calorie burn. (But the real reason we all do it—it's *fun!*)

ABOUT THIS GUIDE

You're restless, right? You've already been up and down your street a few hundred times on your new skates. The nearby church parking lot is getting a little ho-hum, but the roads around town are just too congested and you don't know how to find a flat, smooth path.

Or maybe you travel frequently to different parts of New England. You know how convenient it is to pack your skates, but how inconvenient it is to waste time rolling around an unfamiliar city looking for an appropriate place to skate. Or perhaps you're an accomplished cross-country skier who's having a hard time finding ideal places to train off-season.

This guide is for everyone who's looking for the inside track on the region's best places to skate. We've done the research for you, eliminating the unsuitable routes and finding out everything we could about the outstanding ones. We tell you how to get there and what you'll find once you do. We also offer tips to help you improve your technique.

The chosen 101

We tried to select routes in each New England state that would appeal to a variety of skaters—a few park roads, a rail trail, some long road loops, a short bike path. Safety is one of our major concerns, and we searched for routes without too much traffic or too many steep hills. Smooth pavement is obviously a necessity, and lovely scenery made a route more likely to be chosen. We also looked for skates in areas with other interesting things happening, such as population centers or popular tourist destinations. (See "Points of interest," below.)

Elimination is part of the game. When you limit yourselves to 101 as we did, there's going to be a 102 that was cut, and a 103, and a 104 . . . you get the idea. So there are routes that were not included—maybe we already had too many similar routes in the area, or maybe we had *no* other routes in the area and didn't feel it could stand alone. There are as many reasons to eliminate as there are routes that were cut. But we're confident that we're presenting the 101 *best.*

If you discover a terrific skating route that we didn't include, it doesn't mean it won't make the sequel. Let us know about your favorites!

Our rating system

We ranked the skate routes as Beginner, Intermediate, Advanced, or Expert (and, when they hovered between categories, as Beginner/ Intermediate or Intermediate/Advanced). Often, we included beginner options for an intermediate route or advanced options to add mileage to an intermediate route. Of course, an expert skater can tackle any route in the book—just because we rated it for beginners doesn't mean it won't be enjoyable for a more skilled skater. Similarly, a beginner may read the trip description and route directions for any intermediate or advanced route to see whether there are sections appropriate for novices. It may be that two steep hills near the end of the outbound leg earned it a more advanced rating, but the initial few miles are suitable for anyone. For quick reference, use the chart at the beginning of the book to find tours that suit your needs.

We based the ratings on such factors as terrain, vehicular traffic, surface, and distance. Here's a breakdown:

BEGINNER ROUTES: For the most part, these routes are on paved paths; a limited number follow roads with very light traffic. They are generally flat, with the exception of slight slopes. You're a beginner if you've restricted your skating to parking lots and paths and haven't yet mastered braking and turning skills.

INTERMEDIATE ROUTES: Intermediate routes may include a road with a wide shoulder and light to moderate traffic. You are likely to encounter moderate rolling hills and possibly a steep ascent or descent. Intermediate skaters have solid braking skills but are not confident or comfortable skating on steep hills and in heavy traffic. An intermediate skater might also be someone with advanced technical skills but average or poor cardiovascular conditioning, making the shorter distances of an intermediate route more appropriate.

ADVANCED ROUTES: These trips will take you on roads with little or no shoulder and the potential for moderate to heavy traffic. They often include steep rolling hills and cover greater distances than do intermediate routes. They are appropriate for skaters with excellent skills who are comfortable skating, stopping, and turning in traffic.

EXPERT ROUTES: We have very few exclusively expert routes. These are trips suitable for a skater with an advanced skill level who is a risk taker and seeks a few more thrills than an advanced skate might provide. If you are an expert skater, you know it.

Our "Times to avoid" category
We didn't list winter. We assume that you've noticed how poorly in-line skates roll through slush and snow. We did, however, list times that you may not have thought of, such as days when traffic will be heavier because of seasonal crowds or special events in the area. These are recommendations based on the information we have, not an absolute declaration. If you don't mind skating en masse, by all means visit Misquamicut at noon on a Saturday in July.

Points of interest

Why *would* you drive to Northampton, Massachusetts, from Manchester, New Hampshire, to skate along a 5-mile bike path? Perhaps because of Look Park. You could drop your spouse and kids off there to enjoy the petting zoo, miniature train rides, and paddleboats, while you embark on a (guilt-free) workout. Or, if you are heading to Camden, Maine, you could drop your buddies off at Camden Hills State Park to do a little hiking. How about leaving your folks in Historic Deerfield while you cruise along the Deerfield River? And not one child will complain about spending time at the delightful Montshire Museum in Norwich, Vermont, while you skate the Upper Valley route.

Get the picture? We've listed nearby points of interest so that you will know what to do after your workout or what your nonskating family or friends can do while you're cruising around town on your blades. The lists are by no means complete, but they offer suggestions. Calling a town's chamber of commerce will provide you with other ideas and give you details about the attractions we've listed.

Maps

Routes with more complex trip descriptions are accompanied by maps. (Most rail trails, bike paths, and simple road routes did not require them.) The maps are intended to guide you to the starting point as well as to help you follow the skating directions. In general, they have been simplified to highlight the route and are not intended to replace your road atlas.

Common terms

We've used terms throughout the book that may need further explanation:

CAUTION: An area or situation that requires caution is ahead. Be prepared to stop, slow down, or maneuver. Often our "caution" in the route description is the only warning you'll have about an approaching intersection, steep descent, or other significant route feature.

IN-SEASON: This refers in most cases to summertime (Memorial Day through Labor Day), when beaches, for example, are particularly busy and parking fees are likely to apply. For a ski resort area, in-season likely means the winter. Use the route context and common sense.

RURAL ROAD: A rural road generally has two lanes and no shoulder, is lightly traveled, and has few intersections, stop signs, and traffic lights. These roads often run through lightly populated areas, meaning that you are unlikely to encounter cars entering and exiting driveways, roaming pets, and children dashing into the road.

STEEP HILL: On a descent, a steep hill will always require braking. Ascending a steep slope will be a challenge, demanding a great deal of effort. Short, choppy strokes will take you to the crest.

MODERATE HILL: Intermediate skaters should brake on moderate downhills; advanced skaters may or may not need to. Maintaining a glide up a moderate slope will be taxing for most skaters. It's likely you'll have to slow down and resort to short, choppy strokes.

GRADUAL HILL: Most skaters will be able to cruise down a gradual hill without braking, maintaining a normal stride and rhythm.

ROLLING HILLS OR ROLLERS: Rolling hills consist of a series of short, gradual to moderate hills.

Nothing stays the same

Smooth asphalt today may be choppy pavement tomorrow. A gravel road that signifies the turnaround point may suddenly get paved. A bike path may be extended 2 miles. *Stuff happens.*

We've tried to include the most up-to-date information about road conditions and other route characteristics, but there are always unforeseen changes. We apologize for any discrepancies between our route descriptions and the conditions that exist when you're skating. Please let Countryman Press know of any inconsistencies: PO Box 748, Woodstock, VT 05091. We'll investigate further and make the necessary changes in any future editions.

SKATING SAFE

We want you to have fun. A pulled hamstring (because you forgot to warm up) is not fun. A broken arm from a too-close encounter with a station wagon is not fun. In order to have a safe and enjoyable skate, you need to know a few things about avoiding injuries and accidents.

Warm-up (and -down)

The days of touching your toes before embarking on a 5-mile jog are over. Not only is it nearly impossible to properly stretch a cold muscle, but it also has the potential to be damaging. The best way to warm up for a skate is to do just that—skate! After 5 minutes of slow striding, stop beside the road and grab the nearest tree. Do the three lower body stretches shown below, holding each for at least 10 seconds. (These are not hard to do in skates.)

As you near the final mile of your workout, reduce speed, allowing your heart rate to slow down and return to normal. When you're done, remove your skates and repeat the three stretches.

S. HOOPER

The laws of skating

The International In-Line Skating Association (IISA) has developed guidelines that all skaters should learn and remember.

1 • SKATE SMART: Always wear protective gear and keep all of your equipment in good condition. Be sure you have mastered the basic skating skills (moving, stopping, and turning) before heading out onto the streets.

2 • SKATE ALERT: Control your speed and watch for road hazards such as water, oil, and sand. Avoid areas with heavy vehicular traffic. Be aware of car doors opening and vehicles entering and exiting driveways and parking spaces. And don't wear headphones!

3 • SKATE LEGAL: When on skates, you're under the same obligations as a motorist to obey the traffic regulations, such as stop and yield signs.

4 • SKATE COURTEOUS: Be a good-will ambassador for the sport. Share the path, don't dominate it. Skate on the right and pass on the left, announcing your intentions as you do so, as in: "Passing on your left." Always yield to pedestrians.

Preflight skate check

The IISA also recommends a preflight skate check before you take off. This includes spinning and moving each wheel to be sure that there is no lateral movement. Check to be sure that the nuts that secure the wheels are tight, but not binding. Do the wheels spin easily or is there resistance, indicating the bearings need to be cleaned or replaced? Inspect your brakes for excessive wear and your skates' buckles and laces for frayed or worn pieces and for tightness. Confirm that your protective equipment is on firmly and correctly. (Yes, people have been known to put helmets on backward and switch knee and elbow pads.)

Skating on the road

You know that you're going to turn left at the next intersection. Unfortunately, the driver of the car behind you does not. So, unless you're interested in taking a little ride on his hood, you need to let him know what you're planning. The most effective method of communicating with drivers is sign language. Nothing fancy is required—just point and indicate your intentions. Your best bet is to let any traffic pass, then safely execute your turn.

Many drivers are anxious about passing skaters because we take up more room than cyclists or runners do. So you'll have to give them a little encouragement. Stop stroking, glide, and motion a driver to pass. If you are skating on a street with heavy traffic, make sure that vehicles can safely pass you. Shorten the extension of your stroke so that your span is not as wide—or, in the words of one of the sport's most ardent supporters, Dave Cooper, "Skate skinny."

If you need to cross a street, always stop and wait for the driver behind to signal you. Never assume that other people know what you are going to do.

Hazards

Our best advice on road hazards: Avoid them. Skate around patches of sand, puddles, oil slicks, sticks, potholes, and road grates.

Sometimes, though, you just can't. When your options are skating into the path of an oncoming Winnebago or rolling across a few twigs, you're smart to pick the twigs. To safely skate over most road hazards, position your legs in a "scissor," with one skate forward like an open pair of scissors. For maximum control, keep at least 4 inches between the front and back skates. Keep your hands open and in front of your body, and stay low with your knees bent. If you cannot glide across the hazard, take short steps over it.

THE WELL-DRESSED SKATER

S. HOOPER

One of the best things about in-line skating is that the equipment is relatively minimal and inexpensive. We recommend that you shop in a specialty store rather than a discount or department store. You may spend more money initially, but you're likely to have a greater selection of style and size, purchase durable equipment, and get satisfaction later if a part needs to be repaired or replaced. Knowledgeable salespeople will be able to provide valuable advice about fit and other critical factors.

Skates

There are many types of skates available today—skates for recreational beginners, for racers, for freestyle skaters, for hockey players, even special ones for women and children. Recreational skates, ranging in price from $100 to $500, are the most popular and versatile.

The salespeople in your local skate shop will be able to assess your needs and properly fit your boots. With so many choices in skate styles, you'll want to allow yourself time to shop around. You may even want to rent first. Just remember—skates are like most things in life: You get what you pay for.

BOOTS: Boots are generally made of hard plastic or, in the case of speed skates, leather. Some are vented to keep your feet cooler during a workout. The stiffest, most durable boots are for the types of skating that give a lot of abuse, like ramp riding and freestyle. They should fit snugly, but comfortably. Your toes may be barely touching the front of the boot. If you skate in a correct position with knees bent, your heels will naturally pull to the back of the skate, thus leaving room for your toes at the front of the skate.

BUCKLES AND LACES: The great skating debate: Which are superior, buckles or laces? You may not have a choice. Hockey skates, for instance, nearly all have laces, and many recreational skates have buckles. Buckles fasten quickly (and can be adjusted midskate), they don't fray or wear, and they don't loosen during a workout. Laces provide more uniform pressure on your foot and allow more careful adjustment for a better overall fit. A lace-and-buckle combination is often preferred because it allows the skater to leave the toe area looser while giving tighter and consistent ankle support.

WHEELS: Wheels will have the greatest impact on your performance. Beginners and recreational skaters should choose standard four-wheel skates and avoid five-wheel speed skates. Those with five or more wheels are for racers and are made for speed and stability, providing more stroke and straighter tracking. They are not designed for maneuverability. You are better off mastering your technique on a shorter wheelbase, then graduating to a longer one.

Size and the durometer number are the two significant wheel factors. The durometer number refers to the hardness of the wheel— the higher the number, the harder the wheel. Softer wheels, which absorb shock well, are better for rough surfaces and have greater traction; harder wheels are preferable on smooth surfaces or for anyone weighing more than 200 pounds, but cause disturbing vibrations on rough terrain.

Wheels are measured in millimeters, with most falling between 70mm and 80mm. Recreational skates generally have wheels that are on the smaller side—68mm to 72mm—for a lower center of gravity and greater stability. The larger the wheel, the faster you'll roll.

BEARINGS: Ball bearings are what allow the wheels to spin easily. Bearings are given ratings, or ABEC numbers. In general, those with higher numbers will be faster, longer lasting, and have fewer vibrations. If you skate often and consider speed important (and if you are willing to clean 16 to 20 bearings every week), get bearings with a high ABEC rating. If you are a weekend or vacation skater interested in low-maintenance equipment, opt for sealed bearings with a rating of 1 or 3.

Protective equipment

Even though skating-related injuries do not occur as frequently as those associated with similar outdoor activities, they do happen. Nearly 100,000 people will be treated this year in emergency rooms because of skating injuries. Many of these accidents could have been prevented if skaters had worn protective equipment, honed skills under the supervision of a qualified instructor, and used common sense. Equipment such as a helmet and pads will not only protect you during a fall and help prevent road rash, but will also make you more confident and relaxed, resulting in a more enjoyable workout.

HELMET: Look for a helmet that is ANSI- or SNELL-approved. It should fit well (without a lot of slipping and sliding) and should feel comfortable enough (and look slick enough) so that you are going to want to wear it. (By the way, tossing it on without fastening it doesn't count.)

KNEE PADS: Knee pads are critical because you should drop to your knees first during a fall. Like elbow pads, they should have a hard outer shell so that they will slide—not catch—on the pavement. They must be fastened well enough so that they will not slip during a fall.

WRIST GUARDS: Always try to fall forward when you feel yourself losing your balance. Wrist protection allows you to slide on your wrists, distributing the force of the impact.

ELBOW GUARDS: Elbow pads provide protection in the event of a sideways tumble. And during a forward fall, your elbows will be the last joint to hit the ground, absorbing the full impact of your weight.

TECHNIQUE

We have offered some basic techniques to get you started. This is no substitute, however, for a lesson with a certified in-line instructor.

Ready position

This basic position is the most critical for those just starting out because it ensures steadiness. Most beginner moves start from this "steady ready" position.

Put your skates parallel to each other, hip-width apart. Bend your knees, keeping your arms and hands in front of your body. Focus on a spot 5 feet in front of you.

S. HOOPER

Control position

All too often, skaters forget some of the basics and straighten their legs or put their arms and hands behind their bodies, resulting in a loss of control.

As soon as you feel yourself losing your balance, bend over and grab your knees, staying low. This control position lowers your center of gravity and keeps your weight forward.

Falling

You will fall. Everyone does. So you must know how to fall correctly. Land on your knee pads first. Slide on your wrist guards, then onto your elbow guards. Keep your fingers up and out of the way. Practice—really.

To stand up, start in an all-fours position with hands and knees on the ground and stand up slowly with your heels together and hands in front of your body.

Edges

How you balance on the edges of your skates will determine in which direction you will glide. There are three edges. When the skate is upright, it is on the center edge. When it is angled outward or away from the center of the body, it is on the outside edge. When it is angled inward or toward the center of the body, it is on the inside edge. When one skate is on the inside edge and the other is on the outside edge, the skater is using corresponding edges. As with downhill skiing, this position is used for parallel turns.

S. HOOPER

V-walk (Stride 1)

To start rolling on your skates, assume the ready position. Shift your weight from one skate to the other to become familiar with the sensation of weight transfer. When you pull your heels together so that they form a V and shift your weight side to side, you will begin to roll slowly forward. (Be sure to keep your hands where you can see them.) As you roll forward, bring your skates back to a ready position and repeat. To slow down, point your toes inward or bring your knees together. Think "Shift, shift, shift, glide" as you work on this elementary step. Practice first on the grass and then on smooth pavement, until you are comfortable with the feeling of movement.

Beginner stride (Stride 2)

Once you have perfected the V-walk, move on to the beginner stride (stride 2). This stride is a good starting point for long-distance skating, because it allows you to move forward more comfortably for a longer period of time.

Nearly all skating skills require a support leg and an action leg. The support leg provides stability, while the action leg supplies the power for the move. The components of stride 2 are the stroke and the glide. The stroke is the extension of your leg at a 45-degree angle to the side, which pushes your body forward, creating motion. The glide involves both skates regrouping before proceeding to the next stroke.

From a ready position, bend your knees. With your upper body pitched slightly forward, shift your weight to your support leg, stroke with your action leg, and regroup. For maximum control and efficiency, return to the ready position before stroking on the other side. Stride 2 counts are "Bend knees, stroke, regroup."

Find your natural striding rhythm to help you relax. Swing your arms gently from side to side. As you advance, rest them behind you on your lower back.

Stopping

Achieving a confident and powerful stop is critical to safe skating.

HEEL BRAKE STOP: The heel brake stop is the simplest and most efficient technique. From the ready position, scissor or slide your braking foot forward so that its heel brake is in front of the opposite skate, but still parallel to it. Lift the toe wheel of the braking skate so that the heel brake makes contact with the ground. Then, bend your knees (as if you were going to sit down) until you stop.

To stop immediately and completely, you must apply pressure to the front braking skate even though your natural tendency might be to keep your weight on the back skate. Focus on transferring your weight as you scissor-step your braking foot forward. Sitting on the brake will then bring you to a full stop. Practice again and again until you are confident of your ability to brake automatically in an emergency situation.

S. HOOPER

T-STOP: The T-stop (which looks a whole lot more like an L-stop to us) is a slow-speed stop and is useful for controlling speed. (Do not rely on it, however, for stopping at high speeds.) Assume a ready position, then scissor one foot forward. Turn the heel of the back foot in to meet the heel of the front foot. Roll the back skate to an inside edge with your foot tilted down toward the ground and all wheels on the pavement. Be sure to keep your hips and shoulders squared. To come to a complete stop, increase the pressure on the inside edge of the back foot. Apply pressure from the inside of the foot, not from the knee.

Parallel turning

Turning will add control and mobility to your skating. To make a left turn, start from a ready position; roll your left skate forward. Look left, in the direction of the turn, and rotate your upper body to the left. Your skates will naturally move onto corresponding edges and you will turn left. The more you rotate your upper body, the sharper the resulting turn will be.

Conquering curbs

Skating onto a curb is much like stepping onto one. Shift your weight to one skate while you lift the other onto the curb. Then shift your weight again as you lift the other skate up. To get off a curb, either stop and step down or skate straight off the curb by using a scissors move

SKATING TIP: *Small jumps are fun and can increase your confidence. To start, bend your knees with your arms at chest level. Jump up, keeping your wheels parallel with the ground. Land in a bent—not stiff—position. Practice by jumping over lines on the road.*

S. HOOPER

(one skate in front of the other, like an open pair of scissors) and staying low. (Keep your knees bent and hands low.)

Skating uphill
Shift your weight slightly back when heading up a hill. On a steep slope, use a shorter stroke.

Skating downhill
Beginners and intermediates should keep their heel brakes in contact with the pavement for the entire downgrade. Hands should stay below the waist and in front of the body and knees should be bent. Advanced and expert skaters may not need to brake continuously, but should stay alert to potential hazards.

How to improve your skating ability
To find a qualified in-line instructor, contact the IISA (see Resources), which maintains an Instructor Certification Program to train skating

instructors. The association should be able to provide you with the names of certified instructors in your area.

Have a super time exploring New England on your skates! And stay safe!

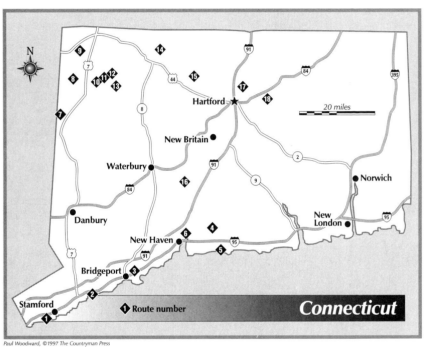

N

9

7

8

10 11 12

13

14

44

15

91

84

395

8

17

Hartford ★

18

20 miles

New Britain ●

2

Waterbury ●

16

91

9

● Norwich

84

Danbury ●

New Haven ●

6

4

New
London ●

95

Bridgeport ●

91

3

5

7

2

Stamford ●

1

1 Route number

Connecticut

Part One

Connecticut

1 •••• *Cove Island Park*

LOCATION: Stamford, CT
RATING: Beginner
DISTANCE: 0.9 mile
TIMES TO AVOID: Midday on summer weekends
TERRAIN: Paved path on a large, circular track
SURFACE: Coarse asphalt
AUTO TRAFFIC: None
POINTS OF INTEREST: Hoyt-Barnum House, Stamford Historical Society, Mianus River Preserve (hiking, biking, fishing), Bartlett Arboretum (ecology trails, swamp walk), Stamford Museum and Nature Center (working farm, trails, planetarium), Whitney Museum of American Art

DRIVING DIRECTIONS: From I-95 in Stamford, take exit 9 (Glenbrook). Head south on Seaside Avenue; drive 0.6 mile to a traffic light. Turn left onto Cove Road, and you'll soon arrive at Cove Park. As you enter the park, turn right and park in the lot on your left. (*Note:* In-season, you must be a Stamford resident to park in Cove Park. Non-residents must park outside the entrance. There is no residency requirement from Labor Day to Memorial Day.)

TRIP OVERVIEW: Cove Park is not for reserved, demure types. Skaters flock to this public park to be seen—to perform, to demonstrate their skills, to show off their fit bodies in the latest skating garb. It's what a fitness gym is to so many athletes: a place not only to work out, but also to socialize with like-minded people.

The loop is short—not quite a mile—but it is common to see skaters rolling around it again and again. Similiar to a running track, with a shoulder for skaters and cyclists, the path is usually crowded with joggers and walkers. The constant ocean breeze makes for a comfortable workout, even on the hottest days.

Conveniently situated less than a mile off I-95, Cove Park also boasts a public beach and boat docks on Long Island Sound, an indoor ice skating rink, and play and picnic areas.

ROUTE DIRECTIONS: From the eastern side of the parking lot, follow a steel footbridge onto the track, which forms a 0.9-mile loop. To avoid a collision, skate in a clockwise direction and stay in the designated skater's path. (There are public rest rooms on your left as you exit the bridge.)

2 •••• Sherwood Island State Park

LOCATION: Westport, CT
RATING: Intermediate
DISTANCE: 1.5 miles
TIMES TO AVOID: Midday on summer weekends
TERRAIN: Path with gentle hills
SURFACE: Smooth asphalt with some broken asphalt
AUTO TRAFFIC: None
POINTS OF INTEREST: Rolnick Observatory, Bowman Observatory, Mill Hill Historic Park, Nature Center for Environmental Activities, Westport Arts Center, Maritime Center Aquarium, Sheffield Island Lighthouse

DRIVING DIRECTIONS: From I-95 in Westport, take exit 18 (Sherwood Island) and turn south onto the Sherwood Island Connector. In 0.6 mile, arrive at the gatehouse. (Pay a moderate-to-high parking fee in-season; parking is free from Columbus Day to Memorial Day.) Park in the lot on your left.

TRIP OVERVIEW: Westport's Sherwood Island State Park—the first state park in Connecticut—is also one of the first in the nation. The park is named for the Sherwood family who moved here in the 1600s from England's Sherwood Forest—the same Sherwood Forest inhabited by Robin Hood and his band of merry men. Sherwood Island's 234 acres include marshes, wooded areas, and more than a mile of beachfront (including a seaside gravel bike path).

Take in expansive views across Long Island Sound as you follow the paved path that runs along the beach, passing the park's nature center and then hugging Compo Cove. Plunge into the woods before returning to the beach. Repeat the loop until you're ready for an ocean swim!

ROUTE DIRECTIONS:

0.0 From the parking lot, head southward toward the pavilion and the beach; turn right onto a paved path.

0.4 Turn left and pump up a short hill; as you crest, turn left. ▼ CAUTION: On a 0.1-mile descent, brake with care on choppy pavement.

0.7 Bear right, pushing up a slight incline.

1.1 ● STOP. Cross the road, heading straight (toward the beach).

1.3 Bear left beyond the pavilion, rolling beside the beach. (Rest rooms, showers, and snacks are available.)

1.5 Return to the parking lot. Repeat!

> **SKATING TIP:** *After skating through a puddle, glide for approximately 4 feet before resuming your stride to allow your wheels to dry off.* ▼ *CAUTION: Wheels are slippery when wet.*

3 •••• *Seaside Park*

LOCATION: Bridgeport, CT
RATING: Beginner
DISTANCE: 2.4 miles (sidewalk route) or 3.0 miles (bike path route)
TIMES TO AVOID: Early morning or late afternoon, midday on summer weekends
TERRAIN: Flat, with some concrete sidewalks and some bike paths on the side of the road
SURFACE: Smooth concrete and coarse asphalt
AUTO TRAFFIC: Most of the route is not open to traffic
POINTS OF INTEREST: P.T. Barnum Museum, Housatonic Museum of Art, Captain's Cove Seaport, Discovery Museum, Beardsley Zoological Gardens, Shoreline Star Greyhound Park Entertainment Complex, Downtown Cabaret Theater

DRIVING DIRECTIONS: From I-95 north in Bridgeport, take exit 27. Turn right onto Myrtle Street; at the first stop sign, turn right onto Gregory Street. Drive two blocks and turn left onto Park Avenue. From I-95 south, take exit 27 and drive through two lights. Turn left onto Park Avenue.

Drive about 0.5 mile to the entrance to Seaside Park, marked by two big arches. Turn right onto Waldmere Avenue and park along the street.

TRIP OVERVIEW: In the midst of a deteriorating urban area, Seaside Park stands as a testament to what used to be. Monuments dot the manicured lawns, ancient trees shade napping visitors, the splendid public beach stretches between stone jetties on Long Island Sound. It isn't hard to imagine what the area must have looked like to P.T. Barnum when, after taking "the Greatest Show on Earth" to every place on earth, he decided to settle down here.

Today, the water is not clean, and the abutting neighborhoods make this an unsafe place after sunset. But you can enjoy what Seaside has to offer during the day (along with lots of other folks, especially on warm weekends): large grassy expanses for throwing a Frisbee, baseball fields for a pickup game, a concrete skating rink for practicing technique, and a beautiful backdrop for any workout.

We've described two routes within the park boundaries. The first, 2.4 miles, runs the length of the smooth concrete sidewalk. The edge of the sidewalk drops off to the beach (and there is no railing), so take it slow if you are not confident with your braking. We recommend this route in the off-season because on sunny summer days, crowds clog the narrow sidewalk.

The second route option, 3 miles, runs the length of the beach access road on an adjacent bike path. The windswept road is rough in places, with bits of broken shells and craggy asphalt making for a bumpy ride. (The incredible views of Long Island Sound compensate.) Auto traffic is sporadic, because the road is closed to cars at certain points.

ROUTE DIRECTIONS:
- *2.4-MILE SIDEWALK ROUTE.* From the Barnum monument, head eastward on the smooth sidewalk.
- 0.5 Rest on this seaside bench or on one of many placed along the sidewalk.
- 1.0 Reach the sidewalk's end. Turn and head back the way you came.
- 2.0 Pass the Barnum monument where you began your skate, continuing to follow the sidewalk.
- 2.1 The sidewalk ends about 25 feet from the beach access road. Turn and head back to the monument. (You do have the option of extending the skate by connecting the sidewalk and beach road loops. Carefully walk across the dirt area to join the beach road described below.)
- 2.4 Return to your starting point and your car nearby.

- *3.0-MILE BIKE PATH/BEACH ROAD ROUTE.* From the Barnum monument, head west along Sound View Road, skirting the beach.
- 0.7 The road opens to beach auto traffic.
- 1.5 The road ends at a marina and fishing area overlooking Black Rock Harbor. Head back the way you came.

4 ••••   *Chatfield Hollow State Park*

LOCATION: Madison and Killingworth, CT
RATING: Intermediate
DISTANCE: 3.0 miles
TIMES TO AVOID: Summer weekends
TERRAIN: Flat path and limited road skating with rolling hills
SURFACE: Coarse asphalt
AUTO TRAFFIC: Off-season, very light; in-season, moderate for 1.5 miles on park access road
POINTS OF INTEREST: Hammonasset State Park, Deacon John Gravehouse, Madison Historical Society, Forster Pond, Hyland House, Whitfield House Museum, Gillette Castle

DRIVING DIRECTIONS: From I-95, take exit 63. Travel north on CT 81 for 5.1 miles to a rotary that joins CT 80. Drive west on CT 80 in Killingworth for 1.2 miles to the Chatfield Hollow State Park entrance on your right. Turn here and park in the lot to your immediate right or left. (Pay a moderate parking fee.)

TRIP OVERVIEW: On sunny summer days, the beach at Chatfield Hollow State Park's Schreeder Pond is littered with brightly colored buckets and shovels and cast-off towels. Children romp along the sand and splash each other in the water. Parking spots are tough to come by, and picnic tables are filled as quickly as they're vacated.

So you'll probably have company as you roll along the park's delightful path—popular with walkers, runners, cyclists, and skaters alike—which winds beside brooks (crossing several) and visits a waterfall and a serene pond. This enchanting area has been appreciated by people for hundreds, maybe thousands, of years. Long ago, Native Americans hunted and fished in this valley, sleeping beneath the rock overhangs and holding tribal meetings in the rocky hills.

If, after a few trips along the path, you decide you'd like to seek solitude, lace up your hiking boots and explore some of the 18 miles of trails that meander through the surrounding woods. Even in the forest, though, you may not be alone: Local legends tell of two mischievous witches, Goody Wee and Betty Wee, who lived in the hollow and enjoyed playing mean-spirited tricks on trespassers! Watch out!

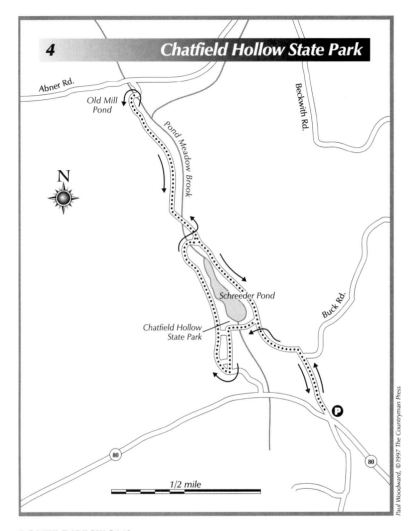

4 Chatfield Hollow State Park

ROUTE DIRECTIONS:

0.0 Head northward along the park access road; brake on a slight decline.

0.1 ▼ CAUTION: Brake on a descent and step or roll slowly over a speed bump. Keep your hands in front of your body and stay low.

0.4 Bear left at a fork and roll over a bridge. Pause to take in the lovely view of Schreeder Pond and the waterfall below.

0.6 At an intersection, turn left.

0.7 At another intersection, head right. ▼ CAUTION: Watch for twigs scattered along the path. Be sure to stay low and loose.

1.0 Before crossing the bridge, look across the lake to check out the beach activity.

1.1 Hop over a bridge and bear left, joining the bank of Pond Meadow Brook.

1.2 Push up a gentle hill for 0.2 mile, passing a weary covered bridge on your right.

1.5 After rolling by Old Mill Pond, pause for a sip of water or to take a photo. When you're ready, turn and head back toward your car.

2.3 Bear left, working up a slight incline.

2.4 ▼ CAUTION: Brake on a gentle descent.

2.5 Glide by the beach on Schreeder Pond on your right and descend easily for 0.1 mile.

2.8 ▼ CAUTION: Negotiate speed bumps. Scissor-skate with hands in front and stay low.

3.0 Exit the park access road and return to the parking lot.

5 •••• *Hammonasset Beach State Park*

LOCATION: Madison, CT
RATING: Beginner
DISTANCE: 3.7 miles (with many side trails)
TIMES TO AVOID: Summer weekends
TERRAIN: Flat path
SURFACE: Smooth asphalt
AUTO TRAFFIC: In-season, heavy but slow (campers); off-season, none
POINTS OF INTEREST: Chatfield Hollow State Park, Deacon John Gravehouse, Madison Historical Society, Forster Pond, Hyland House, Whitfield House Museum, Clinton Crossing (outlet shopping), Gillette Castle

DRIVING DIRECTIONS: From I-95, take exit 62 in Madison (guided by park signs) and follow the Hammonasset Connector south for about 1 mile to the park entrance. From there, follow signs for West Beach parking. In-season parking rates are moderate to high for nonresidents, but no fee is charged during the off-season.

TRIP OVERVIEW: So often, skaters are not welcomed the way walkers, runners, and even cyclists are. Sniff. We're considered a nuisance, lumped together with skateboarders, FORBIDDEN, PROHIBITED, RESTRICTED, or BANNED—take your pick—from using many streets and walkways.

Not here!

In fact, you'll believe that these paths and roads were designed with in-line skaters in mind. (Actually, they were designed with 541 camping sites—and the consequent Winnebagos—in mind.) The pavement is smooth, the interconnecting trails are wide, and the terrain is varied enough to add interest but not so tough as to exclude beginners. In addition to some of the best skating turf we've found, the 900-acre park offers 2 miles of beach on Long Island Sound (the state's largest public beach), a 1.2-mile seaside gravel bike path, picnic areas, baseball fields, playgrounds, rest rooms, and the Meig's Point Nature Center.

Because the best place to skate is the camping area, we strongly recommend that you visit between Labor Day and Memorial Day, when there are few (or no) campers. (If you decide to skate during the busy summer months, be sure to skate with the traffic.) Although we have described a route, we encourage you to create your own from the maze of paths.

ROUTE DIRECTIONS:

0.0 Leave the West Beach parking lot and turn left onto the wide path that is the extension of the park access road.

0.1 Turn right onto a narrower path. ▼ CAUTION: The pavement is choppy for 0.1 mile.

0.2 Enter the campground through wood barriers. ▼ CAUTION: Walk—don't roll—through the barriers, as there is a patch of broken pavement.

From here, explore the paths on your own, or follow the route below:

Inside the barriers, take an immediate right.

0.3 Turn left at the playground.

0.7 At path's end, head right, passing public rest rooms.

0.9 Cruise by an outdoor movie theater.

1.1 ● STOP. At the stop sign, turn left.

1.2 Before you reach an island of trees, go left.

1.4 Turn right at the public rest rooms.

1.5 ● STOP. At the stop sign, cross the main park road.

2.0 At the camp store (on the beach), turn around and begin to head back.

2.2 ● STOP. At the stop sign, turn right.

2.3 ● STOP. At the stop sign, turn left.

2.5 Turn sharply left; do not exit the park.
3.0 Bear left at the rest rooms and follow the (now one-way) traffic to your right.
3.3 ● STOP. At the stop sign, turn right. Shortly, turn left onto Algonquin Road.
3.5 Leave the campground through the wood barriers; turn left onto the park access road.
3.7 Return to the parking lot.

6 •••• *East Shore Park, New Haven*

LOCATION: New Haven, CT
RATING: Beginner
DISTANCE: 2.0-mile loop (with an additional 1.3-mile fitness path)
TIMES TO AVOID: During special events (call ahead: 203-946-8025)
TERRAIN: Flat path
SURFACE: Smooth asphalt with limited sections of coarse asphalt
AUTO TRAFFIC: None
POINTS OF INTEREST: East Rock Park, Edgewood Park, Edgerton Park, Indian Ledge and Pequonnock Valley Park, Shore Line Trolley Museum, Eli Whitney Museum, Fort Nathan Hale and Black Rock Fort, Peabody Museum of Natural History at Yale, Long Wharf Nature Preserve, West Rock Ridge State Park

DRIVING DIRECTIONS: From I-95, take exit 50 (Woodward Avenue). Head south on Woodward Avenue (toward the water) for 0.75 mile to a blinking light. Turn right into East Shore Park and park in the large lot on your left. There is no parking fee.

TRIP OVERVIEW: East Shore Park is a delightful escape from the crowds and concrete of urban New Haven. Comprising 82 acres along New Haven Harbor, the park offers a variety of activity sites, including baseball fields, tennis and basketball courts, playgrounds, picnic areas, and a trail that winds along the shoreline. Adjacent to the parking lot is a smooth concrete skating rink perfect for beginners and children. East Shore Park is also the site of the Special Olympic Summer Games. Perhaps best of all, park facilities are free and accessible to residents and nonresidents alike, making it a terrific (guilt-free!) spot to bring family or friends who may prefer tennis or throwing a Frisbee to skating.

After stretching and taking a few warm-up laps in the rink, you'll follow the main park access path for 0.8 mile—the length of the park—with the option of rolling along the connecting fitness path that skirts the edge of the New Haven Harbor. Take a few laps, then challenge your son or daughter to a game of hoops.

ROUTE DIRECTIONS:

0.0 Warm up in the rink, then head north through the parking lot with Baseball Field II on your left.

0.2 STOP at a chained barrier (banning auto traffic). Step under the chain or sidestep the pole to join the main park path. The fitness path (with great water and city views, but rougher pavement) leaves on your right, parallel to this entrance.

0.7 Pass the main recreational area, which has playgrounds, basketball and tennis courts, and more.

1.0 At the end of the path, turn and head back the way you came. Then repeat!

SKATING TIP: *If you get caught in the rain, don't hurry home! Instead, slow down and keep your strokes short: Do not fully extend your leg. This will help you maintain control on wet roads, which are often slick with oil.*

7 •••• Mt. Algo & the Housatonic River

LOCATION: Kent, CT
RATING: Intermediate
DISTANCE: 5.2 miles
TIMES TO AVOID: None
TERRAIN: Gently rolling
SURFACE: Smooth asphalt
AUTO TRAFFIC: Very light
POINTS OF INTEREST: Appalachian Trail, Kent Falls State Park, Macedonia Brook State Park, Housatonic Meadows State Park and Housatonic Forest, Wyantenock State Forest, Kent's Sloane-Stanley Museum (featuring artist Eric Sloane)

DRIVING DIRECTIONS: From the junction of US 7 and CT 341 in Kent, drive west on CT 341, crossing the Housatonic River. The first paved road on your left after the bridge is Schaticoke Road. Park at the corner of Schaticoke Road and CT 341.

TRIP OVERVIEW: Are you hovering between beginner and intermediate status? Beginner routes seem too easy, but you're not sure you're ready to tackle a significantly tougher route? This is a terrific trip for the up-and-coming intermediate. Cruise along a wide road that winds along the Housatonic River with essentially no traffic. Companions who do not join you for the skate can browse the shops in Kent, just over the bridge. Make a postskate stop at Kent Falls State Park (about 8 miles north on US 7) and enjoy a picnic lunch by the spectacular falls.

ROUTE DIRECTIONS:
  0.0 Head south on Schaticoke Road, gliding up an easy climb.
  0.4 Skate along flatter terrain with the Kent School campus on your left.
  0.7 Roll beside the Housatonic River.
  1.2 Leave the Kent School behind.
  1.6 Dart to the top of a small bluff overlooking the spillwaters of the Housatonic River with Mount Algo visible on your right.
  2.6 Rejoin the Housatonic River just before the road becomes gravel. Reverse direction and head back to your car.

8 •••• *Mudge Pond*

LOCATION: Sharon, CT
RATING: Intermediate or advanced
DISTANCE: 5.4 miles (intermediate); 12.8 miles (advanced)
TIMES TO AVOID: None
TERRAIN: Gently rolling with two long, difficult hills on the advanced segment
SURFACE: Smooth and coarse asphalt
AUTO TRAFFIC: Very light
POINTS OF INTEREST: Gay-Hoyt House Museum, Sharon village, Northeast Audubon Center, Housatonic Meadows State Park and Housatonic Forest, Macedonia Brook State Park, Appalachian Trail, Kent Falls State Park

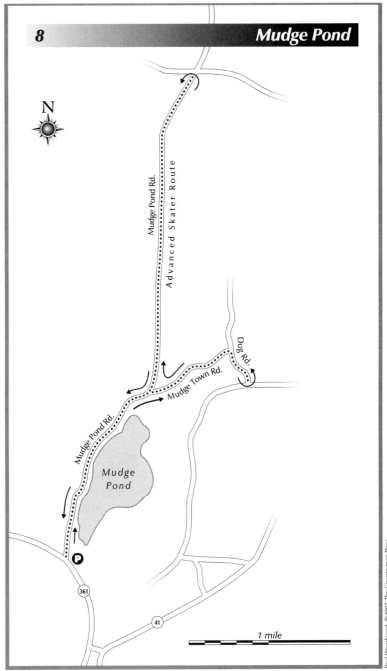

8

Mudge Pond

N

Mudge Pond Rd.

Advanced Skater Route

Dug Rd.

Mudge Town Rd.

Mudge Pond Rd.

Mudge Pond

P

361

41

1 mile

Paul Woodward, ©1997 The Countryman Press

DRIVING DIRECTIONS: From CT 8, take exit 44 (downtown Torrington) to CT 4. Take CT 4 West and, 6.5 miles from CT 8, continue straight through the rotary where CT 4 intersects CT 63. Drive 17.5 miles to a stop sign in Sharon; turn right onto CT 41 North. In 0.1 mile, turn left onto CT 361 West. Drive 0.9 mile, turn right onto Mudge Pond Road, and park on the shoulder.

TRIP OVERVIEW: Roll along wide, straight roads, passing country estates, horse farms, and open pasture. As you skate beside scenic Mudge Pond—about 0.5 mile into the route—intermediate skaters will find the terrain easy to pond's end, although coarse pavement necessitates slower speeds. Beginning at about the 4.2-mile mark, a series of extended climbs (on smoother pavement) presents a challenge for advanced skaters. Your effort is rewarded by the long, straight descents that follow.

Nonskaters (or skaters post-trip) will enjoy exploring the 684-acre Northeast Audubon Center (on CT 4, about 5 miles east of Mudge Pond). Hike along 11 miles of trails (open 7 days, dawn to dusk), enjoy the wildflower gardens, and visit the main building with live natural history displays and a children's discovery room.

ROUTE DIRECTIONS:
- 0.0 Head north on wide, coarse Mudge Pond Road, immediately tackling a moderate hill lined with elegant homes and clipped meadows.
- 0.1 Crest with a view over Mudge Pond to your right; begin a gradual descent.
- 1.3 Pass the town beach area.
- 1.7 Turn right onto narrower Mudge Town Road.
- 2.4 After passing the Mudge Pond headwaters, turn right onto Dug Road.
- 2.7 INTERMEDIATE SKATERS: Turn around at the next intersection and return to your car. You may want to walk the final descent, 0.1 mile from your car.
  ADVANCED SKATERS: Return to Mudge Pond Road.
- 3.7 Turn right onto Mudge Pond Road; embark on a moderate 0.2-mile-long ascent.
- 4.2 Begin a steeper ascent, and cross into Lakeville on smoother pavement.
- 4.5 Continue to climb, now gradually.
- 5.2 Drop down a moderate pitch, and glance north for a view of Bear Mountain and Mount Riga.

5.5 Negotiate moderate rolling hills.

5.9 ▼ CAUTION: Brake on this descent; it's steep and long, though straight.

6.3 Bottom out, and prepare to stop.

6.4 At the stop sign, reverse direction to return to your car.

9 •••• *Salmon Kill Road*

LOCATION: Salisbury and Lime Rock, CT
RATING: Intermediate
DISTANCE: 7.4 miles
TIMES TO AVOID: None
TERRAIN: Gently rolling and flat
SURFACE: Smooth asphalt
AUTO TRAFFIC: Light
POINTS OF INTEREST: Macedonia Brook State Park, Appalachian Trail, Taconic Park, Housatonic Meadows State Park and Housatonic Forest, Cathedral Pines, Lime Rock Park (sports-car road racing), Housatonic Railroad Company

DRIVING DIRECTIONS: From the junction of US 44 and CT 41 in Salisbury, drive 0.3 mile on US 44 West. Park on the south side of US 44 near Salmon Kill Road.

TRIP OVERVIEW: Salisbury and Lime Rock, tucked in the northwest corner of Connecticut and bordered by New York and Massachusetts, is a favorite destination for city folks who seek rural—but elegant—surroundings and a host of recreational activities. Several lakes offer public access for swimming, fishing, and boating. In addition, hikers can follow part of the Appalachian Trail (as well as a number of local paths), which wanders within the town boundaries. From April to October, weekends are action packed at the Lime Rock Park racetrack, which has spotlighted European-style sports-car racing for nearly 40 years.

With all that this area has to offer, you may need a weekend to fit in your skate! On this route, you'll quickly depart busy Salisbury center and dive into a valley rimmed with open pastures, horses and deer outnumbering the cars you'll meet. Salmon Creek will be a nearly constant companion. The road does not have a shoulder but is not well traveled. You'll cruise easily on the outbound route, gradually (and

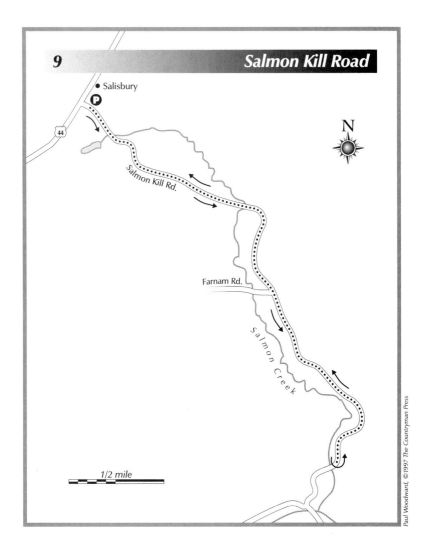

9 **Salmon Kill Road**

• Salisbury

Salmon Kill Rd.

Farnam Rd.

Salmon Creek

N

1/2 mile

Paul Woodward, © 1997 The Countryman Press

nearly indistinguishably) heading downhill. You probably won't recognize the elevation loss until you head back to your car, when you'll have to expend considerably more effort to travel the same distance.

ROUTE DIRECTIONS:

0.0 Follow Salmon Kill Road southeasterly, rolling through a suburban neighborhood.

0.2 Cross a stream as the surroundings turn distinctly rural.

0.6 Roll by a country estate with horses grazing in the adjacent field (and watch for less domesticated animals, too!).

1.1 Stay alert on a short descent with a left-hand bend.

2.0 After rolling over Salmon Creek, continue straight as Farnam Road joins from the right.

2.6 Cruise through a more wooded area as the road trends downward.

3.6 Salmon Creek trickles past on your right.

3.7 Stop at the stream crossing, gather your strength, and head back to your car.

10 •••• *Cornwall Village*

LOCATION: Cornwall, CT
RATING: Intermediate
DISTANCE: 5.0 miles
TIMES TO AVOID: None
TERRAIN: Gently rolling, with one moderate hill near route's end
SURFACE: Smooth and coarse asphalt
AUTO TRAFFIC: Very light
POINTS OF INTEREST: Mohawk Mountain Park and Forest, Cathedral Pines, Cream Hill Lake, Cornwall's covered bridge, White Memorial Foundation and Conservation Center, White Flower Farm, Kent Falls State Park, Haight Vineyard

C. LEWIS

Impressive rural scenery makes this an invigorating trip.

DRIVING DIRECTIONS: From CT 8, take exit 44 (downtown Torrington) to CT 4. Take CT 4 West and in 6.5 miles continue straight through the rotary where CT 4 intersects CT 63. In another 6.2 miles, turn left onto Pine Street. Park in Cornwall village near this intersection.

TRIP OVERVIEW: Cornwall is known for its outdoor variety—from fishing and swimming in Cream Hill Lake to camping in Housatonic Meadows State Park and skiing at Mohawk Mountain. It is also famous—perhaps infamous—for its roller-coaster-like terrain: Steep hills plunge into low valleys that climb back up steep hills and dip again (you get the picture).

The trip described here avoids the most daunting hills but takes in the loveliest scenery. Glide through the quaint and historic downtown, passing the town hall, the library, and a church. Follow a wide, quiet road that rolls through a valley, with pastures and then a hemlock forest stretching to the hills on each side. On the return trip, your approach to town affords a delightful view of the buildings nestled on a knoll, demonstrating once again that the same route looks different on the way back.

ROUTE DIRECTIONS:
- 0.0 Head south through Cornwall center on Pine Street.
- 0.3 Turn left onto Valley Road.
- 0.5 Bear right, still on Valley Road.
- 1.5 A stream trickles alongside the road on your right.
- 1.8 Bear right as Everett Hill Road heads left.
- 2.0 Begin a moderate ascent as the road narrows.
- 2.2 Crest the steeper section, still trending gently upward.
- 2.5 As the road steepens and narrows in a thick hemlock forest, turn around and return to your car the way you came.

11 •••• *Mohawk Mountain Ski Area*

LOCATION: Cornwall, CT
RATING: Intermediate
DISTANCE: 4.8 miles
TIMES TO AVOID: None
TERRAIN: Gently rolling
SURFACE: Smooth and moderate asphalt

If you head to Mohawk Mountain in the spring, you can skate while your family members ski.

AUTO TRAFFIC: Very light

POINTS OF INTEREST: Mohawk Mountain Park and Forest, Housatonic Meadows State Park and Housatonic Forest, Cathedral Pines, historic Litchfield, White Memorial Foundation and Conservation Center, White Flower Farm, Lime Rock Park (sports-car road racing), Macedonia Brook State Park

DRIVING DIRECTIONS: From CT 8, take exit 44 (downtown Torrington) to CT 4. Take CT 4 West and in 6.5 miles continue straight through the rotary where CT 4 intersects CT 63. In another 5.4 miles, turn left onto Great Hollow Road, following signs to Mohawk Mountain Ski Area. Drive 0.3 mile and park in the Mohawk Mountain Ski Area parking lot.

TRIP OVERVIEW: In springtime, skaters and skiers meet at Mohawk Mountain. (We enjoyed this skate while the ski area was in operation!) Follow gently rolling Great Hollow Road, appropriately named with Mohawk's sweeping slope dominating on the left side. The smooth, dead-end road sees little traffic, leaving you free to relax and enjoy the views of the Mohawk Mountain Ski Area and surrounding Mohawk State Forest. It's classified as an intermediate route, but if you're an experienced beginner, give it a try!

Après-skate, be daring: Rent a kayak or canoe (try Clarke Outdoors in West Cornwall), or go horseback riding at Lee's Riding Stable in East Litchfield. And if you feel like a real change of pace, stop by

Lime Rock Park, where the race may be among vintage cars or turbo-charged prototypes.

ROUTE DIRECTIONS:
0.0 From the parking area, turn left onto Great Hollow Road. Begin on gently rolling hills that continue for the route's duration.
1.2 Stay to the right on Great Hollow Road, avoiding Great Hill Road, which veers left.
2.0 Continue straight as Everest Hill Road leaves on your right; begin a brief ascent.
2.4 The road ends; return to your car.

12 •••• *Mohawk State Forest & Mountain*

LOCATION: Cornwall, CT
RATING: Expert
DISTANCE: 5.4 miles
TIMES TO AVOID: Spring (because of sand on the road)
TERRAIN: One long, difficult hill
SURFACE: Smooth and coarse asphalt
AUTO TRAFFIC: Very light
POINTS OF INTEREST: Mohawk Mountain Park and Forest, Cathedral Pines, Cornwall's covered bridge, White Memorial Foundation and Conservation Center, White Flower Farm, Lime Rock Park (sports-car road racing), Kent Falls, Macedonia Brook State Park

DRIVING DIRECTIONS: From CT 8, take exit 44 (downtown Torrington) to CT 4. Take CT 4 West and in 6.5 miles continue straight through the rotary where CT 4 intersects CT 63. Drive 4.1 miles and turn left into the Mohawk State Forest; park in the ample parking lot just off CT 4.

TRIP OVERVIEW: Very few of the New England mountain summits are accessible by road, and only one of these roads is manageable on skates—the road to the top of Mohawk Mountain. Expect to tax your lungs as you push up the narrow park road for 2.5 miles, then prepare to brake—a lot—on the stiff descent. In between these two extremes, though, you'll enjoy lovely views from the summit to far-off Bear Mountain, Connecticut's highest peak (and afterward, you'll have lots to brag about!).

ROUTE DIRECTIONS:

0.0 Skate along the narrow park road through thick woods, trending upward for 1 mile.

0.9 Well water may be available on the right side of the road.

1.1 At a parking overlook, crest, rest, and enjoy distant northwesterly views to Bear Mountain.

1.4 Turn right, still on the park road, as Allyn Road goes left. Follow signs for the picnic area and observation tower.

1.5 As the road bends left, look right to glimpse the top of the Mohawk Mountain Ski Area.

1.7 With a picnic area on your left and a stone tower hidden in the woods on your right, begin a series of upward steps to the summit.

2.3 Pump up a steep ascent that stretches 0.4 mile and leads you to the top.

2.7 Arrive at the summit. Enjoy the panoramas, an energy bar, and a reprieve before heading down the mountain to your car.
     ▼ CAUTION: Significant braking is required on the first 0.4 mile of the descent.

SKATING TIP: *To increase the intensity of a workout, alternate 10 quick short strokes with 10 slow long strokes. Repeat this drill for at least 5 minutes.*

---

13 •••• *Woodridge Lake*

LOCATION: Goshen, CT
RATING: Intermediate
DISTANCE: 7.6 miles
TIMES TO AVOID: None
TERRAIN: Gently rolling, with two moderate hills
SURFACE: Smooth asphalt
AUTO TRAFFIC: Very light
POINTS OF INTEREST: Mohawk Mountain Park and Forest, Housatonic Meadows State Park and Housatonic Forest, historic Litchfield, White Memorial Foundation and Conservation Center, White Flower Farm, Lime Rock Park, Haight Vineyard, Lourdes in Litchfield Shrine Grotto

The roads rimming Woodridge Lake are ideal for skating, running, walking, or cycling.

DRIVING DIRECTIONS: From CT 8, take exit 44 (downtown Torrington) to CT 4. Take CT 4 West. In 6.5 miles, continue straight through the rotary where CT 4 intersects CT 63; in 1.5 miles, turn left onto Beech Steet; in another 0.2 mile, turn right onto Shelbourne Steet. Drive 0.7 mile and turn right onto West Hyerdale Drive. Bear left at all intersections. In 1.7 miles, park in the cul-de-sac.

TRIP OVERVIEW: Less than 30 years ago, the Woodridge Lake resort area was just a river surrounded by pasture in a sleepy farming community. Now it encompasses a 400-acre lake, and strict regulations determine what type of homes will be built within its boundaries (substantial contemporaries only), what color they will be painted (earth tones), and how many trees will be cut down in the building process (very few). The result is a visual feast for anyone who appreciates cutting-edge architecture and magnificent landscaping; it is the antithesis of the typical summer lake community with rustic cabins jockeying for water frontage.

Though the roads are public, the lake is private, and the club-house, beach, and pool are for the use of property owners only. But you will enjoy feeling like part of this special community as you skate along a road that follows the contour of the lake with a row of spectacular homes separating you from the water (but nearly constant water views). The roads have no shoulder but are wide enough to accommodate the skaters, cyclists, and runners who outnumber the cars. At the halfway point, take a break near the spillway and enjoy the peaceful water views before retracing the route to your car.

ROUTE DIRECTIONS:

0.0 Reverse your driving route along West Hyerdale Drive.

0.7 ▼ CAUTION: A challenging little descent drops you down near lake level.

0.9 Regain the elevation you just lost by pushing up a short, tough ascent.

1.1 ● STOP. On a gradual descent, turn right at a stop sign, still on West Hyerdale Drive.

1.3 ▼ CAUTION: The road narrows and descends on a right bend between guardrails.

1.7 As the road widens, continue straight on West Hyerdale Drive as Shelbourne Street turns left.

2.8 As Sherbrooke Road joins from the left, stay straight.

2.9 ▼ CAUTION: Descend, then pass the Woodridge Lake clubhouse entrance. Watch for traffic entering and exiting, especially on weekends.

3.2 Continue straight as Brynmoore Court enters from the left.

3.4 Stay straight as Marshpaug Road joins on your left.

3.5 Continue straight as Woodale intersects Hyerdale on your right.

3.7 Turn right, rolling down Wynwood Court.

3.8 As the road ends, arrive at the spillway. Turn around and return to your car the way you came.

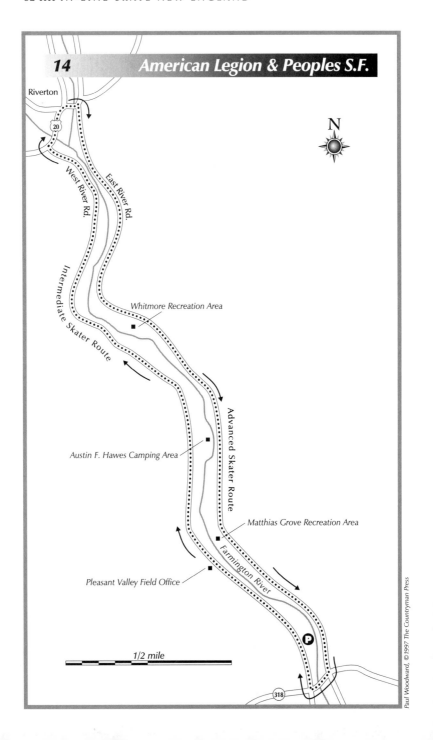

14   *American Legion & Peoples S.F.*

Riverton

20

West River Rd.

East River Rd.

N

Intermediate Skater Route

Whitmore Recreation Area

Advanced Skater Route

Austin F. Hawes Camping Area

Matthias Grove Recreation Area

Farmington River

Pleasant Valley Field Office

1/2 mile

P

318

Paul Woodward, ©1997 The Countryman Press

14 •••• *American Legion & Peoples State Forests*

LOCATION: Riverton, CT
RATING: Intermediate or advanced
DISTANCE: 7.4 miles (intermediate); 8.6 miles (advanced)
TIMES TO AVOID: None
TERRAIN: Flat and gently rolling
SURFACE: Smooth and coarse asphalt
AUTO TRAFFIC: Light
POINTS OF INTEREST: Historic Hitchcock Manufacturing Museum, American Legion and Peoples State Forests (hiking, camping, and picnicking), the Farmington River (fishing and canoeing)

DRIVING DIRECTIONS: From the junction of CT 8 and US 44 in Winsted, head east on US 44. At the blinking yellow light in 3 miles, turn left on CT 318 North (following signs to Bradley International Airport). In 0.8 mile, turn left at the stop sign (before the bridge) onto West River Road, guided by a sign to Riverton. Drive 0.4 mile and park in a gravel turnout on your right.

TRIP OVERVIEW: As you roll along West River Road, you'll pass campers clustered around fires, fishermen casting into the river, and hikers exploring the woods. With the Farmington River on your right and the American Legion State Forest on your left, you'll be surrounded by all types of outdoor enthusiasts. The road, though shoulderless, is relatively straight and wide, with few homes and light traffic. As you skate out—against the flow of the river—the road rises gently. You'll barely notice the gradual elevation gain, but you'll relish the faster, easier skate on the way back. Advanced skaters may elect to return along the road that follows the opposite bank of the Farmington River, winding through Peoples State Forest. This road is quite narrow and has more twists and turns, but it's an option for experienced skaters who prefer to take in different sights on the return leg.

ROUTE DIRECTIONS:
0.0 Roll along West River Road—heading toward Riverton—with the Farmington River rushing beside you on your right.
0.3 Enter the American Legion State Forest and soon begin one of the route's two gradual ascents.
0.7 Pass the Pleasant Valley Field Office on your left as you lose the elevation gained at the 0.3-mile mark.

1.5 On a wider stretch of road, pass the Austin F. Hawes camping area on your right.

2.0 Sweep closer to the river's edge, passing access to hiking trails.

3.1 Emerge from the forest and rejoin civilization, passing a baseball field (Riverton Field) on your right.

3.7 ● STOP. INTERMEDIATE SKATERS should return to their cars via the outbound route. ADVANCED SKATERS may elect to return by way of a different route: Turn right and stay far right on the narrow shoulder of busy US 20 as you endure a short section through Riverton.

4.0 Turn right onto narrow East River Road (following signs to Peoples State Forest), and roll up and over easy hills on twists and turns.

4.4 Approach the river on your right with a precipitous hillside on your left.

4.7 Enter Peoples State Forest.

5.0 Negotiate a moderate, left-bending descent.

5.3 Cruise by Whittemore Recreation Area before passing hiking trailheads.

7.1 Pass Matthias Grove Recreation Area on your right.

7.9 Encounter the first houses on this side of the river.

8.1 ● STOP. Turn right onto CT 181 and cross the bridge over the Farmington River.

8.2 Turn right, now back on West River Road.

8.6 Return to your car.

15 •••• *Farmington Valley Greenway*

LOCATION: Simsbury, CT
RATING: Beginner
DISTANCE: 4.2 miles
TIMES TO AVOID: None
TERRAIN: Flat path
SURFACE: Smooth asphalt with a gravel path running parallel
AUTO TRAFFIC: None
POINTS OF INTEREST: Massacoh Plantation, Talcott Mountain State Park (Heublein Tower), Avon's Living Museum, McLean Game Refuge, Holcomb Farm, Old New-Gate Prison and Copper Mine, Tariffville Gorge (white-water canoeing and kayaking)

DRIVING DIRECTIONS: Less than 0.5 mile north of the intersection of CT 10/US 202 and CT 167/CT 309 in Simsbury, head east on Drake Hill Road. Drive 0.2 mile; turn right onto Old Bridge Road. Park in the small lot near the restored bridge spanning the Farmington River.

TRIP OVERVIEW: As you drive through Simsbury, passing art galleries, chic restaurants, and oh-so-trendy boutiques, you may decide to leave your skates in the backseat for a few hours and explore the town!

When you're ready to swap sneakers for skates, endure a short stint on Old Bridge Road, then a brief roll along a sidewalk, before diving into the woods on the wide, paved Farmington Valley Greenway. It's an easy skate along flat terrain, and with an adjacent dirt path for walkers and runners, you won't be preoccupied with darting around crowds. Pleasant surroundings—the lively Farmington River (which bisects Simsbury) bordered by wildflower meadows—make the 4 miles pass too quickly. The pastoral surroundings may take you by surprise— after all, you're just 20 minutes from the state capital. Simsbury residents are dedicated to maintaining the rural feel of this former farming town—more than one-quarter of the land has been set aside as open space.

Fortunately, the trail may soon become part of the proposed 88-mile Farmington Valley trail system, which will include the Farmington River Trail, Farmington Valley Greenway, and the Farmington Canal Heritage Trail. The plan targets 1999 as the year of completion.

ROUTE DIRECTIONS:

0.0 From the parking lot, head back the way you came to Drake Hill Road, watching for signs for the bike path.

0.2 Cross the street and join the path, which runs along Iron Horse Boulevard (essentially a sidewalk, which is lined with lilies in summer). Watch as you pass the downtown shops, and plan your postskate stops.

0.9 ▼ CAUTION: Watch for entering and exiting vehicles at the access to the Simscroft Farms General Contractors facility.

1.1 The trail splits right (north) into the woods, leaving Iron Horse Boulevard (now running parallel to it). Here the path widens; a gravel path runs alongside it for pedestrians.

1.4 Roll below CT 10/US 202, which runs along the left side of the path. Rest, if you need to, on pathside benches and boulders.

1.6 The road has risen to run alongside the trail; briefly join the Farmington River.

1.8 Enjoy the views across meadows blanketed with wildflowers.

2.1 At the junction of CT 315 and CT 10/US 202, the finished trail ends. Turn and follow the path back to Old Bridge Road and your car. Return to the restored bridge, a perfect spot for a postskate rest.

16 •••• Farmington Canal Linear Park

LOCATION: Cheshire and Hamden, CT
RATING: Beginner
DISTANCE: 3.0 miles or 8.0 miles
TIMES TO AVOID: In-season weekends at midday
TERRAIN: Flat path
SURFACE: Smooth asphalt
AUTO TRAFFIC: None on paths; light at intersections (▼ CAUTION: Cars do not have stop signs)
POINTS OF INTEREST: Farmington Canal, Lock 12 Museum, Bishop Farm (apple orchard and winery), South Brooksvale Park (petting zoo), Mixvale Pond (swimming, picnicking), Cheshire Historical Society's Phillips House

DRIVING DIRECTIONS: From I-84, take exit 26. Follow CT 70 East toward Cheshire to CT 10 South. At the junction of CT 10 South and CT 42 (North Brooksvale Road), turn west and follow CT 42 for about 1 mile past a church and school. Park in the ample lot at Lock 12 on your left.

TRIP OVERVIEW: Completed in 1828, the Farmington Canal stretched 83 miles, linking the busy New Haven seaport with a number of towns from Hamden, Connecticut, to Northampton, Massachusetts. It was a monumental feat for the time, accomplished entirely by men using animals and simple tools. A railroad replaced the canal in 1848. In recent years, the former canal was converted for use by outdoor enthusiasts. Work continues on an extension to the 4-mile southerly path in the town of Hamden.

The flat, 12-foot-wide path that follows the banks of the canal is ideal for skaters of all ability levels. The route's only drawback is its popularity. The well-maintained path is frequently congested on weekends and on weekdays before and after work hours with dog-walkers,

C. BRADLEY

Pause to admire the restored Lock Number 12 in the Farmington Canal Linear Park.

groups of parents and toddlers, birdwatchers, and runners. Skaters must stay alert and expect to shout frequent warnings: "On your left!" or "Heads up!" The trail is open to skaters and others each day from sunrise to sunset (and is plowed in winter).

ROUTE DIRECTIONS:

- *3.0-MILE NORTHERN ROUTE.* From the parking area, head north. Cross the street; locate the designated trail entrance. (Skate on the right-hand side of the path.)
- 0.3 Pass over the wooden bridge.
- 0.5 The path hugs the canal.
- 0.6 ● STOP. Cross Higgins Road. (Cars have a blind rise prior to this intersection; use caution as you cross.)
- 1.4 Cross a second wooden bridge.
- 1.5 The trail ends at Cornwall Avenue. Return to your car the way you came.

- *8.0-MILE SOUTHERN ROUTE.* From the parking lot, skate down the wheelchair ramp and head southward on the path. (Skate on the right-hand side of the path.)
- 0.1 Roll over a stone arch bridge and the restored Lock 12. (Perhaps you'll spot a turtle in the canal below!)

0.4 Relax, if you'd like, on the sandy area on the canal's bank.

0.5 ● STOP. Cross South Brooksvale Road.

1.1 Follow the path over a wooden bridge.

1.3 ● STOP. Cross Mt. Sandford Road (Hamden/Cheshire town line).

1.7 Continue straight as a path exits right to Brooksvale Park. The gravel path paralleling the paved route drifts right, allowing hikers and runners to run directly alongside the canal.

2.5 Pass a Christmas tree farm on your left.

3.1 ● STOP. Cross River Road.

3.5 The path now runs parallel to CT 10 in a commercial area. Several stores and restaurants near the path are especially welcoming to skaters.

3.7 ● STOP. Cross Shepard Avenue.

3.8 Skate over an elegant cedar arch bridge with a brook rushing 20 feet below. Pause for a water break if you need one.

4.0 The trail ends at Todd Street. Return to your car the way you came.

17 •••• *Captain John Bissell Bridge*

LOCATION: Windsor and South Windsor, CT

RATING: Beginner

DISTANCE: 4.0 miles

TIMES TO AVOID: None

TERRAIN: Flat path and quiet country road

SURFACE: Smooth asphalt

AUTO TRAFFIC: None on paths, light on roads

POINTS OF INTEREST: New England Air Museum, Nook Farm (including homes of Mark Twain and Harriet Beecher Stowe), Wood Memorial Library and Indian Museum, Connecticut Trolley Museum, Wadsworth Atheneum, Museum of Connecticut History, Riverside Park

DRIVING DIRECTIONS: From I-91, take exit 34 (CT 159 North). Drive 0.7 mile on CT 159 and turn right onto East Barber Street. In about 1 mile, arrive at the state boat launch on the Connecticut River (with the Bissell Bridge on your left). Park in the ample lot on your left.

TRIP OVERVIEW: As you follow this route, you'll have to keep reminding yourself that you're just 20 minutes from downtown Hartford.

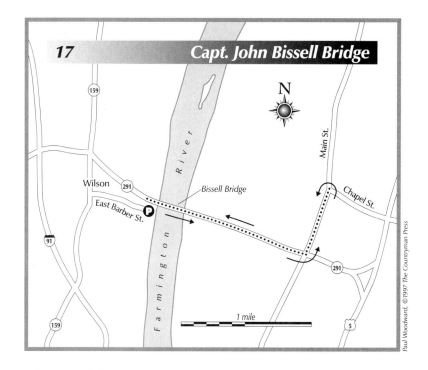

After an exhilarating half-mile skate across the Bissell Bridge (which carries CT 291), you'll roll into South Windsor, a tranquil, unassuming farm town. Cruise leisurely along the wide Main Street, thinking back to a time when everyone's activities revolved around the soda shop, the five-and-dime, and the white-steepled church at the head of the town common.

The path beyond the bridge will eventually join the Captain John Bissell Greenway, which runs 2 miles along CT 291, and the Charter Oak Greenway (Tour 18).

ROUTE DIRECTIONS:

0.0 From the parking lot, skate on the bike path that leads to the Bissell Bridge. Roll along the bridge's pedestrian path, which is well protected from the heavily trafficked CT 291. ▼ CAUTION: The pavement may be sandy.

0.3 Pause to enjoy the views from the bridge and to drink in the cool breeze.

0.5 At the end of the bridge, continue to roll beside the highway on a smooth path.

1.0 Travel along busy CT 291.

1.4 The path intersects with Main Street in South Windsor; turn left. This road, primarily residential, sees little traffic.

2.0 As Chapel Road joins from your right, turn around and return to your car for a total 4-mile loop. (Or, for added mileage, continue to cruise along Main Street before heading back.)

18 •••• *Charter Oak Greenway*

LOCATION: Hartford, East Hartford, and Manchester, CT
RATING: Intermediate
DISTANCE: 11.4 miles
TIMES TO AVOID: None
TERRAIN: Gentle rolling hills on path and short distance on road
SURFACE: Smooth asphalt with some coarse asphalt
AUTO TRAFFIC: None on the path, light on the short stretch of road
POINTS OF INTEREST: Connecticut River, Charter Oak Park (with tennis, basketball, playground), Cheney Homestead, Connecticut Firemen's Historical Society Museum, Lutz Children's Museum, Manchester Historical Museum, Hockanum River (guided walks)

DRIVING DIRECTIONS: From I-91, follow I-84 East to I-384 East. (*Note:* The path is visible from the highway.) Take exit 3 (CT 83) and turn right. At the first traffic light, in 0.1 mile, turn right onto Charter Oak Street. Drive 0.2 mile and turn right into Charter Oak Park (where you'll find plenty of free parking).

TRIP OVERVIEW: The Charter Oak Greenway, leaving from Charter Oak Park in Manchester, is a work in progress. The greenway currently connects with the Captain John Bissell Greenway and will expand as Hartford improves sections of interstate highway. Eventually, this paved path will join the River Front Recapture route along the Connecticut River and the Charter Oak Bridge.

For now, think of the path as a diamond in the rough. As you follow beside I-384 for much of the way, the frequent hills will satisfy anyone looking for some leg burn. The path also skirts parks and the Manchester Community Technical College campus. The route joins the road for 1 mile, but you can avoid that section by starting your trip from the parking lot at the community college.

ROUTE DIRECTIONS:

0.0 From the parking lot, head back the way you came by car. Turn left and ▼ (with CAUTION) cross Charter Oak Street; turn left again.

0.1 Skate along Charter Oak Street, rolling up a short hill to a traffic light. Turn left, and again carefully cross Charter Oak Street to join the sidewalk.

0.2 Skate on a bridge that passes over I-384.

0.4 Immediately after the bridge, join the path on your left.

0.7 Roll beside I-384.

1.0 Pump up the route's steepest hill.

1.3 ▼ CAUTION: Cross Prospect Street.

1.5 Push up a brief, easy ascent.

1.7 The path ends at Keeney Street. Turn right (following the bicycle route signs) and skate over I-384.

1.8 ▼ CAUTION: At the intersection of Keeney Street and Hartford Road, cross Hartford Road and continue on the bike route, which is now along the shoulder of Hartford Road.

2.6 Guided by bike route signs, turn left onto Bidwell Street.

2.7 ▼ CAUTION: Skate gingerly over choppy pavement.

2.8 Turn right into the entrance for Manchester Technical Community College. (*Note:* There is ample parking in the college lot for those who want to join the bike route here, eliminating the road skating.)

3.0 Head up an easy rise as the path cuts through the campus, dodging tennis courts and playing fields.

3.5 Dive into thick woods.

4.0 Cruise alongside I-384.

4.5 ● STOP. Cross Spencer Street, now in a more industrial area.

5.0 Continue straight as a path to Wickham Park splits right. (*Note:* This path intersects with the Captain John Bissell Greenway, about 2 miles of paved paths, which you can explore to add 4 miles to your total trip.)

5.4 You are treated to pleasing views of the Hartford skyline as you pump up a gentle riser. A path leaves on your left for Veterans' Memorial Park.

5.7 The path ends (for now) at Silver Lane. Turn and head back to your car the way you came.

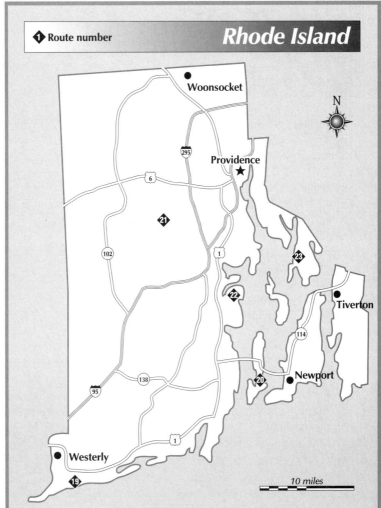

Route number

Rhode Island

Woonsocket

295

Providence

6

21

102

23

1

22

Tiverton

114

138

95

20

Newport

1

Westerly

19

N

10 miles

Paul Woodward, ©1997 The Countryman Press

•••• *Part Two*

Rhode Island

19 •••• *Misquamicut State Beach*

LOCATION: Westerly, RI
RATING: Intermediate
DISTANCE: 6.0 miles
TIMES TO AVOID: Summer weekends (because of increased auto traffic)
TERRAIN: Flat beach road with narrow shoulder
SURFACE: Initially coarse asphalt, then smoother
AUTO TRAFFIC: Heavy (but slow moving) on summer weekends
POINTS OF INTEREST: Westerly beaches, Watch Hill Lighthouse Museum, Watch Hill Beach and Napatree Point, Historic Flying Horse Carousel, Water Wizz (waterslide park), historic Wilcox Park, Block Island Ferry, Ninigret Conservation Area

DRIVING DIRECTIONS: From I-95 in Rhode Island, take exit 1 (Westerly, Hopkington, RI 3). From the exit ramp, follow signs for BEACHES and MISQUAMICUT STATE PARK. In 1.7 miles, drive through the village of Ashaway. At the 4.4-mile mark, turn left at a traffic light onto RI 78 East (also known as the Westerly bypass). Drive 2.3 miles to the junction of US 1 at a traffic light. Drive straight onto Airport Road; 1.2 miles from the junction with US 1, turn left onto Winnapaug Road. In another 0.7 mile, continue straight across US 1A. Drive another 0.8 mile and turn left onto Atlantic Avenue (at a traffic light). In 0.5 mile, turn right into the parking lot for Misquamicut State Beach. (Pay a moderate in-season parking fee.)

TRIP OVERVIEW: The Westerly area, a favorite seaside vacation spot for more than a century, offers something for everyone. Watch Hill, an elegant, Victorian-style village, was once the retreat for Groucho Marx, Douglas Fairbanks, and Clark Gable, among others. Watch Hill Beach and Napatree Point are popular with beachgoers; the historic Flying Horse Carousel takes a steady stream of children up and down and around and around all summer long. Westerly and nearby Pawcatuck, Connecticut, have bustling centers that provide the necessities for visitors, and Misquamicut is crammed with all of the typical touristy shops that appeal to families on vacation. (If this isn't your scene, come during the off-season.)

On this skating trip, you'll leave from an action-packed area, then roll into more peaceful surroundings, passing traditional New England homes covered in weathered shakes with wide porches facing the water. Cruise beside Misquamicut State Beach—a strip of land bisecting

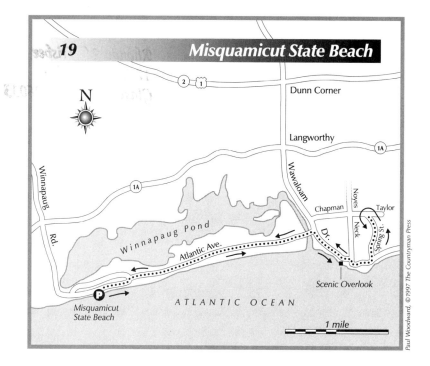

Block Island Sound and Winnapaug Pond—on the shoulder of Atlantic Avenue. Head back when you reach the Weekapaug Inn.

ROUTE DIRECTIONS:

0.0 From the parking lot, turn right onto Atlantic Avenue.

0.6 Pass the Westerly Town Beach on your right.

0.9 Summer cottages line both sides of the road.

1.3 Take in views of Winnapaug Pond.

1.9 Cruise by the Seaside Beach Club on your right.

2.0 Cross the short Weekapaug Bridge spanning the Weekapaug Breachway.

2.1 Turn right onto Wawaloam Drive.

2.3 Arrive at a scenic overlook with views of Block Island Sound (a popular picnic spot).

2.6 ● STOP. At the stop sign, turn right onto Noyes Neck Road, then turn immediately left onto Meadow Avenue, which has more great water views.

2.7 Turn right onto Spring Avenue and curve left.

3.0 The road ends at the Weekapaug Inn. Turn around and head back along the beach.

20 •••• *East Shore Road, Jamestown*

LOCATION: Jamestown, RI
RATING: Intermediate
DISTANCE: 7.8 miles
TIMES TO AVOID: None
TERRAIN: Flat rural road with no shoulder
SURFACE: Coarse asphalt
AUTO TRAFFIC: Light
POINTS OF INTEREST: Beavertail Lighthouse, Quaker meetinghouse, Fort Wetherill State Park, Revolutionary Earthworks Battery (splendid views), Sydney L. Wright Museum, Watson Farm, Fort Getty State Park, Newport mansions, Rhode Island Fisherman and Whale Museum, White Horse Tavern, Newport Aquarium

Rhonda M. Frisbee
17 Upland Way
Glastonbury, CT 06033

DRIVING DIRECTIONS: From I-95 in Rhode Island, take exit 3 (RI 138 East/Newport and Kingsport). Drive 19 miles to the Jamestown-Verrazano Bridge. Drive another 1.8 miles beyond the bridge, still on RI 138 East, and exit at the sign for Jamestown (just before the Newport Bridge). In 0.3 mile, turn left onto East Shore Road. Drive 0.3 mile to the stop sign; continue straight, still on East Shore Road. In another 0.3 mile, at an intersection with Seaview Avenue, park along the side of the road.

TRIP OVERVIEW: At the mouth of Narragansett Bay, Conanicut Island (also referred to as Jamestown, the island's only town) offers a terrific alternative to skating in Newport. (Newport officials are working to institute a ban on skating in the downtown area.) Roll along quiet East Shore Road (speed limit: 25 mph) that flaunts a succession of grand homes and even grander views across the water to downtown Newport. When the road occasionally approaches the shoreline, feel the refreshing breeze and glimpse sailboats whispering across the bay. East Shore Road concludes at the intersection with a private gravel road.

The island has an interesting and checkered past. The Quakers arrived in the 1650s to farm the land and raise sheep. A Quaker meetinghouse, built in 1786, still stands in the center of the island near the Jamestown Windmill. The British occupied the island during the Revolutionary War; Fort Wetherill State Park, on the island's southeastern tip, is the site of an American fort and artillery battery. If you're feeling lucky, visit the park's Pirate Cave after your skate—this is where Captain Kidd is supposed to have stashed some of his booty!

ROUTE DIRECTIONS:

0.0 Head north on East Shore Road.

0.3 Push up a gentle climb for 0.2 mile.

0.5 As RI 138 West intersects on your left, the road becomes more residential.

0.8 Glide by a cemetery on your left.

1.0 Pass Reservoir Circle on your left.

1.1 Roll down a gradual slope with pleasing views of open fields on your left.

1.4 Take in views of Narragansett Bay.

1.6 Cruise by a small beach on your right.

2.4 Pass Holmestead Court on your right.

2.7 Enjoy more bay views.

3.3 Continue along East Shore Road as Fairview Street intersects on your right.

3.6 Enjoy panoramic views of the bay and Newport mansions.

3.9 At the intersection with Summit Road (a gravel road), turn and head back to your car.

SKATING TIP: Consistency is the key to maintaining or improving your fitness level. Aerobic conditioning is recommended three to five times per week for at least 20 minutes each time. This includes skating, running, walking, cycling, and even skipping!

21 •••• *Scituate Reservoir*

LOCATION: Scituate, RI
RATING: Advanced
DISTANCE: 12.0 miles
TIMES TO AVOID: None
TERRAIN: Designated bike path on the shoulder of a rolling country road
SURFACE: Coarse asphalt
AUTO TRAFFIC: Light
POINTS OF INTEREST: Seagrave Memorial Observatory, Benefit Street's Mile of History, Arcade Building, Federal Hill, John Brown House, Roger Williams Landing Place Monument, Roger Williams Park and Zoo, Waterplace Park and River Walk

DRIVING DIRECTIONS: From I-95 in Rhode Island, take exit 15 for Cranston/RI 10. Head straight, following signs for RI 10 TO RI 12 PARK AVENUE; in 0.5 mile, join RI 10 North. Drive 0.5 mile and bear right onto RI 12 West. Drive 9 miles on RI 12 West to the Scituate Reservoir. Park on your right in the area for the Gainer Memorial Dam.

TRIP OVERVIEW: Skating along the water—whether it's a bay, a river, or a pond—is always delightful. But when the water is a reservoir, the surface undisturbed by boats and the shorefront thick with trees rather than cottages, it's a particular pleasure. This spot is made all the more desirable by the fact that a designated bike shoulder runs along RI 12, which is lightly traveled at this point. In addition to the water views, you'll roll by farms and farmland, a number of lovely churches, and some pleasant neighborhoods.

There are two ways to skate this route: You can begin at the dam, soaking in the delightful views, and then embark on the trip; or, if you like to have something to look forward to, follow the skate directions in reverse. Park at the DB Mart and skate (relishing the anticipation) to the dam for the awesome vista.

After the skate, head into Providence for some sight-seeing. The award-winning Roger Williams Park & Zoo houses more than 900 animals, including polar bears and penguins, and has a new tropical rainforest area. Stop by the zoo's Carousel Village and the planetarium before you leave. For art buffs, the highly regarded Rhode Island School of Design runs a Museum of Art that displays masterpieces from the early Middle Ages to the present and a gallery that features students' and professors' artwork. Prospect Terrace, with its panoramic view of the city's skyline, rounds out the city's "something-for-everyone" theme.

ROUTE DIRECTIONS:
- 0.0 From the parking area, turn left onto RI 12 East. (The bike path runs along both sides of the road; be sure to travel with the traffic on both legs of the trip.)
- 0.4 Push up a short, easy hill.
- 0.5 ▼ CAUTION: Cross RI 116 and then embark on a steep 0.4-mile climb.
- 1.0 Roll by farms and neighborhoods.
- 1.2 Pass open fields on your left.
- 1.7 On your right, cruise by Hank and Judy's Homestead.
- 2.0 Glide by the Holy Apostle Church on your left.
- 2.8 Get into a rhythm as you climb gently for 0.2 mile.

3.1 Roll gently downhill.

3.8 ▼ CAUTION: Cross Comstock Parkway.

4.0 Push up a slight hill for 0.2 mile as the road bends right.

4.3 Drop steeply for 0.1 mile.

4.5 RI 12 crosses over I-295.

5.3 Descend steeply for 0.2 mile.

6.0 The bike path ends at the intersection with RI 5 (with a DB Mart on your right). Grab a snack and head back to your car.

SKATING TIP: *In speed-skating technique, when one foot is going forward, the opposite arm should swing forward with it, thumb up.*

---

22 •••• *Goddard Memorial State Park*

LOCATION: East Greenwich, RI

RATING: Beginner

DISTANCE: 3.6 miles

TIMES TO AVOID: Summer weekends

TERRAIN: Flat park road

SURFACE: Smooth asphalt

AUTO TRAFFIC: Light

POINTS OF INTEREST: Goddard Memorial State Park, General James Mitchell Varnum House Museum, Varnum Military Museum, Benefit Street's Mile of History, the Arcade Building, Rhode Island School of Design's Museum of Art, Roger Williams Park and Zoo, Waterplace Park and River Walk

DRIVING DIRECTIONS: From I-95 in Rhode Island, take exit 8A/B (East Greenwich RI 2/RI 4). Drive 0.1 mile on RI 2 and turn left onto RI 401 East. In 2.5 miles, turn right onto US 1 South. Drive 0.5 mile and turn left onto Forge Road, following a sign for Goddard State Park. Turn left in 2 miles at the park entrance. Drive 0.2 mile to the gatehouse and pay a moderate (out-of-state) fee. Beyond the gatehouse, drive 0.1 mile and bear right, following signs for the beaches. Pass the Carousel Performing Arts Center in 0.2 mile and bear right. Park in the beach parking lot.

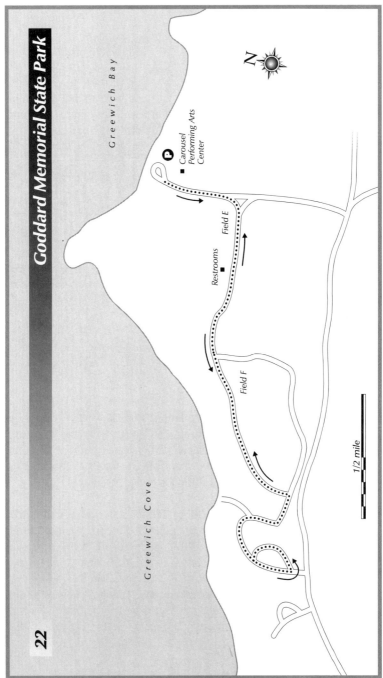

TRIP OVERVIEW: More than a century ago, a man named Henry Russell began to plant trees on his property along the barren shore of Greenwich Cove. For 30 years he coaxed seedlings into taking root in the sandy soil. After his death, another man dedicated to private forestry, Colonel Goddard, continued the effort for two more decades. Today the 500-acre Goddard Memorial Park is the result, a lovely public area that welcomes hikers, horseback riders, swimmers, picnickers, golfers, boaters, concertgoers, cross-country skiers, and, most important to us, in-line skaters.

Our route loops through the park on smooth asphalt, passing all of the park's facilities, including the golf course, the Carousel Performing Arts Center, and the fishing area. The impeccable grounds exude an air of opulence, more like a private club than a state-operated park. If you prefer to go it on your own (you won't get lost, promise), then grab a park map at the gatehouse. Beginning skaters (and nonskaters who come with them) will be delighted with this spot!

ROUTE DIRECTIONS:

0.0 From the parking lot, turn left, passing the Carousel Performing Arts Center.

0.3 Bear right at Field E.

0.4 Roll by (or visit!) rest rooms on your right.

0.7 Cruise along the golf course on the left side of the path.

0.8 At Field F, continue straight.

1.0 Roll down a gentle pitch for 0.1 mile.

1.1 The road bends left.

1.3 Now the road curves to the right.

1.5 Dip briefly; pass the boat-launch and fishing area on your right as the road bears left.

1.7 Continue to bear left with the road (as you loop back toward the boat-launch area).

2.2 Déjà vu: Cruise by the boat-ramp and fishing area again, this time on your left.

2.3 Climb a gentle hill.

2.7 Pass a picnic area on your left.

3.3 ● STOP. At a stop sign, bear left.

3.5 Pass the Carousel Performing Arts Center on your right.

3.6 Return to the parking lot.

23 ••••   *East Bay Bike Path*

LOCATION: East Providence, Barrington, Warren, and Bristol, RI
RATING: Beginner for most of the route; intermediate for the last mile
    in East Providence
DISTANCE: 27.4 miles (wow!)
TIMES TO AVOID: None
TERRAIN: 10-foot-wide paved path
SURFACE: Smooth asphalt
AUTO TRAFFIC: None
POINTS OF INTEREST: Coggeshall Farm Museum, Colt State Park,
    Blithewold Mansion and Gardens, Herreshoff Marine Museum,
    Haffenreffer Museum of Anthropology, Roger Williams Park &
    Zoo, Waterplace Park and River Walk, Crescent Park Carousel,
    Hannaway Blacksmith Shop, Barrington Civic Center Historic
    District, Maxwell House

DRIVING DIRECTIONS: From I-95 in Rhode Island, take exit 20 for I-195 East (Cape Cod). Drive about 5 miles on I-195 East to exit 7 (East Providence/RI 114). From the exit ramp, drive 0.3 mile and bear right onto RI 114 South. Drive 11 miles on RI 114 South and bear right onto Thames Street. In 0.1 mile, park on your right in the small parking lot for Independence Park.

    To begin the skate in East Providence, take I-95 in Rhode Island to exit 20 for I-195 East (Cape Cod). Drive about 2 miles to exit 2 (East Providence). As you exit, turn left onto Wickenden Street. Drive 0.6 mile and turn right onto Gano Street. Drive 0.1 mile and watch for the path entrance under I-195 on your left. Park along the road or at the nearby Days Inn Hotel. (*Note:* Just 0.2 mile from the path entrance is India Point Park on the Providence Harbor, with picnic sites and open fields.)

TRIP OVERVIEW: Rhode Island may be small, but like the other New England states, it offers a wide variety of terrain and scenery—from the flatter southern and eastern parts of the state to the more mountainous and thickly wooded areas to the north and west. Islands and many miles of coastline provide even more diversity. The state's two rail trails exemplify the contrasts, with the Trestle Trail cutting through woodlands and marshes in western Rhode Island (with a surface inappropriate for skaters) and the East Bay Bike Path traveling along the shore of Narragansett Bay through a number of urban areas with access to several state parks.

Follow the well-maintained bike path edged in wildflowers past Bristol Harbor and the Seekonk River, skirting beaches and exclusive waterfront neighborhoods. With a number of parking options, you can shorten the trip if you don't feel up to the entire 27.4 (whew!) miles. If you enjoy the offbeat, bustling Wickenden Avenue area near the campuses of Brown University and the Rhode Island School of Design, park there to begin the route. If you favor a more sedate locale, design your route to begin and end in Bristol, the town that brags about having the nation's oldest Fourth of July parade. (In fact, the dividing lines on the town's streets are red, white, and blue!)

If you decide to begin in East Providence, you will be required to skate up (and down, on the return trip) several ramps to reach the Washington Bridge, carrying I-195. You'll then need to skate 0.5 mile across the bridge (on a narrow path) and manage a steep descent. Beyond the bridge, you'll have to endure another 0.5 mile of road skating before reaching the paved path.

No matter where you begin, you'll be faced with a number of grade crossings (40 in all on this route). The larger intersections are mentioned in the route directions; the less significant ones are not.

ROUTE DIRECTIONS (FROM BRISTOL):
0.0 The East Bay Bike Path begins 0.1 mile north of the parking area.
0.2 Enjoy views across Narragansett Bay.
0.3 Grade crossing: Poppasquash Road.
0.9 Grade crossing: Asylum Road. (Alternative parking can be found at Colt State Park. *Note:* Skating is not permitted within the park.)
1.2 Grade crossing: Fales Road. As you enter a residential area, the path rolls by upscale bayside homes on your left.
1.4 Roll up a slight ascent for 0.1 mile.
1.8 Grade crossing: Gibson Road. Enjoy panoramic bay views.
2.8 Grade crossing: North Farm Drive. Enter the town of Warren.
3.6 Pass Burris Hill Park on your left, with shaded picnic sites and a town beach.
3.8 ▼ CAUTION: At a busy intersection, cross RI 114 and reconnect with the path on the other side of the street.
3.9 Grade crossing: Cherry Street and Franklin Street.
4.3 ▼ CAUTION: At a busy intersection, cross Child Street (RI 103).
4.6 Roll beside RI 114, behind Warren's downtown area.
4.7 Roll across the Palmer River Bridge (wooden, but skater-friendly), and enter the town of Barrington.
4.9 Grade crossing: New Meadow Road.

5.0 Head over the Barrington River Bridge; the path runs across the Barrington peninsula and rejoins the coast of Narragansett Bay.

5.5 ▼ CAUTION: At a busy intersection, cross RI 114 (Country Road).

5.8 Grade crossing: West Street.

6.2 Roll beside Brickyard Pond and Veterans' Memorial Park.

6.8 Grade crossing: Middle Highway.

7.5 Grade crossing: Washington Road. Enter a residential area.

7.8 Grade crossing: Bay Spring Avenue.

8.2 Grade crossing: Narragansett Avenue. Follow the path through Haines State Park (picnic tables and rest rooms available).

8.6 ▼ CAUTION: At a busy intersection, cross Crescent View Avenue. Roll through a wooded area abutting a neighborhood.

9.5 Grade crossing: Turner Avenue. Reach a market area called Riverside Square.

9.7 Grade crossing: Washington Street.

10.0 Revel in the views of Providence Harbor and the Cranston and Providence skylines.

10.8 Cruise alongside Providence Harbor.

10.9 Roll over the Burgess Cove Bridge.

11.6 Travel along a causeway dividing Providence Harbor and Watchmoket Cove.

11.9 Curve sharply to the right and undertake a steep 0.2-mile climb, staying on the right side of the path to avoid those descending.

12.1 Alternative parking is available off Veterans' Memorial Parkway.

12.8 Pass another alternative parking site.

12.9 ▼ CAUTION: A steep 0.2-mile descent leads to a grade crossing.

13.0 The path ends; INTERMEDIATE SKATERS should turn left onto First Street. BEGINNERS should return along the path to Independence Park.

13.1 Grade crossing: Mauran Avenue.

13.2 ▼ CAUTION: At a busy intersection, cross Warren Street.

13.3 Head across the Washington Bridge. ▼ CAUTION: Watch out for other skaters, joggers, and cyclists. Allow others to pass at the two places where you can step to one side. Also, avoid sandy patches in early spring.

13.6 ▼ CAUTION: At the end of the bridge, roll down a series of five ramps on your left (with handrails). If you are hesitant to use the ramps, take off your skates and walk down the stairs.

13.7 Skate back to your car or to Indian Point Park, 0.2 mile south on Gano Road.

SKATING TIP: *Extended periods of aerobic exercise will increase demand for oxygen. This type of exercise trains the cardiovascular system to process and deliver oxygen quickly and efficiently to every part of the body. As the heart muscle becomes stronger and more efficient, it pumps more blood with each beat. An athlete with an aerobically fit cardiovascular system will be able to work longer and more vigorously and recover more quickly.*

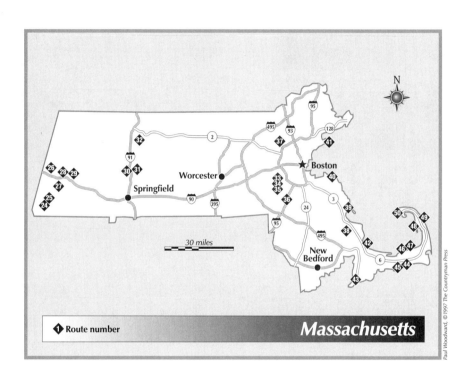

Route number

Massachusetts

Part Three

Massachusetts

24 •••• *Monument Valley Road*

LOCATION: Great Barrington, MA
RATING: Advanced
DISTANCE: 9.0 miles
TIMES TO AVOID: None
TERRAIN: Rolling hills on rural road with no shoulder
SURFACE: Coarse asphalt
AUTO TRAFFIC: Light
POINTS OF INTEREST: Monument Mountain Reservation, Beartown
    State Forest, Great Barrington State Forest, historic Stockbridge,
    Norman Rockwell Museum, Mission House (built in 1739—the
    first mission to the Mahican tribe), Berkshire Botanical Garden,
    the Red Lion Inn (1773), Indian burial grounds, Shaker Hancock
    Village

DRIVING DIRECTIONS: From I-90, take exit 2 (Lee/US 20) and turn
onto US 20 East. Drive 0.1 mile (under I-90) and turn right onto MA
102 West. In 4.5 miles, reach the center of Stockbridge. Turn left onto
US 7 South and drive another 2.5 miles to the parking lot for Monument Mountain Regional High School on your right.

TRIP OVERVIEW: This trip will not be a disappointment to those eager
for a solid workout. The hills are continuous along this challenging
route, but so are the spectacular views: You will have Monument
Mountain as a constant companion. The mountain gained attention
when poet William Cullen Bryant wrote about the Indian maiden who
long ago leaped off the summit when the man she loved rejected her.
(On the mountain's southern slope is a stone cairn said to have been
built in her memory by sympathetic members of her tribe.) In the summer of 1850 (or 1851—accounts vary), a group of notable authors,
including Herman Melville and Nathaniel Hawthorne, were caught in
a thunderstorm during a climb to the Monument summit. They passed
the hours downing champagne and reciting Bryant's poem as the storm
rumbled by. If you enjoy hiking (or literary history) as much as skating,
plan to visit in late July when the event is commemorated with the
annual Monument Mountain Author Climb. The hike to Squaw Peak
(at 1642 feet, the highest point in the reservation) offers super views of
the eastern valley and the Berkshires.
    If you're traveling with beginners, don't despair: The smooth
parking lot at Monument Mountain Regional High School is terrific turf

for skaters who need a little practice. (Tennis courts and a track are also available here for public use.)

ROUTE DIRECTIONS:

0.0 From the parking lot, return to US 7 and turn left. Stay on the left side of road because the right side has no shoulder.

0.1 Turn left onto Monument Valley Road, with the jagged cliffs of Monument Mountain on your right.

0.4 Muddy Brook Road turns right.

1.2 Pump up a steep incline and then execute a descent.

1.3 Roll by a dairy farm on your left. Mooo!

1.7 ▼ CAUTION: Tread carefully on sections of rough pavement.

2.0 Stony Brook Road intersects on your left.

2.8 Blue Hill Road joins on your right.

4.1 ▼ CAUTION: Watch for more chopped-up pavement.

4.5 At the intersection with MA 23, turn around and return to your car.

---

25 •••• *Housatonic River*

LOCATION: Great Barrington and Housatonic, MA

RATING: Intermediate

DISTANCE: 4.6 miles or 5.4 miles

TIMES TO AVOID: None

TERRAIN: Rural road with no shoulder and a few rolling hills

SURFACE: Smooth asphalt with some choppy sections

AUTO TRAFFIC: Light

POINTS OF INTEREST: Beartown State Forest, Great Barrington State Forest, Chesterwood (home/studio of sculptor Daniel Chester French), Norman Rockwell Museum, Naumkeag (historic mansion), Berkshire Botanical Garden, Hawthorne Cottage (home of Nathaniel Hawthorne), Hancock Shaker Village, Ice Glen (hiking), Laura's Tower, Berkshire Scenic Railway Museum, Kennedy Park, Pleasant Valley Wildlife Sanctuary

DRIVING DIRECTIONS: From I-90, take exit 2 (Lee/US 20) and turn onto US 20 East. In 0.1 mile, turn right onto MA 102 West. Drive 4.5 miles into the center of Stockbridge. Turn left onto US 7 South and drive about 4.5 miles to the junction with MA 183 North. Turn right onto MA 183 North. In 1.0 mile, park at the Tafts Farm on your left.

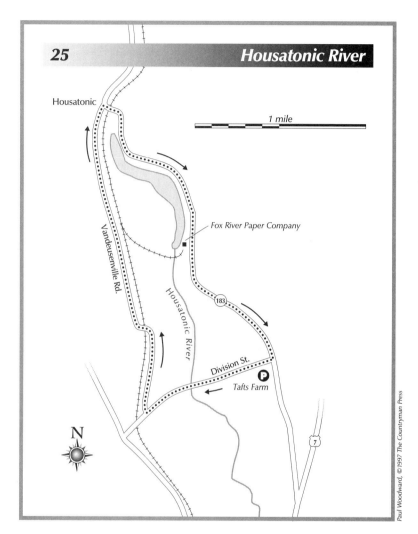

25 **Housatonic River**

Housatonic

1 mile

Fox River Paper Company

Vandeusenville Rd.

Housatonic River

183

Division St.

Tafts Farm

7

N

TRIP OVERVIEW: Peace and quiet . . . just what you came to the Berkshires to find! The tranquillity of the countryside will lull you into a lazy rhythm as you skate by farms and beside the Housatonic River. There are plenty of inviting spots along the riverbank where you might want to rest or have a snack. Because the road is lightly traveled, encourage skating friends who normally shy away from street skating to join you.

Great Barrington itself is not quite as charming as some of the other nearby towns, like Stockbridge and Lenox. It features a busy downtown with no-nonsense brick buildings, but there are a few local shops where you might find a treasure or two—particularly a neat antiques shop and a wonderful bakery.

ROUTE DIRECTIONS:

0.0 From the Tafts Farm parking lot, turn left onto Division Street.

0.4 Cross a concrete bridge over the Housatonic River.

0.6 Pump up a slight incline.

0.8 Turn right onto Vandeusenville Road, passing an unusual Gothic church on the corner.

1.1 Descend gently with pleasing views of the western hills and a farm.

1.3 ▼ CAUTION: Skate carefully over a railroad crossing.

1.7 Roll beside the railroad tracks.

2.2 Pass a cemetery on your left.

2.7 Vandeusenville Road ends in the town of Housatonic. (Turn left if you want to breeze through this small village.)
For the easier return leg, head back at this point the way you came. For an alternative (and slightly harder) return trip, continue by turning right and skating over a concrete bridge.

2.8 Turn right onto MA 183 South. (*Note:* The speed limit is 35 mph and traffic is light.)

3.2 Take in views of the Housatonic River on your right.

3.8 Pass the Fox River Paper Company on your right.

4.2 Cruise by a ball field on your right.

4.5 Roll down an easy hill.

4.6 At the intersection with Division Street, skate back to Tafts Farm and your car.

26 •••• *Swamp Road*

LOCATION: West Stockbridge, MA
RATING: Intermediate
DISTANCE: 10.0 miles
TIMES TO AVOID: None
TERRAIN: Flat with limited gradual hills on a rural road with no shoulder
SURFACE: Smooth asphalt
AUTO TRAFFIC: Light
POINTS OF INTEREST: Chesterwood, Norman Rockwell Museum,

Mission House (built in 1739), the Red Lion Inn (dating from 1773), Hawthorne Cottage, Lenox village, Tanglewood, The Mount (Edith Wharton's home), Kennedy Park, Pleasant Valley Wildlife Sanctuary

DRIVING DIRECTIONS: From I-90 traveling west, take exit 1 (West Stockbridge) and turn right onto MA 41 North. Drive 0.2 mile and turn left onto MA 102 West. In 0.5 mile, reach the small center of West Stockbridge. Park anywhere in the village.

From I-90 traveling east, take exit B-3 (Canaan, New York) and turn left onto NY 22 South. Drive 0.75 mile and turn left onto MA 102 East. In about 5 miles, arrive in the small village of West Stockbridge and park downtown.

TRIP OVERVIEW: Okay. We'll admit it. We do have our favorites. And this is one of them: our favorite Berkshire skate. Begin in the quiet hamlet of West Stockbridge (population: 1596), then roll on smooth pavement into the glorious countryside. The road is just flat enough, and the views of the local hills are breathtaking. You'll cruise by working farms and trademark Berkshire "cottages" before returning to town.

Of course the cottages in Stockbridge, West Stockbridge, and Lenox are not much like the summer cottage that your folks rented on Sunset Lake when you were 10 years old. That one smelled like a basement and had two sets of bunk beds shoved into the only bedroom. These cottages have servants' quarters and in-ground pools, landscaped gardens and cascading fountains. During the Gilded Age, the Berkshires became *the* place for wealthy industrialists to build extravagant summer mansions. By the end of the 19th century, the Stockbridge area was known as inland Newport because of the 100-plus "cottages" that had been built here. (About 30 are still standing).

Intermediate skaters who embark on this trip should be comfortable descending: There is one significant hill.

ROUTE DIRECTIONS:
0.0 From West Stockbridge center, head west on MA 102.
0.1 Turn right onto Swamp Road.
0.5 Enjoy lovely views of mountains on your left.
0.6 ▼ CAUTION: The road drops steeply for 0.3 mile and curves to the left where Cone Hill Road intersects from the left.
1.2 Roll by picturesque farms, meadows, and hills.
1.8 Pass Stevens Glen Road on your right.
2.0 Continue straight as Dublin Road intersects on your left.

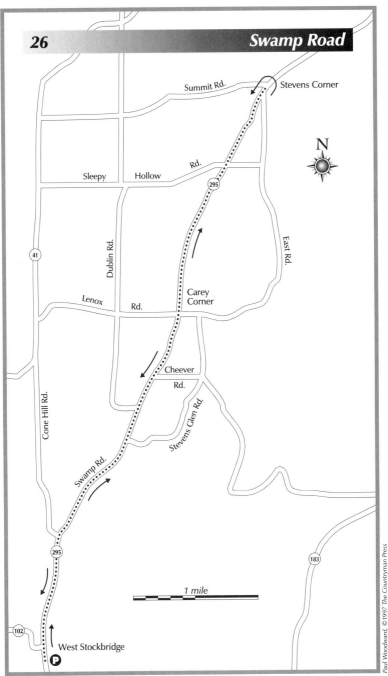

26   *Swamp Road*

Summit Rd.

Stevens Corner

Hollow   Rd.

Sleepy   Hollow

N

295

East Rd.

41

Dublin Rd.

Carey
Corner

Lenox   Rd.

Cheever

Rd.

Cone Hill Rd.

Stevens Glen Rd.

Swamp Rd.

295

183

1 mile

102

West Stockbridge

P

Paul Woodward, ©1997 The Countryman Press

2.3 Cruise by the junction with Cheever Road on your right.

2.7 ▼ CAUTION: Stop at the flashing light, then head straight through the intersection with Lenox Road.

4.1 Pass Sleepy Hollow Road on your left.

4.7 Head straight as East Road joins from your right.

5.0 ▼ CAUTION: Stop at the intersection with Summit Road (MA 295). INTERMEDIATE SKATERS should turn and head back to West Stockbridge on Swamp Road. ADVANCED SKATERS can continue along MA 295 before turning around; be aware that the road becomes hilly and the traffic increases.

27 •••• *Stockbridge Golf Course*

LOCATION: Stockbridge, MA
RATING: Advanced
DISTANCE: 3.0 miles
TIMES TO AVOID: None
TERRAIN: Rolling hills on a rural road with no shoulder
SURFACE: Coarse asphalt
AUTO TRAFFIC: Light
POINTS OF INTEREST: Chesterwood, Norman Rockwell Museum, Mission House (built in 1739), Naumkeag (historic mansion), Berkshire Botanical Garden, the Red Lion Inn (dating from 1773), Indian burial grounds, Hancock Shaker Village, Ice Glen (hiking), Laura's Tower

DRIVING DIRECTIONS: From I-90, take exit 2 (Lee/US 20). Drive 0.1 mile on US 20 East (cross under I-90) and turn right onto MA 102 West. Drive 4.5 miles into the center of Stockbridge. Continue straight on MA 102 West (Main Street); 0.5 mile from Stockbridge center, bear left onto Glendale Middle Road as MA 102 veers right. In another 0.1 mile, park on your left in a dirt turnout.

TRIP OVERVIEW: Even if you haven't been to Stockbridge, you've seen it. You've seen it in the work of Norman Rockwell, who captured the town's essence (and many of its citizens) in his well-known paintings. A trip to the area would be incomplete without a stop at the Norman Rockwell Museum to admire more than 600 of the artist's original paintings.

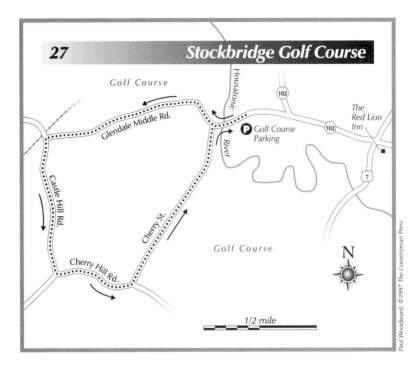

There are a number of other postskate stops you'll want to make in this charming New England town, so rich in history and tradition. The Red Lion Inn, at the intersection of Main and South Streets, served as a meeting place in pre-Revolutionary days. The Hawthorne Cottage was home to one of the Berkshires' most celebrated authors, Nathaniel Hawthorne, who wrote *The House of the Seven Gables* while he lived there. And Chesterwood, summer residence of the country's foremost traditional sculptor, Daniel Chester French, is open daily from May through October. When you've had your fill of history, head to Ice Glen. This naturally "air-conditioned" ravine is a perfect place to visit on a steamy summer day (or on Halloween, when residents journey through the maze of boulders carrying torches!).

Once you've seen how delightful Stockbridge center is, you may opt for a leisurely skate around town. But if you want a challenge (or if you want to add miles to the end of an in-town skate), follow our route. Leave from the Stockbridge Golf Course (the nation's fifth oldest, dating from 1895), and loop back via rolling country roads. Great local views punctuate the route, and it's short enough to leave you plenty of time to enjoy the area sites.

ROUTE DIRECTIONS:

0.0 From the parking lot, turn left onto Glendale Middle Road.

0.2 Roll over Tuckerman's Bridge, which spans the Housatonic River.

0.3 Bear right, still on Glendale Middle Road; push up a short hill. Peer over the stone wall on your right for pleasant views of the golf course.

0.5 Drop down a gentle hill.

0.9 ▼ CAUTION: Negotiate a steep descent. At the base of the hill, turn left onto Castle Hill Road. (*Note:* If you cross the railroad tracks, you've gone too far.)

1.2 Climb a steep 0.2-mile hill.

1.6 As Castle Hill Road ends, turn left onto Cherry Hill Road. (*Note:* The intersection is unmarked.)

1.8 Turn left onto Cherry Street and endure a short section of choppy pavement.

2.5 ▼ CAUTION: Be alert at a railroad crossing.

2.6 Skirt the edge of the golf course on your right.

2.7 Turn right onto Glendale Middle Road and cross the bridge.

3.0 Return to your car.

28 •••• *Spring Street*

LOCATION: Lee, MA
RATING: Intermediate
DISTANCE: 4.8 miles
TIMES TO AVOID: None
TERRAIN: Gently rolling hills on a rural road with no shoulder
SURFACE: Coarse asphalt
AUTO TRAFFIC: Light
POINTS OF INTEREST: Monument Mountain Restoration, Beartown State Forest, Great Barrington State Forest, Chesterwood, Norman Rockwell Museum, Mission House (built in 1739), Naumkeag (historic mansion), Berkshire Botanical Garden, the Red Lion Inn (dating from 1773), Indian burial grounds

DRIVING DIRECTIONS: From I-90, take exit 2 (Lee/US 20). Follow US 20 West into Lee and at the first stop sign proceed straight (as US 20 turns right) onto West Park Street (which will turn into Stockbridge Road). Drive 1 mile and park at the Devonfield Inn on your left.

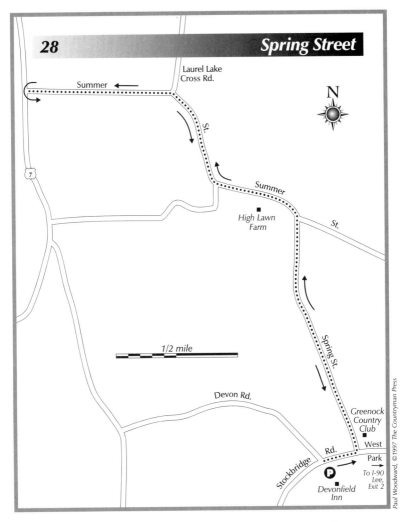

28 | **Spring Street**

Laurel Lake Cross Rd.

Summer

N

St.

Summer

High Lawn Farm

St.

7

Spring St.

1/2 mile

Devon Rd.

Greenock Country Club

West

Rd.

Park

Stockbridge

To I-90 Lee, Exit 2

Devonfield Inn

Paul Woodward, © 1997 The Countryman Press

TRIP OVERVIEW: The Berkshires are appropriately named. Because the original Berkshire is in England, *Berk* is from the British and Welsh and means "forest" and "summit"; *shire* stands for "hilly country." The town of Lee, the "Gateway to the Berkshires," proudly declares itself a "real town" (as opposed to a tourist stop) with a barbershop, hardware store, drugstore soda fountain, and a five-and-dime clustered in the downtown. (Lee's Main Street is listed on the National Register of Historic Places.)

Follow this "road less traveled" in an area near downtown Lee that tourists often overlook, passing dairy and horse farms and a lake with pleasant views of the countryside. The road is relatively flat with only gentle hills, and the lack of traffic makes for a peaceful trip.

Simple. Relaxing. Uplifting.

ROUTE DIRECTIONS:

0.0 From the Devonfield Inn (check out the views from its back-yard!), turn right onto Stockbridge Road.

0.1 Turn left onto Spring Street, passing the Greenock Country Club on your right.

0.5 On your right, roll by St. Mary's Cemetery.

0.7 On a slight descent, cruise by pastures with grazing horses.

1.0 ● STOP. Bear left onto Summer Street.

1.3 Pass High Lawn Farm on your left; check out the interesting clock tower.

1.5 Take time to admire the delightful surroundings: Pastures car-peted in wildflowers stretch to the distant hills.

1.9 Roll by Laurel Lake Cross Road and lakeside condominiums.

2.4 At the intersection with US 7, turn around and return to the Devonfield Inn.

29 •••• *Old Stockbridge Road*

LOCATION: Lenox and Stockbridge, MA
RATING: Intermediate
DISTANCE: 4.2 miles
TIMES TO AVOID: None
TERRAIN: Gently rolling hills with one steep hill on a rural road with no shoulder
SURFACE: Smooth asphalt with limited sections of coarse asphalt
AUTO TRAFFIC: Light
POINTS OF INTEREST: Naumkeag (historic mansion), Berkshire Botan-ical Garden, Indian burial grounds, Lenox village, Tanglewood, The Mount (Edith Wharton's home), Ice Glen (hiking), Laura's Tower, Berkshire Performing Arts Theater at the National Music Center, Berkshire Scenic Railway Museum, Kennedy Park, Pleas-ant Valley Wildlife Sanctuary
DRIVING DIRECTIONS: From I-90, take exit 2 (Lee/US 20). Drive 4.1 miles on US 20 West to the junction with US 7 in Lenox. In another 0.2

C. BRADLEY

Be sure to spend some time in historic downtown Lenox after you skate.

mile, turn left at the intersection with MA 183 (Walker Street). Drive 1.1 miles to the center of Lenox (marked by the Paterson monument). Park in a designated space in the downtown area.

TRIP OVERVIEW: Something about this skate says "Sunday morning" to us. Awaken as the sun splashes across the comforter of your wrought-iron bed in your favorite Berkshire bed & breakfast. Grab a warm muffin from the kitchen, strap on your wheels, and head out into the crisp, early-morning air. Cruise into the center of Lenox and turn onto Old Stockbridge Road. Pass fields and wooded areas—and, of course, lovely homes and "cottages"—before turning around at the intersection with US 7 and returning to Lenox.

After your "official" skate, explore the smooth paths that wander through the downtown area, and stop at one of the great eateries for a big (well-deserved) breakfast!

ROUTE DIRECTIONS:

0.0 From the Paterson monument in the center of Lenox, head southwest on Old Stockbridge Road.

0.2 ▼ CAUTION: Steep decline.

0.9 Roll by Windin Hill residential area on your right. (*Note:* The road leading to this development is private.)

1.6 Roll by the Hillcrest Educational Center on your right (starched collars, anyone?).

2.1 At the intersection with US 7, turn and head back to your car.

> *SKATING TIP:* When you begin to see more wear on one side of your wheels, it's time to rotate them. (Turn the front wheel 180 degrees and move it to the back; turn and move each of the other wheels up one place.) Doing so will lengthen the life of your wheels.

30 •••• *Northampton Bikeway*

LOCATION: Northampton, MA
RATING: Beginner
DISTANCE: 5.2 miles
TIMES TO AVOID: None
TERRAIN: Flat, paved path
SURFACE: Smooth asphalt
AUTO TRAFFIC: None
POINTS OF INTEREST: Look Memorial Park, Barrett Street Marsh Conservation Area, Yankee Candle Company, the Robert Frost Hiking Trail, Emily Dickinson House, Smith College Museum of Art, Summerside at Mt. Tom, Lyman Plant House and the Botanic Garden at Smith College, Thornes Marketplace

DRIVING DIRECTIONS: If you're heading north on I-91, take exit 19 in Northampton and drive straight through the light at the base of the exit ramp onto Damon Road. In 0.7 mile, head under I-91; at 1 mile, cross US 5/MA 10. Continue straight on Bridge Road for 2.2 miles and turn left onto MA 9 West. Turn left, then immediately turn right to enter Frank Newhall Look Memorial Park (at a large sign). Park in the lot for a minimal fee.

If you're traveling south on I-91, take exit 20 in Northampton and join US 5 and MA 10 South. In 0.1 mile, turn right onto Bridge Road. Drive 2.2 miles to the intersection with MA 9 West. Turn left, then immediately turn right to enter Frank Newhall Look Memorial Park (at a large sign). Park in the lot for a minimal fee.

The Northampton Bike Path is popular with local couples and families as well as the many students in the five-college region.

TRIP OVERVIEW: If you're traveling with children, plan to spend the day here. Look Park, where the trail begins, has a miniature train (an authentic replica of the 1863 C.P. Huntington gives 1-mile rides), playgrounds (including two giant playscapes), pedal boats to use on Willow Lake, the Christenson Zoo (with a petting zoo), miniature golf (18 holes), tennis, fishing, camping, walking trails, picnic sites . . . maybe you'll need 2 days! For teens, downtown Northampton is funky and fun, with offbeat restaurants and shops—don't miss Thornes Marketplace. The elegant Smith College campus abuts the downtown area. Wander among the stately mansions (used as dorms) and visit the Lyman Plant House and the Botanic Garden near Paradise Pond.

The Northampton Bikeway travels along the outskirts of Northampton, ending just 1 mile from the start of the Norwottuck Rail Trail. (There are plans to connect the two via a bike route.) You'll roll through residential and industrial areas along a flat path that's ideal for new skaters (with less pedestrian and other traffic than on the Norwottuck). There are a number of intersections at quiet neighborhood streets with little vehicular traffic.

ROUTE DIRECTIONS:

0.0 From the entrance of Look Park, cross MA 9 and head east on Bridge Road. Immediately turn right and join the trail.

0.3 Roll behind a busy neighborhood.

0.5 ▼ CAUTION: Cross Oak Street.

1.1 Embark on an extended (but gradual) descent.

2.2 Skate through a tunnel under Jackson Street.

2.4 A gravel path splits left for the Barrett Street Marsh Conservation Area: Birdwatchers, take note!

2.6 Reach the trail's end as it intersects with State Street. Turn and follow the path back to your car.

31 •••• *Norwottuck Rail Trail*

LOCATION: Northampton, Hadley, and Amherst, MA
RATING: Beginner
DISTANCE: 17.0 miles
TIMES TO AVOID: None
TERRAIN: Flat paved path with gentle hills
SURFACE: Smooth asphalt
AUTO TRAFFIC: None
POINTS OF INTEREST: Yankee Candle Company, the Robert Frost Hiking Trail, Look Memorial Park, Emily Dickinson House, Smith College Museum of Art, Lyman Plant House and the Botanic Garden at Smith College, Academy of Music, Northampton Center for the Arts, Thornes Marketplace, Historic Deerfield

DRIVING DIRECTIONS: If you're heading north on I-91, take exit 19 in Northampton; drive straight through the traffic light at the base of the exit ramp, now on Damon Road. Continue less than 0.1 mile and turn right into Elwell State Park. (Signs guiding you to the Norwottuck Rail Trail are plentiful.)

If you're heading south on I-91, take exit 20 in Northampton; join US 5/MA 10 South. In 0.1 mile, turn left onto Damon Road. Drive about 1 mile to the Elwell State Park entrance on your left. There is no parking fee.

TRIP OVERVIEW: The Norwottuck Rail Trail—the state's newest—is also one of the best from a skater's perspective. Its unique features, including a half-mile stretch on a truss bridge spanning the Connecticut River, make this path popular with local college students as well as out-of-towners. The smooth path rolls by campuses and town commons and through farmland and forests. Wildlife abounds (especially birds), so keep your head up if you want to catch sight of a hawk or a heron. The distant views are also impressive, with the Holyoke Range stretching across the southern horizon.

The rail line was active for nearly 100 years, intended for delivering people from the Pioneer Valley to the state capital. The Great Depression brought an end to the daily passenger service to Boston, and eventually even freight traffic dwindled, until the line was abandoned altogether in 1980. Now it has been granted a second life as a recreational path, and probably serves more people than at any other time in its history.

ROUTE DIRECTIONS:

0.0   The path begins at the northern end of the parking lot. (There is a sign marking the entrance.) Roll across the bridge spanning the Connecticut River. Look south to see the Calvin Coolidge Bridge, named for the president who made his home in Northampton. ▼ CAUTION: Roll slowly over the bridge's metal dividers.

0.4   ▼ CAUTION: Cross Cross-Path Road.

1.7   ▼ CAUTION: Cross West Street by the historic Hadley common. (You may want to leave the trail to skate around the common. Years ago, residents were permitted to graze their animals here.)

2.0   ▼ CAUTION: Cross Middle Street and glide through open farmland, taking in southerly views of the Holyoke Range (Can you spot the historic Summit House atop Mount Holyoke?) and northerly views of Mount Toby and Mount Sugarloaf.

2.4   ▼ CAUTION: Cross East Street.

2.9   Dart into a tunnel under Spruce Hill Road.

3.4   Follow the trail under MA 9, then pass shopping malls and more farmland. Look farther south to see the Seven Sisters hills.

4.3   ▼ CAUTION: Cross South Maple Street with the Hampshire Mall on your left.

5.3   Cruise by Hickory Ridge Country Club on your right.

5.7   Roll across a bridge over Snell Street. As the trail nears Amherst center, it leads over two small, concrete tunnels, originally used as cattle crossings when the railroad was in operation.

6.0   Skirt the Amherst College campus and roll through a conservation area owned by the college and the town of Amherst.

7.5 Skate across the bridge spanning the Fort River. Pause to scan the riverbanks for muskrats and beavers.

8.0 Tour several wetlands, watching for wildlife. If you've brought a picnic, here's the spot to spread it out!

8.5 The trail ends at Station Road in Amherst (where there is also parking available). The railbed continues across the street. There are plans to extend the paved path into Connecticut.
Turn around here, and head back to your car.

SKATING TIP: *To increase the intensity of a workout, incorporate the upper body into your skating moves. Using your arms will help to raise your heart rate and condition your cardiovascular system.*

S. HOOPER

32 •••• *Historic Deerfield*

LOCATION: Deerfield, MA
RATING: Intermediate
DISTANCE: 4.4 miles or 10 miles
TIMES TO AVOID: None
TERRAIN: Rural roads with some rolling hills
SURFACE: Smooth asphalt
AUTO TRAFFIC: Light

POINTS OF INTEREST: Memorial Hall Museum, Wright House, Ashley House, Park and Russell Silver Shop, Sheldon-Hawks House, Hall Tavern, Dwight-Barand House, Wells-Thorn House, Wilson Printing House, Helen Feier Flynt Fabric Hall, Asa Stebbins House, Pocumtuck Ridge

DRIVING DIRECTIONS: Heading north on I-91, take exit 24 North (Deerfield). Heading south, take exit 25 south (Deerfield). From the exit ramp, follow signs for US 5/MA 10 North. (There is a tourist information center on your right about 0.5 mile from the exit ramp.) Follow MA 5/10 for 5 miles and turn left onto Old Deerfield Road at the sign to Historic Deerfield. Follow the road for about 0.5 mile and turn right into the visitors parking area (with a visitors information center) directly across from the Deerfield Inn.

TRIP OVERVIEW: Deerfield residents brag that their main street is three centuries long. Settled in the mid-1600s by English farmers, Deerfield has endured for more than 300 years. For more than a century, townspeople have been working to preserve the area's history. Old Deerfield Street is lined with 200-year-old elms and old homes, mostly Colonial-style, that reveal what life was like for early New England settlers as well as for later, wealthier residents. Visitors to this National Historic Landmark wander through houses filled with tens of thousands of objects made or used between 1650 and 1850, including furniture, glass, and silver.

We bet you won't take this trip alone—even if you don't have any skating friends, most people would love to hitch a ride to Deerfield and explore the town while you're working out. Our delightful route begins in the center of Historic Deerfield and heads into the countryside, passing farms, fields, and hillsides. On the way home, drive down MA 5/10 and stop at any one of the farm stands to load up on Deerfield corn, maple syrup, tomatoes, apples, and cider.

ROUTE DIRECTIONS:
0.0 From the parking lot, turn left onto Old Deerfield Road.
0.1 Pass solemn Deerfield Academy (a preparatory school founded in 1797) on your right.
0.3 Pass Memorial Hall Museum on your left.
0.4 Head straight at the junction with Wells Road.
0.5 ▼ CAUTION: On a slight downhill, bear right at a fork onto Mill Village Road. Watch for oncoming traffic.

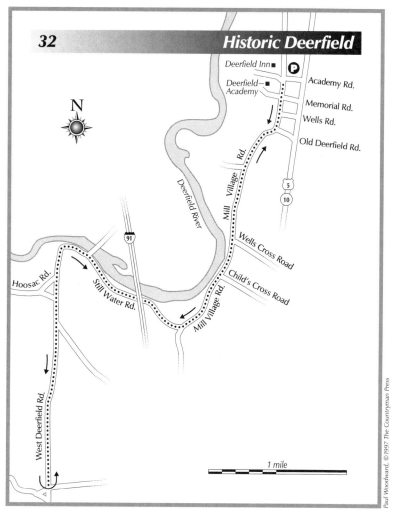

32

Historic Deerfield

Paul Woodward, © 1997 The Countryman Press

0.7 Take in pleasant farm views.

1.1 Glide by a tree farm on your left.

1.9 With a dairy farm on your right, roll into a more residential area.

2.0 ▼ CAUTION: The road begins to twist and turn.

2.2 Turn right onto Still Water Road. (This is a the turnaround point for the 4.4-mile trip, or for anyone not excited about a half-mile climb at the 3.1-mile mark and mirror-image downhill on the return leg.)

2.6 The road passes under I-91 beside the Deerfield River.

3.1 Work up a gradual 0.4-mile climb; as the road curves left, it turns into West Deerfield Road.

3.5 Continue straight as Hoosac Road bears right.

4.7 Cruise through a neighborhood.

5.0 ● STOP. At a stop sign, turn and head back to your car. (If you continue straight here, you will intersect with busy MA 116.)

33 •••• *Dover (Intermediate Loop)*

LOCATION: Dover, MA
RATING: Intermediate
DISTANCE: 2.5 miles
TIMES TO AVOID: Weekdays between 5 and 7 PM
TERRAIN: Flat, with one manageable climb
SURFACE: Smooth asphalt
AUTO TRAFFIC: Light
POINTS OF INTEREST: Broadmoor Wildlife Sanctuary, Stony Brook Wildlife Sanctuary, Rocky Woods Reservation State Park, pleasant rural scenery, nearby city activities

DRIVING DIRECTIONS: From I-95 (MA 128), take exit 19B (Highland Avenue/Needham). Head west toward Needham. At a light 1.7 miles from I-95, bear right onto Chestnut Street (which becomes Dedham Street in Dover). Four miles from the highway, bear left at the stop sign onto Centre Street and park along the common in Dover.

TRIP OVERVIEW: Relish the rural setting as you roll through the pages of *House and Garden* magazine, passing magnificent homes and open fields that reach to the distant tree line. You'll cruise along four stretches of road in Dover with few cars and fewer houses. (The roads that are busier are wide and straight with excellent visibility from the driver's point of view.) If this area becomes a favorite and you feel capable of tackling a more advanced route, check out Tours 34 and 35, two challenging, longer routes also in Dover.

ROUTE DIRECTIONS:
0.0 Skate up Springdale Road, passing the Dover Congregational Church.

0.4 Glide past the Dover recreational area on your right.

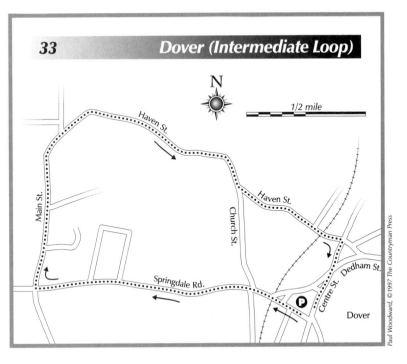

Paul Woodward, ©1997 The Countryman Press

0.8 Turn right onto Main Street (at a sign for Natick).

1.2 Climb the route's only hill, then glance right to see Needham's radio towers.

1.5 At a Y-intersection, bear right onto Haven Street.

2.0 The road narrows and becomes more rural, but still presents a good skating surface.

2.2 At the intersection with Church Street, continue straight on Haven Street, which is bordered by lofty pine trees.

2.4 Negotiate a set of railroad tracks.

2.5 ● STOP. At a stop sign, turn right onto Centre Street and return to your car parked in Dover center.

34 •••• *Dover (Advanced Loop)*

LOCATION: Dover, MA
RATING: Advanced
DISTANCE: 7.6 miles
TIMES TO AVOID: Weekdays between 5 and 7 PM
TERRAIN: Gently rolling, with two moderate hills
SURFACE: Smooth asphalt
AUTO TRAFFIC: Light
POINTS OF INTEREST: Broadmoor Wildlife Sanctuary, Stony Brook Wildlife Sanctuary, Rocky Woods Reservation State Park, pleasant rural scenery, nearby city activities

DRIVING DIRECTIONS: From I-95 (MA 128), take exit 19B (Highland Avenue/Needham). Head west toward Needham. At a light 1.7 miles from I-95, bear right onto Chestnut Street (which becomes Dedham Street in Dover). Four miles from the highway, bear left at the stop sign onto Centre Street and park along the common in Dover.

TRIP OVERVIEW: Skating along the country roads of Dover, you'll find it hard to believe that you're just 20 miles from the hustle and hubbub of downtown Boston. Fields outlined with stone walls and dotted with grazing horses stretch to acres of woodlands. The houses you'll see from the road are spectacular; the ones you can't see behind clipped hedges or down seemingly endless driveways are even grander. Because it's a local favorite, you'll share this route with runners, cyclists, and fellow skaters on most pleasant weekends. Be careful, however, as you're also sharing the road with vehicular traffic—there is little or no shoulder on these moderately wide roads.

ROUTE DIRECTIONS:
0.0 Head south through the traffic light onto Centre Street. Pass the fire station on your left.
1.0 Warm up on gently rolling terrain for the first mile.
1.5 Push hard up a short, steep incline.
2.0 Glide easily on more rolling terrain with open fields to your left and right.
2.2 Control your speed down a moderate descent followed quickly by a mirror-image ascent.
2.5 Cross into the town of Medfield.
2.7 Enjoy views of stately horse farms.

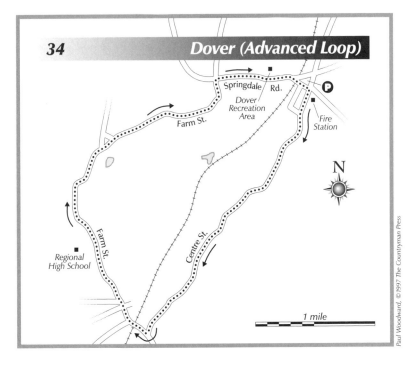

34 — *Dover (Advanced Loop)*

3.0 ● STOP. Make a hard right turn at an intersection onto Farm Street, a narrower but more rural road.

3.2 Heading uphill, negotiate a railroad track crossing and pump up a brief, but steep, hill.

3.6 Enter the town of Dover on a gradual but continuous climb.

4.0 Note the regional school on your left.

4.6 ▼ CAUTION: Brake, with knees bent and hands in front of the body, on a sharp descent, curling to the right.

5.4 Continue to roll downward. The road is rimmed with stone walls.

5.5 Pass a sprawling mansion on your left.

6.2 ▼ CAUTION: Brake on a stiff descent, hooking left.

6.7 Turn right onto Springdale Road, following signs to Dover.

7.2 Skate past the Dover recreational area on your left.

7.5 Tackle the final short climb to Dover center.

7.6 ▼ CAUTION: Cross railroad tracks as you return to the center of town.

35 ••••   *Dover (Expert Loop)*

LOCATION: Dover, MA
RATING: Expert
DISTANCE: 9.8 miles
TIMES TO AVOID: Weekdays between 5 and 7 PM
TERRAIN: Long, gradual hills and two steep downhills
SURFACE: Mostly smooth, with some coarse and broken asphalt
AUTO TRAFFIC: Moderate
POINTS OF INTEREST: Broadmoor Wildlife Sanctuary, Stony Brook Wildlife Sanctuary, Rocky Woods Reservation State Park, pleasant rural scenery, nearby city activities

DRIVING DIRECTIONS: From I-95 (MA 128), take exit 19B (Highland Avenue/Needham). Head west toward Needham. At a light 1.7 miles from I-95, bear right onto Chestnut Street (which becomes Dedham Street in Dover). Four miles from the highway, bear left at the stop sign onto Centre Street and park along the common in Dover.

TRIP OVERVIEW: You're on cycling turf here! This route is a favorite of Boston-area bicyclists and is destined to become popular with skilled skaters, too. Warm up on gently rolling terrain for the first 3 miles, then tackle a formidable, three-tiered climb. Crest, but don't relax, because next you'll plunge down a pair of hair-raising descents. Catch your breath midroute on a narrow road with tolerable traffic (stay alert, though, and keep to the right). Begin the final leg along a busy stretch leading to Dover center. Once you complete the final climb, you can sail into town on a brisk but manageable downhill.

ROUTE DIRECTIONS:
- 0.0 From Dover center, skate back the way you came by car on Centre Street.
- 0.1 Bear right onto Dedham Street.
- 1.0 Glide down an easy descent, passing manicured farms.
- 2.0 Continue to rise and fall over small hills.
- 2.5 ▼ CAUTION: Turn right onto Westfield Street as Chestnut Street veers left. Be sure to stay right and watch for traffic on this relatively busy road.
- 2.8 Pass an equestrian center on your left.
- 3.2 Turn right onto Summer Street, following signs to Westwood.
- 3.3 Cruise beside a golf course that encompasses the land on your left.

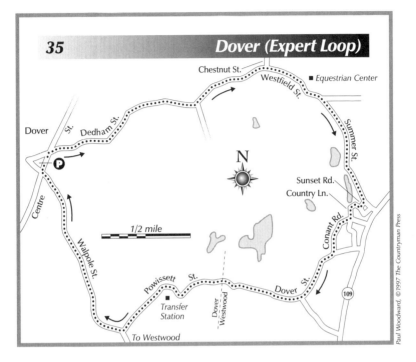

35   *Dover (Expert Loop)*

3.4 Begin the first (and easiest) section of a three-tiered ascent, with fields and fences bordering the road.

3.6 Push up the route's most challenging climb.

3.9 As a pond becomes visible through woods on your right, negotiate the third tier.

4.3 The road levels; turn right onto Sunset Road, entering a suburban neighborhood.

4.4 ▼ CAUTION: Turn right onto Country Lane and plunge down a challenging left-bending curve that requires braking.

4.5 Let a sharp uphill check your speed as you approach a ● STOP sign; turn right onto Conant Road.

4.6 Drop down a second sharp descent, still in a neighborhood setting. Skilled skaters can gather speed on the downhill because the road soon flattens and straightens.

5.0 ▼ CAUTION: Turn right onto rural Dover Street. This road, with light traffic and posted 25 and 20 mph speed limits, is narrow and twisting to mile 7.0.

6.1 Reenter Dover (Dover Street is now called Powissett Street) and watch for limited rough pavement.

6.6 Roll past the Dover transfer station on your left.

7.5 Bisect a sprawling farm with fields and outbuildings on both sides of the road.

7.7 ▼ CAUTION: Turn right onto well-traveled Walpole Street at a yield sign; be sure to stay right.

8.3 Crest a 0.4-mile-long gradual ascent.

8.5 ▼ CAUTION: Drop down a descent that may require braking.

9.7 A traffic light marks the intersection with Centre Street in Dover center. Return to your car. Whew!

36 •••• *Moose Hill*

LOCATION: Sharon, MA
RATING: Expert
DISTANCE: 9.5 miles
TIMES TO AVOID: Weekdays between 5 and 6 PM
TERRAIN: Two major climbs and descents
SURFACE: Smooth and coarse asphalt
AUTO TRAFFIC: Light, with about 1 mile of moderate traffic
POINTS OF INTEREST: Moose Hill Sanctuary, Kendall Whaling Museum, Foxboro Stadium and Raceway, Great Woods

DRIVING DIRECTIONS: From I-95, take exit 9 to US 1 (Foxboro Stadium and Raceway). In less than 0.5 mile on US 1 South, turn left (at the first traffic light) onto Old Post Road. Park on the shoulder near the highway overpass.

TRIP OVERVIEW: The course follows primarily rural roads with terrain varying from smooth, flat sections to narrow and grainy hills. The expert rating is the result of two descents that demand superior braking skills and two ascents that will tax even the hardiest endurance athletes. Exercise caution on the section of busy MA 27 that connects rural Moose Hill Road with Moose Hill Turnpike: There is little shoulder and plenty of traffic.

Enjoy the distant views of Great Blue Hill and the occasional deer, chipmunk, and porcupine sightings within the sanctuary boundaries. Incorporate a visit to Moose Hill Wildlife Sanctuary to extend your day or for nonskating family members or friends who accompany you. The sanctuary, owned by the Massachusetts Audubon Society, maintains 25

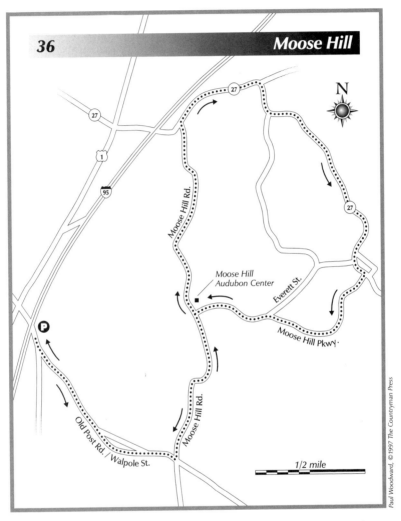

miles of hiking trails. Also consider stopping by the Kendall Whaling Museum on Everett Street.

ROUTE DIRECTIONS:

0.0 Head east on wide, smooth Old Post Road/Walpole Street (with an ample shoulder).

0.1 Do not bear right onto the narrow side street.

1.0 Turn left onto Moose Hill Road, a narrow rural road with a rougher surface.

1.4 Push up a tough, twisting ascent for 0.2 mile, watching for patches of broken pavement. (*Note:* This will be an equally challenging *descent* on the return trip.)

2.0 Continue straight as Moose Hill Parkway heads right, passing the Moose Hill Audubon Center.

2.2 Look right beyond the field for a glimpse of Great Blue Hill.

2.6 ▼ CAUTION: Brake on a sweeping (right) descent, then drop gradually for 0.8 mile.

3.4 ● STOP at the intersection with MA 27. (If you prefer, turn around here for a total 6.8-mile trip, thus avoiding the busiest section.) Skate on the generous shoulder of smooth, moderately traveled MA 27.

3.9 ● STOP. Turn right, still on MA 27, now a narrower road with moderate traffic.

5.7 ▼ CAUTION: Brake on a short, steep descent. As the hill bottoms out, turn right (note the Massachusetts Audubon Society sign) onto Moose Hill Parkway, a rural road with light vehicular traffic and some pedestrian traffic because of the sanctuary.

6.5 Begin a gradual climb.

6.7 Bear left following a Moose Hill sign.

7.1 Embark on a steep climb to the Moose Hill Center.

7.5 Turn left onto Moose Hill Road and reverse the original 2.0 miles to your car.

7.9 ▼ CAUTION: Remember to brake on the stiff descent.

9.5 Return to your car.

37 •••• *Minuteman Bikeway*

LOCATION: Bedford, MA
RATING: Beginner/intermediate
DISTANCE: 17.8 miles
TIMES TO AVOID: Busy summer weekends and holidays
TERRAIN: Flat, wide path
SURFACE: Smooth asphalt
AUTO TRAFFIC: None, except at well-marked street crossings
POINTS OF INTEREST: Lexington green, Lexington Visitors Center, Walden Pond, Buckman Tavern, Longfellow and Thoreau Concord sites, historical bridge in Concord, route taken by Paul Revere

This family cruises safely over the congested interstate highway by way of an overpass.

DRIVING DIRECTIONS: From I-95 (MA 128) in Bedford, take exit 31B (for MA 4 North and MA 225 West) and head toward Bedford center. In 1.9 miles, turn left onto Loomis Street. At the junction of South and Loomis Streets in 0.3 mile, park in a lot for the Minuteman Bikeway at the intersection. The bikeway leaves from this intersection.

TRIP OVERVIEW: "Listen, my children, and you shall hear / Of the midnight ride of Paul Revere . . ." Or, in this case, hear of the skating route that travels through the area where Paul called out his warning about the Redcoats more than 200 years ago. The Minuteman Bikeway also strays near the Lexington green, where the "shot heard round the world" was fired.

It's not just the area's rich history that draws people to this path, though. For hundreds of daily commuters, it's an alternative to an agonizingly slow drive on the congested highways that feed into metropolitan Boston. Although the bikeway winds through populated areas, it avoids the crowds and the traffic of Bedford, Lexington, and Arlington. Built in 1993 at a cost of $2.7 million, the Minuteman Bikeway is reported by the *Boston Globe* to be "spawning clones" because of its tremendous popularity—an estimated 9000 people use it on an average weekend day. But don't let the path's popularity discourage you. Because it's in a semiurban area, walkers, skaters, and cyclists know how to share the road: You can learn from their techniques. Pace off faster skaters, or join a slower group. And don't miss an opportunity to relax along the way and people-watch—we guarantee quite an interesting variety!

ROUTE DIRECTIONS:

0.0 Skate by the old Bedford Depot railroad station under shade trees, initially through a residential neighborhood.

1.0 ● STOP. Cross Wiggins Avenue, then a bridge over the Shawsheen River.

1.3 ● STOP. Cross Westview Street.

1.5 ● STOP. Cross Hartwell Avenue as the path meanders through open surrounds in Topsham Swamp.

2.0 Cross I-95 on an elevated bridge and return to thick woods.

2.7 ● STOP. Cross busy Bedford Street.

3.1 ● STOP. Cross quiet Revere Street.

3.7 ● STOP. Cross Hancock Street, with the Lexington green to your right.

3.9 ● STOP. Cross Merriam Street.

4.3 ● STOP. Cross Fletcher Avenue.

4.4 Angle across Hays Lane, then stop before crossing Woburn Street. From here the trail gently twists and turns for about 1 mile.

5.4 Duck under Maple Street's wooden bridge.

6.2 ● STOP. Cross Fotler Avenue.

6.4 ● STOP. Cross Bow Street.

7.1 Pass under the bridge that carries Park Avenue. (Note the wooden "boxed pony truss" design.)

7.2 Pass under another similar bridge for Lowell Street.

7.5 Cruise by a playground and baseball field on your left.

7.9 Glide over a Washington Street bridge.

8.3 Skate past impressive Arlington High School on your right.

8.5 ● STOP. Cross Mill Street.

8.7 ● STOP. Cross Water Street.

8.9 ● STOP. Reverse direction to return to your car at the intersection with MA 4 and MA 225 in Arlington.

38 •••• *Myles Standish State Forest*

LOCATION: Plymouth, MA
RATING: Intermediate
DISTANCE: 7.1 miles
TIMES TO AVOID: None
TERRAIN: Flat and rolling with many curves
SURFACE: Primarily smooth asphalt
AUTO TRAFFIC: Very light to light
POINTS OF INTEREST: The *Mayflower*, Plymouth Rock, Plimoth Plantation

DRIVING DIRECTIONS: From the west, take I-495 to exit 2 (MA 58/Carver/W. Wareham); note the sign for Myles Standish State Forest. Head east on MA 58, and 3.3 miles from I-495 turn right onto Cranberry Road following the STATE FOREST signs. Drive another 3 miles and park at the headquarters parking area.

From Plymouth, take MA 3 to exit 5. Head west on Long Pond Road, following the signs for Myles Standish State Forest. In 3.7 miles, turn right and enter the forest. Drive another 1.8 miles and bear left, guided by the sign to the park headquarters. In 3.5 miles, park in the headquarters parking lot on your right.

TRIP OVERVIEW: Chubby Checker would have a lot to sing about along the roads of Myles Standish State Forest. "The Twist"—an apt nickname for this trip—begins in the shade of lofty pine trees, sweeping right and left on fairly wide roads (with no shoulders, but minimal traffic). You'll curl around ponds and wind through scrub pine woods before leaving the shelter of the forest to skate along exposed and windswept highlands. On steamy summer days you'll be grateful for the abundance of swimming spots here: We recommend College Pond, about 3 miles into the loop. If you're an advanced skater, invite your mountain biking friends to join you and show them how fast those R3 bearings truly are!

ROUTE DIRECTIONS:
0.0 From the headquarters parking lot, turn right onto East Head Road, then right again onto Lower College Pond Road (guided by a sign to CURLEW POND/BARRET POND).
0.2 Take note of the fire tower on your left: The next time you see this landmark, you'll be at the trip's halfway point.
0.5 Twist and turn, passing Barret Pond on your left.
0.9 Curve along an upper section of East Head Pond on your right.

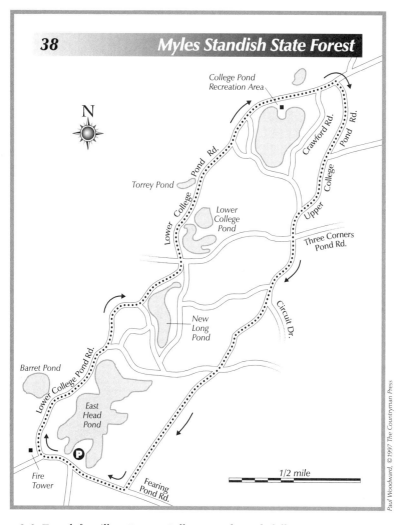

38   *Myles Standish State Forest*

College Pond
Recreation Area

N

Crawford Rd.

Pond Rd.

Lower College Pond Rd.

Torrey Pond

Upper College

Lower
College
Pond

Three Corners
Pond Rd.

Circuit Dr.

New
Long
Pond

Barret Pond

Lower College Pond Rd.

East
Head
Pond

P

1/2 mile

Fire
Tower

Fearing
Pond Rd.

Paul Woodward, ©1997 The Countryman Press

1.0   Turn left, still on Lower College Pond Road (following CURLEW and
COLLEGE POND signs).

1.2   At the intersection, follow a COLLEGE POND sign.

1.5   Flirt with the edge of New Long Pond on your right.

2.6   Glance left to see tiny Torrey Pond.

2.8   At the intersection with an unmarked side street that heads right,
continue straight.

3.3   Skate past the College Pond Swimming/Recreation Area on your
right.

3.5 At the intersection, continue straight as Crawford Road goes right.

3.6 Before reaching a stop sign, turn right onto wider and straighter Upper College Pond Road. (This road is busier, but automobiles have good visibility.) Begin a short, sharp climb on the roughest section of pavement.

3.8 As you crest, look right to see the fire tower, with distant views over the area you just traveled.

4.5 At the intersection with Three Corners Pond Road, continue straight.

4.7 Cruise by a parking area for hiking and mountain biking trails on your right.

5.1 At the intersection with Circuit Drive, continue straight, following a sign to the forest headquarters.

5.7 Continue straight at the junction with an unmarked road, rolling along a straight section of open road: Expect to feel the effects of direct sun and a strong, steady breeze.

6.5 Turn right at a T-intersection onto Fearing Pond Road, skating toward the forest headquarters.

6.7 Climb up a short, moderately difficult hill.

6.8 On a moderate descent, advanced skaters need not brake.

7.1 Turn right into the parking area. Strip to your swimsuit and take a dip!

39 •••• *Powder Point*

LOCATION: Duxbury, MA
RATING: Intermediate
DISTANCE: 3.3 miles
TIMES TO AVOID: Summer weekends (because of heavy traffic)
TERRAIN: Gently rolling with one moderate hill
SURFACE: Smooth asphalt (route includes a skateable wooden bridge)
AUTO TRAFFIC: Light (but heavy on summer weekends)
POINTS OF INTEREST: Duxbury Beach, Standish monument, Plymouth Rock, Plimoth Plantation, the *Mayflower,* Myles Standish State Park on Goose Point, Fort Standish

DRIVING DIRECTIONS: From MA 3, take exit 11 to Duxbury and MA 14 East. In 0.7 mile, bear right, still on MA 14. Three miles from MA 3, bear left onto Powder Point Avenue. Turn right in 0.25 mile onto King Caesar Avenue; park on the shoulder.

TRIP OVERVIEW: You've probably marveled at skaters who plunge down flights of stairs, lunge over cracked pavement sprinkled liberally with stones, and leap on and off curbs. For a mile along this route, you'll have a chance to show off what appears to be a daring maneuver of your own, though it's actually quite simple. You will cross Duxbury Bay along the wooden Gurnet Bridge. Despite any initial qualms, you'll soon discover how well your skates roll over the worn boards—there's a soft feel to this surface that's a welcome change from asphalt. After this trip, you may be inspired to try out some of those other "trick" maneuvers!

Start by winding beside the bay on moderately wide King Caesar Avenue, a road with no shoulder but not much traffic. On some of the tighter corners, watch for cyclists and pedestrians as well as the occasional car. Cross the bridge to reach Duxbury Beach, where you may want to take a swim or just hang out for a while. (The beach is public, but the parking area is not, so you may be one of the few "strangers" there.) When you're heading back to your car on Powder Point Road, you'll encounter more traffic, although the road is straighter and frequented by athletes.

ROUTE DIRECTIONS:
0.0 Skate along Duxbury Bay on King Caesar Avenue with elegant homes on your left.
0.4 Pass a small bayside park.
0.5 Bear right as Weston and Upland Roads head left; climb a slight hill.
0.9 Roll up and over an easy hill as the eastern end of Upland Road joins from the left.
1.1 ▼ CAUTION: Descend gently to the intersection with Powder Point Road (and parking for access to Duxbury Beach). Roll across wooden Gurnet Bridge. (The bridge's sidewalk is not as skater-friendly as is the roadway.)
1.7 Arrive at Duxbury Beach.
2.3 Return to the Powder Point Road/King Caesar Avenue intersection and bear right on Powder Point Road.
2.8 Crest a gentle hill.
3.3 At the intersection with King Caesar Avenue, turn left to return to your car.

40 •••• *Wompatuck State Park*

LOCATION: Hingham, MA
RATING: Beginner
DISTANCE: 6.6 miles
TIMES TO AVOID: Early spring, when the path may have scattered debris
TERRAIN: Flat to gently rolling roads and paths
SURFACE: Smooth asphalt
AUTO TRAFFIC: Very light on the road; none on the path
POINTS OF INTEREST: World's End Reservation, Nantasket Beach, John F. Kennedy Museum

DRIVING DIRECTIONS: From MA 3, take exit 14 (Rockland/Nantasket), following signs to Wompatuck State Park. Drive north on MA 228 and in 3.7 miles turn right onto Free Street. In 1 mile, turn right into the park. Park your car in the Mason A. Foley Visitor Center lot on your right or in the lot across the street.

TRIP OVERVIEW: This route follows a smooth cycling and skating path that winds through pleasant park woods. You'll encounter roads built during World War II, when the park was a munitions storage area, and roll by mounds of granite, reminders of the years this area was quarried. Two miles from the start, the path opens onto an extensive paved lot, a popular gathering spot for skaters. From there you'll follow the race loop used by the Skating Club of Boston and local cyclists before returning to your starting point on the park road. You may be tempted to veer off course and explore some of the old roads through Wompatuck that are inaccessible to vehicular traffic, but be warned: Many are not suitable for skaters. The trip we've described includes the paths and roads with surfaces that are most appropriate for skating.

ROUTE DIRECTIONS:
0.0 From the parking lot across the street from the Foley Visitor Center lot, locate the smooth paved bike/skate path, blazed with white arrows on the asphalt.
0.3 Roll over a small bridge and turn right, now on a wider road.
0.4 Turn left, returning to a narrow path. Push up two short, steep climbs. (You will not be retracing your steps, so you need not worry about descending these hills later!)
2.0 After winding along the woods path marked with white arrows

(and avoiding a number of side roads and paths), you'll reach an expansive parking area where skaters congregate to practice and refine their techniques and to size up the skills of others.

2.1 As you leave the parking area, turn left onto the main park road, where you'll encounter light, slow-moving traffic.

2.2 Cruise by the Mount Blue Spring area on your right.

2.6 Turn right onto the gated road that leads to the south loop (as the park road continues for another 0.1 mile up a moderate climb).

2.8 Roll by a pond and a hiking/mountain biking trail access on your right.

2.9 Join the south loop, following it in a counterclockwise direction.

3.0 Cross the start/finish line for the 1.3-mile loop used by cyclists and skaters.

4.3 Turn right to return to the main park road.

4.6 Turn left onto the park road.

5.6 Roll up and over an easy hill.

6.6 Return to your car.

SKATING TIP: *Skating in rhythm makes a workout more relaxing and enjoyable. Count the steps of each stroke or think "Bend, push, and ... bend, push, and ..." while striding.*

---

41 •••• *Marblehead Neck*

LOCATION: Marblehead, MA
RATING: Intermediate
DISTANCE: 4.1 miles
TIMES TO AVOID: None
TERRAIN: Wide, rolling suburban road
SURFACE: Smooth asphalt
AUTO TRAFFIC: Light
POINTS OF INTEREST: Fort Sewall, Chandler Hovey Park and Marblehead Light, Devereux Beach, Abbot Hall, House of Seven Gables

DRIVING DIRECTIONS: From US 1 in Lynnfield, take MA 129 East toward Swampscott and Marblehead. Follow MA 129 East to Marblehead. Just before the junction with MA 114, turn right at a traffic light

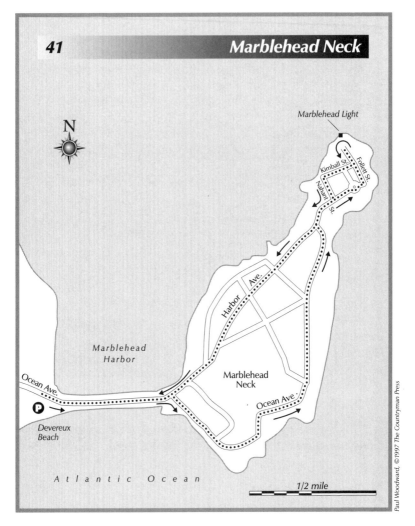

onto Ocean Avenue. In 0.4 mile, turn right into parking for Devereux Beach.

TRIP OVERVIEW: This route will appeal equally to the skating and the nonskating members of your family—no one compromises here! While you're tackling a challenging 4-mile skate, your spouse and children (or your nonskating friends) won't even notice your absence. They'll be enjoying Devereux Beach, a lovely sandy beach on the Atlantic Ocean that boasts a super playground (and proximity to Boston as well). After swimming and sunbathing, your gang can visit the lighthouse at Chandler Hovey Park (on Marblehead Neck) or Fort Sewall (across Marblehead Harbor from the skating route).

Meanwhile, you'll skate along a bike route on wide, gently rolling seaside roads with plenty of sight-seeing opportunities: Terrific ocean views to the Boston skyline and stunning homes compose the landscape. Expect to get a solid workout on the way out *or* on the way back—depending on how the wind is blowing, you'll fight it along the exposed causeway between Marblehead and Marblehead Neck.

ROUTE DIRECTIONS:

0.0 Skate across the causeway with picturesque Marblehead Harbor on your left and the Atlantic Ocean on your right.

0.6 Bear right onto Ocean Avenue, taking in views of the Boston skyline on your right.

1.0 Leave the ocean and trudge up a steep but short hill as the road widens and offers skaters a modest shoulder.

1.7 ▼ CAUTION: Brake on a descent after rolling through an elegant residential area.

1.8 At a rotary, bear right—still on Ocean Avenue—following a BIKE ROUTE sign.

2.1 Turn left onto Follett Street. (Chandler Hovey Park and Marblehead Light are both at the end of this street.)

2.2 Turn left onto Kimball Street.

2.4 At the base of an easy descent, turn left onto Nahant Street.

2.5 Turn right, now back on Ocean Avenue.

2.7 Bear right onto Harbor Avenue, guided by the BIKE ROUTE sign.

2.8 ▼ CAUTION: Apply your brakes on a moderate descent.

3.2 ▼ CAUTION: Brake on another moderate descent.

3.5 Reach the intersection with Ocean Avenue; turn right and skate 0.6 mile to your car across the causeway.

42 •••• *Scusset Beach*

LOCATION: Sagamore, MA
RATING: Intermediate
DISTANCE: 3.6 miles or 7.2 miles
TIMES TO AVOID: None
TERRAIN: Gently rolling on streets of varying width; one moderate hill
SURFACE: Smooth and coarse asphalt
AUTO TRAFFIC: Light through the first 2 miles; very light at route's end
POINTS OF INTEREST: Scusset Beach State Reservation, Plymouth, Myles Standish State Park, Cape Cod Canal Trail, Shawme-Crowell State Forest, Massachusetts State Fish Hatchery

DRIVING DIRECTIONS: From the rotary north of the Sagamore Bridge, take MA 3A (Meetinghouse Lane). In 0.1 mile, bear right onto Meetinghouse Lane as MA 3A splits left. Drive to the end of Meetinghouse Lane (which turns into Scusset Beach Road) and pay a minimal parking fee to enter Scusset Beach State Reservation. (Free parking may be available off Meetinghouse Lane.)

TRIP OVERVIEW: Many skaters relish the companionship of other athletes and head for popular spots like the Cape Cod Canal Recreational Trail (a wonderful place to explore on skates). This trip to Scusset Beach, however, is for the solitary skater. Enjoy a 3.6-mile skate through a quiet neighborhood and along a narrow dead-end road lined with homes overlooking Sagamore Beach. When the road ends at Scusset Beach, you have a few options. If you are done, you can remove your skates and walk back to your car along a sandy path. To extend the trip, you can return the way you came (for a 7.2-mile total) or you can join the "canal trail" at the Scusset Beach area. We recommend this trip for anyone who is accompanied by nonskating family members or friends—they can relax at the beach while you're working out.

ROUTE DIRECTIONS:
0.0 From the state park entrance, skate out the way you drove in, ascending gradually on wide Scusset Beach Road.
0.5 Turn right onto Williston Road, beginning a 1-mile skate through pleasant neighborhoods.
1.1 ▼ CAUTION: Brake on a descent; pass Marsh Pond Road on your right.

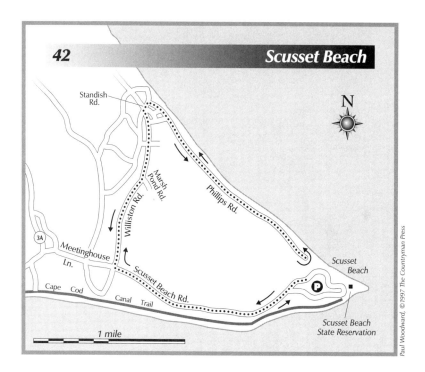

42 — **Scusset Beach**

Paul Woodward, ©1997 The Countryman Press

- 1.3 Roll through the Marsh Pond wetlands as the road begins to narrow.
- 1.8 Turn right onto Standish Road.
- 1.9 Turn right onto narrow Phillips Road and cruise along Cape Cod Bay.
- 3.6 Arrive at a cul-de-sac. Retrace the route to return to your car or follow the sandy path that exits the turnaround to arrive at the parking area for Scusset Beach.

43 •••• *Shining Sea Trail*

LOCATION: Falmouth, MA
RATING: Beginner
DISTANCE: 5.2 miles or 6.6 miles
TIMES TO AVOID: Busy summer weekends and holidays
TERRAIN: Flat, wide path
SURFACE: Smooth asphalt

How often do you have the opportunity to skate for a mile along the ocean, taking in the sunbathers, the sounds of the breaking waves, and the smells of salty air and seaweed?

AUTO TRAFFIC: Moderate at crossings; light at the parking lot at the end of the route

POINTS OF INTEREST: Falmouth, Woods Hole Oceanographic Institute, ferry to the islands, Nobska Light, Quissett Beach

DRIVING DIRECTIONS: From the Bourne Bridge, travel south on MA 28 to Falmouth. In 9.6 miles, continue straight onto Locust Street as MA 28 South goes left. In another 0.4 mile, park in the dirt lot on your right. The bikeway is across the street.

TRIP OVERVIEW: You *could* arrive at dawn to nab one of the limited parking spaces near popular Quissett Beach . . . or you could skate to the beach any time of the day along the Shining Sea Trail. Follow the wide, smooth path from Locust Street that cuts through woodlands then travels along a substantial section of Quissett Beach and Oyster Pond. After diving behind seaside homes, it ends near Vineyard Sound and the ferry to the islands. Expect to be buffeted by blustery ocean breezes along the unprotected half-mile section of path directly on the beach. As you roll past the sun worshipers and sand-castle architects, gaze across Nantucket Sound for a view of distant Martha's Vineyard.

ROUTE DIRECTIONS:

0.0 ▼ CAUTION: From the parking area, cross Locust Street and locate the designated trail entrance. Begin by skating through a residential area.

0.5 Rest, if you'd like, on a trailside bench. On your left, signs point the way to Salt Pond.

1.0 ● STOP. Cross Elm Road with Falmouth Beach on your left.

1.2 ● STOP. Cross Beach Road. Here Quissett Beach belongs to the skaters, cyclists, and hikers who crowd the paved path that cuts through the sand just 50 feet from the water's edge.

1.5 Cross a short, manageable wooden bridge.

2.0 Roll over a second wooden bridge.

2.5 In thick woods, cross a third bridge.

2.6 A final wooden bridge presents no difficulties as the trail narrows and opens onto a parking area for the island ferry. Turn around and return to your car.

Or, if the parking area is not congested, skate through the lot and continue for an additional 0.7 mile on this prime skating path.

3.0 Glance to your left for a view of scenic Little Harbor.

3.3 Conclude your trip as the path ends at the Woods Hole, Martha's Vineyard, and Nantucket Steamship Authority ferry. Return to your car the way you came.

44 •••• *Davis Beach*

LOCATION: West Dennis, MA
RATING: Beginner
DISTANCE: 2.2 miles
TIMES TO AVOID: No skating between 8 AM and 5 PM mid-June through Labor Day
TERRAIN: Generous, flat, parking-lot access road
SURFACE: Smooth and coarse asphalt
AUTO TRAFFIC: Light (for beach parking only)
POINTS OF INTEREST: West Dennis Town Beach, Davis Beach, Hyannis, Quaker Meetinghouse and Burial Ground, Nantucket Sound, Cape Cod Colosseum, MA 28 shops and restaurants

DRIVING DIRECTIONS: From MA 6, take exit 9 (MA 134). Travel south on MA 134 to MA 28. Turn right on MA 28 and drive 1 mile to

School Street. Turn left onto School Street; in 0.6 mile, turn right onto Lighthouse Road. Drive 0.2 mile to the West Dennis Town Beach entrance. (Parking is free after 5 PM; a moderate fee is charged between 8 AM and 5 PM.)

TRIP OVERVIEW: Are you a skater who favors parking lots over paths or roads? Let us introduce you to the ultimate in parking-lot skating! This wide asphalt strip stretches for more than a mile along West Dennis and Davis Beaches with parking on your left and right and a broad two-way travel lane in between. Skating is taboo from 8 AM to 5 PM, but swimming, tanning, using the play equipment, and visiting the snack bar are not. When the clock strikes 5, head for the parking lot with the other skaters, runners, and cyclists who reign during the off-peak hours. (If you enjoy road skating too, exit the beach area and head generally east. Old Wharf Road off Lower County Road provides additional good skating in this area.)

ROUTE DIRECTIONS:
- 0.0 From the beach area entrance, skate west along the beach on what is known as Davis Beach Road.
- 0.6 The road surface becomes coarser. Dunes separate you from Nantucket Sound on your left. To your right is Davis Beach at the mouth of the Bass River.
- 1.1 Reverse direction at the turnaround where the peninsula ends.

45 •••• *Cape Cod Rail Trail, Dennis*

LOCATION: Dennis and Harwich, MA
RATING: Beginner
DISTANCE: 9.6 miles
TIMES TO AVOID: None
TERRAIN: Flat path with many street crossings
SURFACE: Moderately coarse asphalt
AUTO TRAFFIC: None, except at street crossings
POINTS OF INTEREST: Cape Playhouse, Cape Museum of Fine Arts, Bass River and Swan River boat rides, Nantucket Sound, Cape Cod Bay beaches

DRIVING DIRECTIONS: From MA 6 in Dennis, take exit 9 to MA 134 South. In 0.4 mile, turn left into the parking lot for the Cape Cod Rail Trail.

This vintage 1930s train rumbled along what is now the Cape Cod Rail Trail.

TRIP OVERVIEW: The skate stops here . . . so far. This route covers the western end of the Cape Cod Rail Trail, although extensions of the trail toward Provincetown, the Cape Cod Canal, and Chatham are under consideration. You'll enjoy a delightful 9.6-mile skate through quiet forests and past a few small ponds. The only drawbacks are numerous street crossings and coarse pavement—an indication that this trail is relatively old (the first section was paved in 1978) and designed for cyclists and walkers. But the skating is certainly first-rate, and you can look forward to probable trail improvements and additions.

If time permits, take an after-skate drive along MA 6A. At one time, nearly 400 sea captains lived in Dennis, and many of their stately homes still grace the main streets in town.

ROUTE DIRECTIONS:
0.0 Join the trail at the back of the parking area.
0.2 Cross a dirt bike trail.
0.7 ● STOP. Cross Duck Pond Road.
0.8 ● STOP. Angle across Great Western Road.
1.4 ● STOP. Cross Depot Street.
1.5 Skate past a section of Bell's Neck Pond before the trail slips between excavated mounds.
2.1 Cruise by the western end of Bell's Neck Pond with Sand Pond on your left.
2.3 ● STOP. Cross Great Western Road.

2.8 ● STOP. Cross Lothrup Avenue and enter a commercial area.
3.3 Dip into a tunnel under Main Street.
3.5 Look right to see Island Pond and left to take in Flax Pond.
3.8 ▼ CAUTION: Skate with care over sand at a dirt bike crossing.
4.3 ● STOP. Cross Old Queen Anne Road.
4.4 Push up one of the few (gentle) hills along the rail trail.
4.8 At the junction of MA 124, the trail section ends. Turn and head back to your car.

SKATING TIP: *Remember the talk test: If you can sing "Old MacDonald had a farm, E-I-E-I-O" in one breath, then you should increase your intensity. If you need to take a breath after every word, then you should slow down. You are working at an appropriate fitness level if you must take a breath after every three or four words.*

46 •••• Cape Cod Rail Trail, Brewster

LOCATION: Brewster, MA
RATING: Beginner
DISTANCE: 10.8 miles
TIMES TO AVOID: None
TERRAIN: Flat rail trail with many street crossings
SURFACE: Coarse asphalt
AUTO TRAFFIC: None, except at street crossings
POINTS OF INTEREST: Nickerson State Park (boating, camping, swimming, bicycling, rest rooms), Cape Cod Museum of Natural History, Fort Hill, Point of Rocks Beach, Brewster Historical Society Museum, New England Fire & History Museum, Bassett Wild Animal Farm, sandy beaches on two ponds

DRIVING DIRECTIONS: From MA 6 in Brewster, take exit 12 to MA 6A guided by a sign to Nickerson State Park. Follow MA 6A East for 1.4 miles to the Nickerson State Park entrance. As you enter the park, drive into the lot on your right and leave your car there.

TRIP OVERVIEW: While your daring companions test their skating skills in Nickerson State Park, you can enjoy a more leisurely skate along the

The eastern portion of the Cape Cod Rail Trail includes many sections of dense, shaded woods.

Cape Cod Rail Trail. Such a parting of the ways will involve no complicated arrangements because both routes are accessible from the same parking lot! Your beginner route is wooded, providing good protection from the sun and wind. Although you'll encounter a number of street crossings, use them to help set goals: Skate continuously until you reach the next one. Before you embark on the return trip, relax at one of the sandy beaches just off the trail or grab a drink or a snack at a popular country store.

ROUTE DIRECTIONS:

0.0 Begin at the rear of the parking lot where two cement posts near the rest room building mark the access to the rail trail. Turn left onto the trail.

0.3 ▽ CAUTION: Heads up at a four-wheel-drive crossing.

0.6 ▽ CAUTION: Stop at a busy intersection with Millstone Road.

1.3 Dip into a tunnel under Underpass Road.

2.2 ● STOP at a street crossing.

2.3 ● STOP at a street crossing.

2.6 ● STOP and cross Long Pond Road (MA 137). (Ample parking here offers an alternative starting point.)

3.0 Push yourself on this long, straight stretch.

4.0 ▼ CAUTION: Stop on a slight descent at a street crossing.

4.5 ▼ CAUTION: Stop and cross MA 124, with an eye out for fast-moving traffic.

4.6 Skate beside Seymour Pond's sandy beach.

4.8 ▼ CAUTION: Stop and cross busy MA 124 again. Roll past a beach on Long Pond.

5.2 ● STOP and cross a side street.

5.4 The route ends at a store that has become a popular stop for skaters and cyclists. Return to your car the way you came.

Note: As an alternative, park across the street from the store and skate from the store to the state park and back. This lot is accessible from exit 10 on MA 6.

47 •••• Nickerson State Park

LOCATION: Brewster, MA
RATING: Expert
DISTANCE: 6.2 miles
TIMES TO AVOID: Autumn (leaves will make the skating slippery)
TERRAIN: Twisting, hilly, narrow path
SURFACE: Smooth asphalt
AUTO TRAFFIC: None, except at two crossings (very light)
POINTS OF INTEREST: Nickerson State Park (boating, camping, swimming, bicycling, rest rooms), Cape Cod Museum of Natural History, Fort Hill, Point of Rocks Beach, Historical Society Museum, New England Fire & History Museum, Bassett Wild Animal Farm

DRIVING DIRECTIONS: From MA 6 in Brewster, take exit 12 to MA 6A guided by a sign to Nickerson State Park. Follow MA 6A East for 1.4 miles to the Nickerson State Park entrance. As you enter the park, drive into the lot on your right and leave your car there.

TRIP OVERVIEW: Here's an analogy that may take you by surprise: Auto racing is to Le Mans as in-line skating is to _____. Give up? Nickerson State Park! Even for the expert skater, this route is downright hairy—but it's a must-do! There's no other place like it! You'll travel through dense woodlands on a well-maintained paved path, careering down short, steep hills that twist and turn, sometimes more than 90 degrees. On some sections of the course, you'll cascade down multistep hills and—if you dare to maintain your speed—fly around blind corners. (Be aware that the path will be littered with leaves in fall and pine needles in spring.)

If the skate doesn't leave you too weary, explore Brewster, a town unfamiliar with the term "off-season." If you visit in the spring, you will be enchanted by the clusters of roadside daffodils—your trip may coincide with the annual Brewster in Bloom Festival. In summertime, the town is bustling, with gourmet meals and elegant accommodations offered at mansions once owned by local sea captains. In the fall, a drive down MA 6A will reward you with a vivid display of autumn colors.

ROUTE DIRECTIONS:

0.0 Pick up the trail on your right, just before the park road exits onto MA 6A. Pump up a short, steep hill.

0.3 ● STOP. Cross the main park road and turn left onto Deer Park Trail.

0.5 Negotiate a brief but abrupt hill.

0.8 Bear left on Deer Park as Middle and Cedar Trails head right.

1.5 ● STOP. Cross the park road and join the Nook Trail.

1.6 ▼ CAUTION: Brake on a lengthy and steep, two-tiered descent.

1.9 ● STOP. Cross the park road and stay right, now on the Ruth Pond Trail.

2.0 Continue to follow the Ruth Pond Trail, avoiding the Overlook Trail.

Expect to encounter some challenging slopes along the twisting path that cuts through Nickerson State Park.

2.2 Push up some hills, passing Ruth Pond on your left.

2.4 ▼ CAUTION: Brake on a twisting descent.

2.6 Take on more short, tough climbs.

3.0 ▼ CAUTION: Braking will be necessary on another challenging descent.

3.1 Turn left on the Nook Trail, following a sign to the MAIN ENTRANCE.

3.5 ▼ CAUTION: Brake on a quick, two-tiered descent.

3.8 Turn right. Cross the park road and head back to the Deer Park Trail.

4.2 Cross the park road and turn left on the Ober Trail as Deer Park splits right.

4.3 ▼ CAUTION: Brake on this moderate descent.

4.6 Continue straight as Cedar Trail goes right.

5.1 Continue straight as Middle Trail bears right.

5.3 ▼ CAUTION: Brakes are absolutely required on this fast, two-tiered descent.

5.7 ▼ CAUTION: Brake on a steep downhill.

5.9 Link up with the Deer Park Trail. Cross the park road and head for your car.

6.2 Your car!

48 •••• *Cape Cod Rail Trail, Wellfleet*

LOCATION: Wellfleet, MA

RATING: Beginner or intermediate

DISTANCE: 10.2 miles (beginner); 11 miles (intermediate)

TIMES TO AVOID: None

TERRAIN: Wide, flat path

SURFACE: Very smooth pavement

AUTO TRAFFIC: None, except at infrequent crossings

POINTS OF INTEREST: Wellfleet Wildlife Reservation, Cape Cod National Seashore Headquarters, Marconi Beach, Marconi Wireless Station (with its display of the *Titanic*'s distress signal), Nauset Beach Lighthouse, Salt Pond Visitor Center, Great Island, Audubon Bird Sanctuary

DRIVING DIRECTIONS: From MA 6 South in Wellfleet (at mile marker 99.5), turn right onto LeCount Hollow Road. Continue straight at an

T. LEWIS

If you're looking to skate in the sunshine, head for the more exposed western sections of the Cape Cod Rail Trail.

immediate fork. One-tenth of a mile from MA 6, turn right into the parking lot for the Cape Cod Rail Trail.

TRIP OVERVIEW: Not until 1873, when the Old Colony Railroad Company extended tracks to Provincetown, were the isolated folks living at the outer reaches of the Cape finally linked to the East Coast. Suddenly, the grueling stagecoach trip from Boston was replaced by a brief 5-hour jaunt by train, and visitors flocked to the Cape on summer days as they continue to do today.

The 25-mile-long Cape Cod Rail Trail, enjoyed year-round by crowds of skaters, cyclists, walkers, and cross-country skiers, follows the old railway bed. The trip described here is the stuff skaters' dreams are made of, covering the smoothest section of the rail trail (and the smoothest skating surface you'll encounter anywhere). Because the route closely parallels power lines and the accompanying wide clear-cut, you'll fight fierce winds in one direction, then get a helpful push in the other. Rest at street crossings and on cement benches tucked among the trees.

If time permits, explore the art galleries along the main streets of Wellfleet or the tranquil marshes and moors of the Wildlife Sanctuary on Wellfleet Bay.

ROUTE DIRECTIONS:

0.0 Join the rail trail heading south toward Eastham.

0.1 Bisect a marsh created by Blackfish Creek.

0.5 Climb one of the few gradual ascents.

0.9 ● STOP at a street crossing that leads to the seashore headquarters.

1.5 Continue along the windswept path.

2.0 Crest a second gentle rise and commence a long, straight stretch.

3.6 After veering away from the power lines, ● STOP and cross Nauset Road.

4.2 Skate through a more protected section, then ● STOP and cross Brackett Road. Now, power lines are on your right.

5.1 ● STOP and cross Old Orchard Road. (BEGINNERS should reverse direction and return to the start.) ▼ CAUTION: Descend through a tunnel under MA 6.

5.2 ● STOP at a fifth street crossing: Kingsbury Beach Road.

5.5 ● STOP at Locust Road. As the new section of trail ends, return to the start the way you came.

49 •••• *Head of the Meadow*

LOCATION: Truro, MA
RATING: Beginner
DISTANCE: 3.8 miles
TIMES TO AVOID: None
TERRAIN: Flat, narrow, winding path
SURFACE: Coarse asphalt, some broken
AUTO TRAFFIC: None
POINTS OF INTEREST: Head of the Meadow Beach, Highland Beach, Highland Light, Truro

DRIVING DIRECTIONS: On MA 6 in Truro (shortly after mile marker 110), turn right onto Head of the Meadow Road following a sign to Head of the Meadow. In 0.9 mile, bear left and enter the Head of the Meadow Beach parking area (where you'll pay a moderate day-use fee). If you're visiting off-season, you may want to park at the Truro Town Beach (Highland Beach), where fees are charged only during July and August.

As an alternative, from MA 6 take gravel High Head Road (2

Sand encroaches on the path where skaters glide between sand dunes.

miles beyond Head of the Meadow Road) and park in a sandy parking area near the end of the trail.

TRIP OVERVIEW: Art aficionados already know Truro. The paintings of Edward Hopper convey the beauty of its gentle hills and expansive, sandy beaches. If you stand atop a dune in Truro, you'll be able to see the ocean on one side and the bay on the other. Truro is the Cape's narrowest town, less than a mile wide at some spots.

Rolling along this narrow, twisting, sometimes bumpy path will make a beginning skater feel as if he or she is tackling a more advanced route. The terrain exaggerates speed and forces the novice to exercise some control. In reality, the route is not challenging, and the grainy pavement helps check speed. Do be aware, however, that cyclists race around the blind corners. Another tip: Take water. Although there are shady sections, this is a very dry trail. (There is a rest stop and picnic area with rest rooms at Pilgrim Heights, about halfway into the trip.)

ROUTE DIRECTIONS:
- 0.0 The trail begins just short of the Head of the Meadows Beach parking area entrance. Initially the trail is wide and smooth with occasional bumps.
- 0.2 The tree canopy creates the illusion of a tunnel as the path winds through the woods.

0.5 Look for the 0.5-mile marker painted on the pavement.

1.0 The 1-mile mark is also noted on the path.

1.2 To your left, a small picnic area nestles in the woods at Pilgrim Heights. Curve to the right through a brief section of cracked pavement.

1.5 Roll along one of the route's only straight stretches.

1.8 As the trail opens up, enjoy views of distant dunes.

1.9 When the trail ends, reverse direction to return to your car.

50 •••• *Race Point*

LOCATION: Provincetown, MA
RATING: Intermediate
DISTANCE: 8.1 miles
TIMES TO AVOID: Summer weekend afternoons (because of increased traffic)
TERRAIN: Gently rolling, wide roads with two moderate hills
SURFACE: Smooth asphalt
AUTO TRAFFIC: Light
POINTS OF INTEREST: Provincetown, Pilgrim Monument, art galleries, whale-watch cruises, sand dune tours, bike trails, beaches

DRIVING DIRECTIONS: At a traffic light on MA 6 in Provincetown (just after mile marker 116), turn right onto Race Point Road following a sign to Race Point. (*Note:* Ignore another sign indicating that Race Point is straight ahead.) In 0.4 mile, turn left into the Beach Forest parking and picnic area.

TRIP OVERVIEW: Famous for its offbeat population, bustling Province-town (known as the Cape's fist) boasts a unique setting. Surrounded by spectacular beaches and impressive tufted sand dunes, "P-town" is an ideal spot for the skater who travels with nonskating relatives or companions.

Begin this trip in lush woods, then quickly enter the high dunes of the Province Lands. You'll encounter a number of gently rolling hills, along with some moderate inclines. As with other spots on the shore, expect to be blown about by strong gusts. Because the leg to Herring Cove Beach travels through arid country, be sure to have enough water

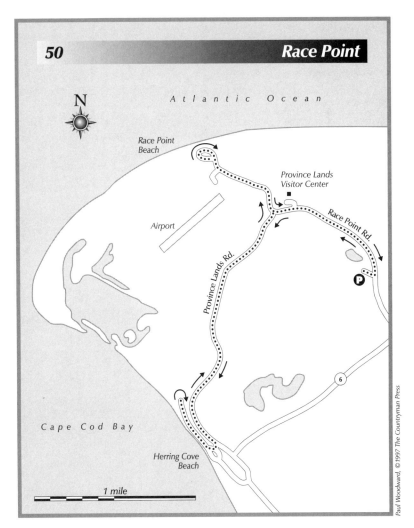

to last for the entire route. Once at the beach, you can enter the parking area free of charge (skaters avoid the fee; cyclists may not!). There you'll find toilet facilities, a snack bar, walking trails, and a bike path. (*Note:* In-line skaters are not permitted to use the bike path because of the many steep descents and sharp turns.) Return by way of Race Point Beach, where whale sightings are not uncommon. During the summer months, we recommend that you skate in the morning, when the traffic and winds are light and the temperature is lower.

ROUTE DIRECTIONS:

0.0 From the parking area, return to Race Point Road and turn left, skating under a deciduous canopy.

0.6 Begin a moderate ascent.

0.8 Crest. Pass the Province Lands Visitor Center entrance as the tree cover vanishes.

1.0 Turn left onto Province Lands Road, guided by a sign to Herring Cove.

1.2 Begin to climb moderately up a sand dune hill.

1.9 Roll over more dunes.

2.7 Skate through a depression bracketed by tall dunes. To your left, the Pilgrim Monument rises in the distance.

3.3 Turn right into Herring Cove Beach. (Explore, if you'd like, the half-mile of paved parking lot that is part of the Province Lands Trail.) Then retrace your route along Province Lands Road.

5.5 At the intersection with Race Point Road, turn left.

5.6 Head down a moderate 0.1-mile descent.

6.3 Enter the Race Point Beach parking area. After scanning the horizon for whale tails, return to your car (1.8 miles away) along Race Point Road.

S. HOOPER

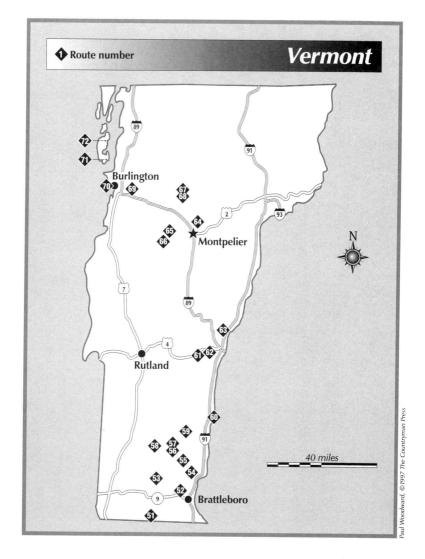

Part Four

Vermont

51 •••• Town Common

LOCATION: Whitingham, VT
RATING: Intermediate (with option for advanced loop)
DISTANCE: 4.0 miles (with option for longer route)
TIMES TO AVOID: None
TERRAIN: Rolling hills on a country road with no shoulder
SURFACE: Coarse asphalt
AUTO TRAFFIC: Light
POINTS OF INTEREST: Harriman Reservoir, North River Winery, Brigham Young monument, Brattleboro Museum and Art Center, Brooks Memorial Library in Brattleboro, Manchester center (outlet shopping), Hildene (Lincoln's son's retreat in Manchester), Skyline Drive to the summit of Mount Equinox

DRIVING DIRECTIONS: From I-91 in Brattleboro, take exit 2 to VT 30 West. Follow VT 30 West to Wilmington and the intersection with VT 100 South. Turn left onto VT 100 South and drive 6 miles to Jacksonville. From the junction of VT 100 and VT 112, continue on VT 100 for another 1.2 miles and park at the Whitingham School on your left.

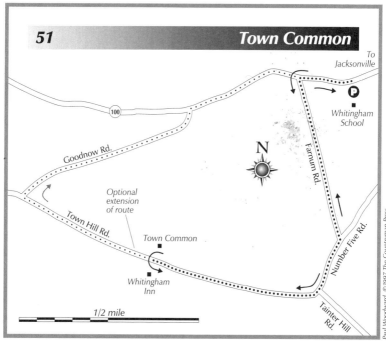

TRIP OVERVIEW: New York has the Empire State Building, Chicago has the Sears Tower, and Whitingham, Vermont, has the Brigham Young monument to honor the birthplace of the famous religious leader. What makes Whitingham different from New York and Chicago (aside from a few million inhabitants) is that the monument is about all it has—which, if you're looking for a quaint and quiet spot for a skate, should please you. This is backcountry Vermont at its best. Not far away, Wilmington and Stratton welcome the tourists, but Whitingham seems content with cows outnumbering cars and stores that sell milk and bread rather than souvenir T-shirts.

On this trip you'll roll by the village common and several dairy and horse farms, all the while treated to splendid views of layer upon layer of hills. You'll return from this skate relaxed, not exhausted. And that's what an escape weekend is all about.

ROUTE DIRECTIONS:

0.0 From the parking lot, return to VT 100 and turn left. Skate 0.1 mile and turn left onto Farnum Road.

0.2 Work up a short hill.

0.5 Bear right, now on Number 5 Road.

0.9 Dip, and then roll uphill.

1.5 ▼ CAUTION: Descend steeply, carefully.

1.4 Bear right, now skating on Town Hill Road; pump up a short hill.

2.0 Reach the Whitingham Town Hill common with the Whitingham Inn on your left.

Note: There are rest rooms, a playground, and a picnic area here, as well as the Brigham Young monument. This marks the turn-around point for INTERMEDIATE skaters. ADVANCED skaters may extend the trip by continuing straight past the Whitingham Inn and bearing right onto Goodnow Road in about 0.3 mile. At the intersection with VT 100, turn right and skate about 3 miles back to your car.

---

52 •••• *West River*

LOCATION: Brattleboro, VT
RATING: Intermediate
DISTANCE: 17.0 miles
TIMES TO AVOID: None (but beware of cars parked along the shoulder)
TERRAIN: Flat, with one moderate hill at about the halfway point

The riverside route is a favorite among area speed skaters, cyclists, and runners.

SURFACE: Smooth asphalt
AUTO TRAFFIC: Moderate (but road has a wide shoulder)
POINTS OF INTEREST: Connecticut River boat tours, Brattleboro shops and restaurants, Living Memorial Park (playground), Fort Dummer State Park, various pick-your-own fruit farms

DRIVING DIRECTIONS: From I-91 in Brattleboro, take exit 3 to VT 9 East. In 0.1 mile, at the traffic light, turn right onto US 5 South (Putney Road), following a sign to VT 30. Drive 2 miles and turn right onto Park Place, again guided by a sign for VT 30. In 0.1 mile, turn right onto VT 30 North. Drive 0.3 mile and park in the wide paved turnout just past the Brattleboro Retreat.

TRIP OVERVIEW: This route is popular among serious in-line enthusiasts, who enjoy racing down the wide shoulder of the "skating superhighway" at a cyclist's pace. You'll follow the southern bank of the West River from its wide, sluggish mouth near the junction with the Connecticut River to a swift, slender section just a few miles east of historic Newfane and the Four Columns Inn. Because you're in Vermont (and, as the T-shirts say, VERMONT AIN'T FLAT), dramatic hills bracket the river, though the road itself, slicing through the river valley, is relatively flat. The setting is quite pleasant, and you'll even pass a lengthy covered bridge. Strong winds will likely be a factor on the outbound leg, but remind yourself as you're pumping hard that the skate back—with a tailwind and general downhill trend—will be quick.

If you're skating the West River on a Thursday evening, expect to share the road with cyclists racing a long-standing time trial organized by Putney's West Hill Shop. And no matter what the day of the week, skate with your head up because anglers park along the road's shoulder.

ROUTE DIRECTIONS:

0.0 Skate on the wide shoulder of VT 30 North, initially on a quick descent. Soon join the "flats" of the West River.

1.0 Pass under the bridge carrying I-91.

3.0 Roll up and over an easy hill.

4.9 The shoulder is squeezed a bit as VT 30 crosses a stream. (You're nearly 5 miles into the route as you pass the metal bridge spanning the river.)

6.5 Continue straight as a covered bridge stretches across the West River.

7.0 Pass the Maple Valley ski area and begin a moderate ascent that soon eases.

7.4 Rest as the hill peaks and levels.

8.5 ▼ CAUTION: At a side road that heads left to Dover, cross VT 30 and reverse direction to return to your car.

53 •••• *Mount Snow*

LOCATION: West Dover, VT
RATING: Advanced
DISTANCE: 5.2 miles
TIMES TO AVOID: Midday in summer
TERRAIN: Rolling hills on a country road with no shoulder
SURFACE: Smooth asphalt with some coarse asphalt
AUTO TRAFFIC: Light
POINTS OF INTEREST: Mount Snow Resort, Haystack Golf Course, Wilmington center, Manchester center, Hildene (Lincoln's son's retreat in Manchester), Skyline Drive to the summit of Mount Equinox, Stratton Mountain Village and gondola ride, Bromley Alpine Slide

DRIVING DIRECTIONS: From I-91 in Brattleboro, take exit 2 to VT 30 West. Follow VT 30 West to the intersection with VT 100 North in downtown Wilmington. Turn right onto VT 100 North and drive approximately 9 miles to a blinking light in West Dover. Turn left onto the access road to the Mount Snow Resort. Pass the Snow Lake Lodge on your right and, 0.5 mile from the light, turn left onto Handle Road. Drive about 1 mile, following signs for the Carinthia Base Lodge, and turn right into the lodge parking area.

TRIP OVERVIEW: We eliminated some skating routes from our *101 Best* list simply because they are so remote. Similarly, we include routes because of their proximity to popular areas. This is one of those. Though ski resort towns are not known for their flatlands and smooth asphalt, we found some skater-friendly turf in West Dover just right for experienced bladers. After all, thousands visit this area during July and August—and we just know that a good percentage of them pack their skates. (In the wintertime, Wilmington's population swells from 3000 to 33,000!)

You'll cruise from the Carinthia Base Lodge of the Mount Snow Ski Area to the access road leading to the Haystack Ski Area, rolling over some significant but skateable hills along the way. The asphalt is in good condition and if you head out early in the morning, you'll encounter little or no traffic.

ROUTE DIRECTIONS:
- 0.0 From the parking area, turn right onto Handle Road, initially on very smooth pavement. (The speed limit here is 35 mph.)
- 0.3 ● STOP. At a stop sign, continue straight.
- 0.8 Head uphill for 0.2 mile.
- 1.1 Reap your reward as you glide down a gradual descent.
- 1.3 ▼ CAUTION: Negotiate a steep descent.
- 2.0 ▼ CAUTION: The road curves sharply left.
- 2.6 At the entrance to the Haystack Ski Area (on your right), turn around and head back to your car.
  Note: You can skate to VT 100, about 6 miles away. The road becomes quite hilly, and the pavement is average.

SKATING TIP: *For speed skating, your head should remain on a level plane with your back and show no bobbing motion.*

54 ••••   *River Road, Putney*

LOCATION: Putney, VT
RATING: Advanced
DISTANCE: 7.6 miles
TIMES TO AVOID: None
TERRAIN: Rolling hills on a rural road with no shoulder
SURFACE: Coarse asphalt
AUTO TRAFFIC: Light
POINTS OF INTEREST: Basketville (US 5), Santa's Land, Green Mountain Spinnery, Putney Nursery (known for its wildflowers), the Putney Inn (with an information booth listing local events), Putney General Store, Harlow's Sugar House

DRIVING DIRECTIONS: From I-91 in Putney, take exit 4 to US 5 North. Follow US 5 North through Putney village. Pass Basketville (a large factory store) on your right and take the first right onto River Road, guided by the sign for Landmark College. Drive 0.1 mile and turn left into the dormitory parking lot.

TRIP OVERVIEW: Everyone loves a happy ending. We know that. So be patient.

After River Road passes through an industrial district (you won't need your camera for this section—promise), it rolls through pastures and farms that stretch to the Connecticut River (that's the happy ending part). The views of the hills are spectacular. In fall, when the hordes of leaf-peepers crowd the highways, escape to River Road for some solitary gazing. And once you've arrived at the turnaround point, you'll agree that the happy end justifies the initial means.

Don't head out without poking around Putney. This offbeat artists community just north of Brattleboro has loads of funky shops, galleries, and restaurants. It is also recognized for its apples (producing 10 percent of the state's crop) and its athletes (like Olympian Bill Koch). And if you're looking for a basket (any shape, size, or color) or a tourist (any shape, size, or color), you'll find lots of both at Basketville.

ROUTE DIRECTIONS:
- 0.0 From the parking lot, return to River Road, heading slightly uphill.
- 0.3 ▼ CAUTION: Two speed bumps have been removed, leaving a 3-inch rut stretching across the road. Stop and step over.

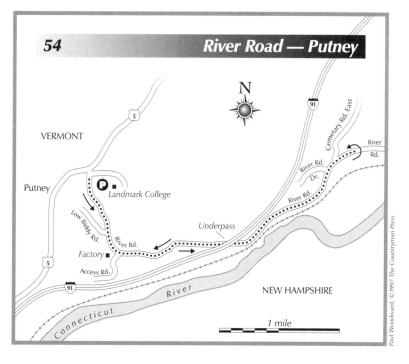

54 *River Road — Putney*

Paul Woodward, © 1997 The Countryman Press

0.4 Turn left onto River Road.

0.5 Drop down a gradual slope for 0.1 mile. Pass a Quaker Oats factory on your right.

0.8 Pass Low Biddy Road on your right.

1.0 ▼ CAUTION: A factory access road turns right along a sharp curve to your left. Watch for vehicles entering and exiting.

1.2 As you head steeply downhill for 0.2 mile, pass a farm on your right with pleasing local views.

1.3 ▼ CAUTION: Negotiate a tight curve.

1.8 Pass the Tavern Hill Pet Care Center on your right on a gradual decline.

1.9 Cruise easily along flat, straight pavement.

2.0 Roll under I-91, avoiding sections of rough pavement.

2.3 As you embark on a gradual ascent, enjoy great views of the Connecticut River and the surrounding hills.

2.4 Skate beside a railroad bed with pretty rolling hills ahead.

2.8 Enjoy smooth asphalt on level ground.

2.9 Continue straight as River Road Drive heads left.

3.0 Glide along flat pavement for 0.2 mile, passing a dairy farm on your right.

3.3 Roll by River View Farm on your right.

3.4 Cemetery Road East leaves on your left.

3.8 As the road turns to gravel, stop and rest (and enjoy the great river views) before retracing the route back to your car, exercising caution on the two sharp curves and watching for the "missing" speed bumps near route's end.

7.6 Take time to roll through the campus of Landmark College on paths totaling about 1.5 miles; pretty views extend to the Connecticut River Valley.

55 •••• Townshend Dam

LOCATION: Townshend, VT

RATING: Beginner

DISTANCE: 1.0 mile

TIMES TO AVOID: None

TERRAIN: Flat dam access road

SURFACE: Smooth asphalt

AUTO TRAFFIC: Light

POINTS OF INTEREST: Newfane village, the Newfane Flea Market (Sundays, spring through fall), Manchester center, Mount Snow Resort, Skyline Drive to the summit of Mount Equinox, Stratton Mountain Resort, Stratton Pond Country Club

DRIVING DIRECTIONS: From I-91 in Brattleboro, take exit 3 to NH 9 East. In 0.1 mile, at the traffic light, turn right onto US 5 South (Putney Road), following a sign to VT 30. Drive 2 miles and turn right onto Park Place, again guided by a sign for VT 30. In 0.1 mile, turn right onto VT 30 North. Drive 18.5 miles on VT 30 North and turn left following a sign to Townshend Lake Recreation Area. Drive across the dam and turn right into a small parking lot, where the route will begin. (*Note:* Public rest rooms are available here.)

TRIP OVERVIEW: What do these things have in common: a Tootsie Roll, a child's prayer, this peaceful trek across the Townshend Dam? Give up? They are all short, but sweet!

Follow the access road that runs atop the dam, overlooking a small public beach and the surrounding hills. The pavement is smooth, the road flat, and you're not likely to encounter many—if any—cars or people. It's a terrific spot to bring new skaters or anyone interested in practicing and improving skating techniques. The setting is lovely, and the location is great (just off VT 30). Bring bathing suits so that you can hit the town beach afterward. If you're not a swimmer, drive through the village of Newfane: Do you recognize the Four Columns Inn? A Rice-A-Roni commercial made it famous!

For a full weekend of skating, combine this route with nearby Jamaica State Park (Tour 56) and Ball Mountain Dam (Tour 57).

ROUTE DIRECTIONS:
0.0 From the parking lot, head back onto the dam access road.
0.5 At the end of the access road, turn around and repeat.

> **SKATING TIP:** *If your shins and knees ache during and after a workout, you may not be skating in the proper position. Be sure that your knees are over your toes when skating. Also, concentrate on using your upper leg muscles for power when you're stroking, not just your lower leg muscles (below the knees). Failing to use these large muscles for power will put added pressure on your joints.*

56 •••• *Jamaica State Park*

LOCATION: Jamaica, VT
RATING: Beginner
DISTANCE: 2.3 miles
TIMES TO AVOID: None
TERRAIN: Flat rural road with no shoulder
SURFACE: Coarse asphalt
AUTO TRAFFIC: Light
POINTS OF INTEREST: Manchester center, Mount Snow Resort (West Dover), Hildene (Lincoln's son's retreat in Manchester), Skyline Drive to the summit of Mount Equinox, Stratton Mountain Village and gondola ride, Bromley Alpine Slide, Newfane village

DRIVING DIRECTIONS: From I-91 in Brattleboro, take exit 3 for NH 9 East. In 0.1 mile, turn right at the traffic light onto US 5 South (Putney Road), following a sign to VT 30. In 2 miles, turn right onto Park Place, again following a sign to VT 30. Drive 0.1 mile and turn right onto VT 30 North; drive 25.6 miles to Jamaica center and Depot Street on your right. Park along the road in front of the Jamaica Community Church.

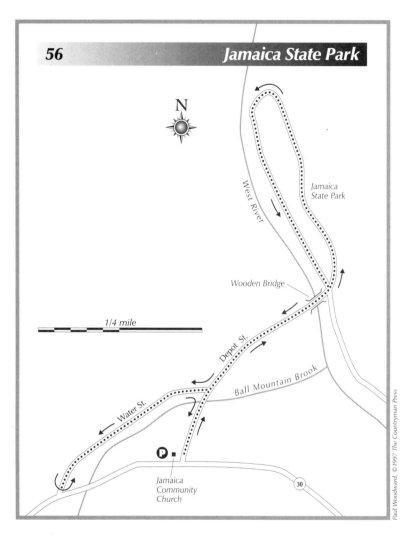

56 *Jamaica State Park*

N

Jamaica
State Park

West River

Wooden Bridge

1/4 mile

Depot St.

Ball Mountain Brook

Water St.

P

Jamaica
Community
Church

30

Paul Woodward, ©1997 The Countryman Press

TRIP OVERVIEW: Many beginning skaters shudder at the thought of Vermont terrain: hills, bigger hills, and mountains. But Vermont has a few—and just a few—flat areas, and we found one. Begin by carefully crossing an old bridge on weathered wooden boards. Roll through the camping area at Jamaica State Park and then cruise through a peaceful, unassuming neighborhood. This is not intended to be a knock-yourself-out workout, but an easy skate, perfect for a lazy weekend.

Jamaica State Park boasts that it is "Home of the West River Water Championships." (If you visit in October, you may catch some of the rafting and tubing races.) It is also home to hiking trails (one leads to scenic Hamilton Falls), prime fishing spots, camping and picnicking sites, and a playground. In the West River, visitors can swim or launch a canoe or kayak—a terrific place for the family to hang out while you skate!

ROUTE DIRECTIONS:

0.0 From the Jamaica Community Church, return to Depot Street and head north, rolling beside a row of cottages. (*Note:* The speed limit here is 15 mph, so you shouldn't have to worry about fast-moving traffic.)

0.3 ▼ CAUTION: Roll slowly over the warped wooden bridge. Pause to take in pleasing views of the West River.

0.4 Bear left at a sign and enter the Jamaica State Park Campgrounds. (*Note:* A minimal day-use fee may be charged upon entering the park.)

0.5 ▼ CAUTION: Hop over speed bumps.

0.6 Follow the campground road as it makes a U-turn and passes campsites.

0.8 Exit the park and turn right onto Depot Street.

0.9 ▼ CAUTION: Again, roll slowly over the bridge.

1.2 Turn right onto quiet, residential Water Street, which runs parallel to VT 30 and along a brook.

1.6 At the intersection with VT 30, we recommend that you return to the intersection of Water and Depot Streets.

2.0 Turn right onto Depot Street and cross the bridge.

2.3 Return to your car.

57 •••• *Ball Mountain Dam*

LOCATION: Jamaica, VT
RATING: Intermediate
DISTANCE: 3.4 miles
TIMES TO AVOID: None
TERRAIN: Gradual rolling hills on a gatehouse access road with no shoulder
SURFACE: Smooth asphalt
AUTO TRAFFIC: Light
POINTS OF INTEREST: Manchester center (outlet shopping), Mount Snow Resort (West Dover), Hildene (Lincoln's son's retreat in Manchester), Skyline Drive to the summit of Mount Equinox, Stratton Mountain

Ball Mountain Dam is your destination, with spectacular views of Stratton Mountain and other local parks.

DRIVING DIRECTIONS: From I-91 in Brattleboro, take exit 3 for NH 9 East. In 0.1 mile, turn right at the traffic light onto US 5 South (Putney Road), following a sign to VT 30. In 2 miles, turn right onto Park Place, again following a sign to VT 30. Drive 0.1 mile and turn right onto VT 30 West; drive 25.6 miles to Jamaica center. Drive an additional 1.5 miles on VT 30 and turn right at the marked entrance to Ball Mountain Lake. Immediately on your left, pull in and park near a white building with a three-car garage (the Ball Mountain Lake Flood Control Reservoir office). The area is open 7 AM to 8 PM.

TRIP OVERVIEW: You'll want to charge along this park access road at top speed to reach the trip's climax: a heart-pounding stretch along a 200-foot-long expanse leading to the Ball Mountain Dam gatehouse.

But you won't be able to.

Exhilarating views—especially at the 0.7-mile mark—will distract you, causing you to stop by the side of the road and gape. Stratton Mountain and the Green Mountains tower over you, and the West River flows through the valley far below.

When you're saturated with scenery and ready to roll, you'll glide along smooth pavement on relatively flat terrain for nearly 2 miles before reaching your destination. If you dare, skate along the narrow walkway (180 feet above the water!) to the gatehouse, which holds the electronic equipment needed to operate the flood-control gates. If you suffer from a fear of heights, your churning stomach may prevent you from venturing out over the river. But for the bravest souls, the views from the gatehouse are worth a few butterflies. Below is the Ball Mountain Dam, which cannot be accessed on skates.

You'll want an excuse to spend some time in this area, so be sure to pack a picnic lunch.

ROUTE DIRECTIONS:

0.0 From the parking area, turn left, trending upward on the access road.

0.7 Take a break at Overlook Point, which offers superb water and mountain views. If you've brought lunch or a snack, spread it out on one of the cliffside tables.

1.1 Roll downhill for 0.2 mile.

1.3 Pass public rest rooms on your right.

1.7 Arrive at the walkway leading to the gatehouse. Skate out to the tower, or enjoy the views from the safety of terra firma.

58 •••• *Stratton Sun Bowl*

LOCATION: Stratton, VT
RATING: Advanced or expert
DISTANCE: 4.4 miles (advanced): 5.2 miles (expert)
TIMES TO AVOID: None
TERRAIN: Rural road with rolling hills
SURFACE: Coarse asphalt
AUTO TRAFFIC: Light
POINTS OF INTEREST: Manchester center (outlet shopping), Mount Snow Resort (West Dover), Hildene (Lincoln's son's retreat in Manchester), Skyline Drive to the summit of Mount Equinox, Stratton Mountain Resort (Stratton Village Square, the gondola, golf, tennis, hiking, mountain biking), Stratton Pond Country Club

DRIVING DIRECTIONS: From I-91 in Brattleboro, take exit 3 for NH 9 East. In 0.1 mile, turn right at the traffic light onto US 5 South (Putney Road), following a sign to VT 30. In 2 miles, turn right onto Park Place, again following a sign to VT 30. Drive 0.1 mile and turn right onto VT 30 West. Drive 30.2 miles to Bondville and turn left onto Stratton Mountain Road. Drive 3.5 miles to the resort entrance on your right, and park in the large parking lot.

TRIP OVERVIEW: The first crop of in-line skaters took to parking lots about as quickly as Cro-Magnon man took to caves. And why not? Parking lots—wide, paved, and usually abutting something interesting—are a terrific place to practice tricks and technique. Some of the biggest parking lots happen to belong to ski areas, which also happen to be relatively empty during the warmer months (exceptions are during special summer events and concerts).

The parking lot below the Stratton Village Lodge is popular with the skating crowd and perfect for beginning and intermediate skaters. For those who crave challenging terrain, follow the Sun Bowl route described below that begins and ends at the parking lot, but includes a few miles of roller-coaster roads in between. If your group of skating chums includes beginners as well as experts, pile everyone in the car and head to Stratton Mountain—southern Vermont's highest peak! (*Note:* Coauthor Carolyn Bradley's SkateFit™ video was filmed in this area and along this route.)

ROUTE DIRECTIONS:
0.0 From the main parking lot, turn right onto the access road.
0.4 Roll by the Stratton Sports Center on your left.
0.5 ▼ CAUTION: Embark on a steep 0.3-mile hill.
1.0 At a sign for the Sun Bowl Base Lodge, turn right.
1.4 Cruise past the Sun Bowl Base Lodge on your right.
2.0 ▼ CAUTION: Drop steeply downhill for 0.3 mile.
2.2 As you approach a steep ascent, ADVANCED SKATERS should turn around. EXPERT SKATERS continue: Climb a formidable 0.4-mile hill.
2.6 Enjoy spectacular hilltop views before reversing direction and descending with caution. Return to your car the way you came.

SKATING TIP: *For maximum power when speed skating, your back should be parallel to the ground: You should be able to cup your hands over your toes.*

59 •••• Main Street, Grafton

LOCATION: Grafton, VT
RATING: Beginner or intermediate
DISTANCE: 3.0 miles (beginner); 6.4 miles (intermediate)
TIMES TO AVOID: None
TERRAIN: Gentle rolling hills on a rural road with no shoulder
SURFACE: Coarse asphalt
AUTO TRAFFIC: Light
POINTS OF INTEREST: Historic Grafton village, Brick Meeting House, the Old Tavern Inn, W.C. Putnam State Forest, Grafton Village Cheese Company, the Green Mountain Flyer (scenic train rides), Grafton Historical Society Museum

DRIVING DIRECTIONS: From I-91 in Westminster, take exit 5. At the end of the ramp, head west. In 0.1 mile, turn right onto Back Westminster Road. In 3 miles, bear left onto VT 121 North. Travel approximately 9 miles to the village of Grafton. Turn left onto Main Street and park immediately on your left at the Old Tavern Inn.

TRIP OVERVIEW: You'll have to glance down at your skates every once in a while to convince yourself that it is indeed the modern era. In the restored 19th-century town of Grafton, the common is edged with historic homes, two steepled churches from the 1830s, and the Old Tavern Inn (built in 1801). The Grafton Historical Society exhibits hundreds of photographs that tell the Grafton story from the early 1800s, when sheep outnumbered people seven to one, through the latter part of the century, when a soapstone quarry, logging operations, cheese and maple syrup production, and the manufacture of carriages and sleighs brought prosperity to this small village. And talk about tradition: If you visit on a Sunday evening in the summertime, you'll hear the Grafton Cornet Band playing—just as it has every Sunday evening since 1867!

Join the tourists who visit in droves, although instead of roaring into town on a bus, you can explore on your own via your skates with no dirty windows to impede the view. Our route takes you by charming cottages, past the well-known Grafton Village Cheese Company, and beside the pleasant Saxtons River. Beginners can handle the initial 1.5 miles to the first bridge; then, more twists and turns demand intermediate skills.

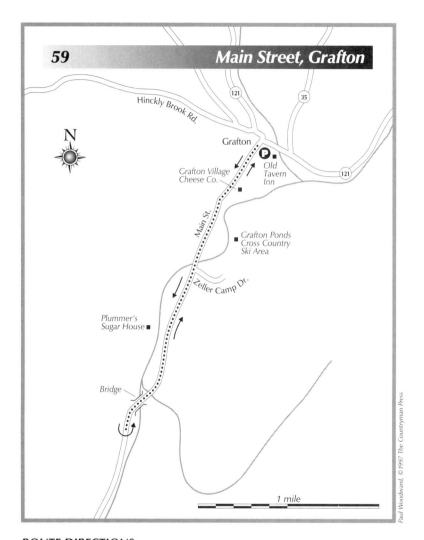

59 *Main Street, Grafton*

ROUTE DIRECTIONS:

0.0 From the Old Tavern Inn in Grafton center, head west on Main Street.

0.2 Cruise by an information center on your left.

0.3 Roll down a gentle slope, winding beside the Saxtons River.

0.5 On your left, pass the Grafton Village Cheese Company, producer of Covered Bridge Cheese. (Main Street turns into Townshend Road here.)

0.8 Glide past Grafton Ponds Cross-Country Ski Area on your left.

1.4 Stay straight as Zeller Camp Drive leaves on your left.
1.5 As you approach a bridge, BEGINNER SKATERS should turn around and return the way they came. INTERMEDIATES: Roll over the small bridge and continue.
2.0 Push up a slight incline.
2.3 Cross a brook on a short bridge.
2.8 With Plummer's Sugar House on your right, pause for a sight-seeing break: Take in views of the rolling countryside beyond the sugarhouse.
3.2 As a minor brook joins on your left, take a break before turning around and heading back the way you came.

60 •••• *Old Connecticut River Road*

LOCATION: Springfield, VT
RATING: Beginner
DISTANCE: 3.4 miles
TIMES TO AVOID: None
TERRAIN: Flat rural road with no shoulder
SURFACE: Coarse asphalt
AUTO TRAFFIC: Light
POINTS OF INTEREST: Historic Grafton village, Grafton Village Cheese Company, the Green Mountain Flyer (scenic train ride), Eureka Schoolhouse, Baltimore Covered Bridge, Springfield Art and Historical Society, Fort at No. 4 (Charlestown, New Hampshire), Wilgus State Park, Ascutney State Park

DRIVING DIRECTIONS: From I-91, take exit 7 in Springfield. Head west on VT 11, following signs for US 5 North. In less than 1 mile, turn left just before the Charlestown Toll Bridge onto US 5 North. Drive about 1 mile to Old Connecticut River Road on your right. Park along the side of the road.

TRIP OVERVIEW: Tired of sight-seeing by car, scenery slipping past the window before you even have a chance to point and exclaim? Hop off I-91 in Springfield and take in the sights, sounds, and scents of rural Vermont and the Connecticut River on your skates. Follow a flat, quiet road that winds along the riverbank, paralleling US 5.

Postskate, load your camera and drive to Springfield center (about 3 miles northwest). Stop by the state's oldest one-room schoolhouse, the Eureka Schoolhouse, east of Springfield on VT 11. The nearby Baltimore Covered Bridge was built in 1870. It spans Great Brook, connecting Springfield with Baltimore.

ROUTE DIRECTIONS:
   0.0 Head north on Old Connecticut River Road, taking in views of the New Hampshire hills across the river.
   0.9 Cruise by a tree farm on your left.
   1.0 Enjoy the river and hill views that surround you in an open area.
   1.7 Intersect with VT 5. Turn around and return the way you came.

SKATING TIP: *If you experience lower-back pain during extended workouts, relax every few minutes by stretching your lower-back muscles as illustrated. Also, remember to engage your abdominal muscles while skating for more lower-back support.*

S. HOOPER

61 •••• *Pomfret Road*

LOCATION: South Pomfret, VT
RATING: Advanced
DISTANCE: 9.4 miles (with options for a 7.4- or a 5.4-mile route)
TIMES TO AVOID: None
TERRAIN: Rolling hills on a rural road with no shoulder
SURFACE: Coarse asphalt
AUTO TRAFFIC: Light
POINTS OF INTEREST: Woodstock village, Billings Farm and Museum,

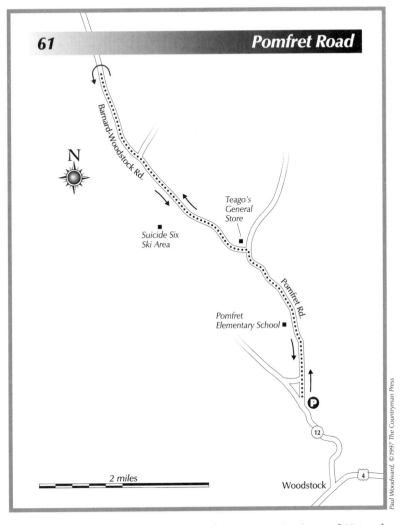

61   *Pomfret Road*

Barnard-Woodstock Rd.

N

Teago's
General
Store

Suicide Six
Ski Area

Pomfret Rd.

Pomfret
Elementary School ■

℗

12

2 miles

4

Woodstock

Paul Woodward, ©1997 The Countryman Press

the Vermont Raptor Center at the Vermont Institute of Natural
Science, Dana House (Woodstock historical museum), Mount
Tom and Mount Peg hiking trails, Silver Lake State Park, Suicide
Six Ski Area

DRIVING DIRECTIONS: From I-89 in White River Junction, take exit
1 (Woodstock/Quechee/US 4). Turn onto US 4 West and drive 10 miles
to the town of Woodstock. As US 4 and VT 12 split, bear right onto VT
12 North. At a stop sign, turn right and continue 0.9 mile on VT 12

North, then turn right into a gravel parking lot across the street from the Mount Tom School.

TRIP OVERVIEW: This area exemplifies all that is good about New England: unspoiled views of the region's signature rolling hills, stately historic homes, centuries-old farmlands. The route itself follows Pomfret Road, a lightly traveled country road, and offers three starting points that allow you to alter the trip to suit your endurance level. If you are anxious about sharing the road with cars, we recommend you begin your trip at Teago's General Store, because the traffic diminishes as you travel farther north.

Nearby Woodstock (known as New England's prettiest village) has drawn prosperous residents for centuries, residents who've always understood the importance of retaining the town's history and tradition and resisting the urge to update and modernize. In fact, what is *missing* is perhaps most important to the Woodstock image: Billboards are forbidden (a hand-lettered message on the chalkboard in the town center announces local events). Telephone and electrical wires are not strung overhead, but run underground. A weary bridge over the Ottauquechee River was replaced not by a modern steel expanse, but by an authentic covered bridge (held together by wooden pegs!). And when you hear church bells chime in Woodstock, chances are the bells were cast by Paul Revere. The only drawback to an excursion into Woodstock is the traffic: US 4, the state's major east–west route, runs by the green and through the town center, making for crowded roads and few empty parking spots in town.

In nearby Pomfret, the same sense of historical significance reigns: Not long ago, residents fought to retain the unspoiled views of the town's trademark hills, instituting zoning rules that confine new construction to existing roads and away from hilltops. Pomfret fruit orchards, abundant a century ago, still flourish, with pick-your-own harvests. Horses, cattle, and sheep roam open pastures, and sugar maples are tapped each spring for syrup.

ROUTE DIRECTIONS:

0.0 From the parking lot, turn right, heading north on VT 12.

0.1 At Thompson's Garage, bear right onto Pomfret Road, following signs for South Pomfret and the Suicide Six Ski Area.

1.0 Pass the Pomfret Elementary School on your left. (*Note:* Park here for a 7.4-mile trip.)

2.0 Roll by Teago's General Store. (*Note:* Park here for a 5.4-mile trip.)

Bear left onto Barnard-Woodstock Road, trending uphill from here to the turnaround point.

2.2 ▼ CAUTION: Watch for a tight corner on a descent.

2.7 Pass the Suicide Six Ski Area on your left, with lovely hill and pasture views typical of the Upper Valley region.

4.7 When the road becomes rough gravel, turn around and retrace the route, now on a gradual descent to Teago's General Store.

7.2 ▼ CAUTION: Tackle a tight corner on an ascent: Skate skinny!

7.4 Pass Teago's on your left.

8.4 Cruise by the Pomfret Elementary School on your right.

9.4 Return to the parking lot.

62 •••• *Quechee Golf Course*

LOCATION: Quechee, VT
RATING: Intermediate
DISTANCE: 5.0 miles
TIMES TO AVOID: None
TERRAIN: Flat rural road with some rolling hills
SURFACE: Coarse asphalt
AUTO TRAFFIC: Light
POINTS OF INTEREST: Quechee Gorge, Quechee Gorge Village, Quechee Covered Bridge (and waterfall), Theron Boyd Homestead, Old Meeting House, Hartland Dam (swimming and picnicking), White River tubing, Taftsville Covered Bridge, Woodstock village, Billings Farm and Museum, Vermont Raptor Center at the Vermont Institute of Natural Science, the Montshire Museum of Science

DRIVING DIRECTIONS: From I-89 in White River Junction, take exit 1 to US 4 West. Drive 1 mile and turn right onto Clubhouse Road. Travel 3 miles to the Quechee Golf Course with the clubhouse on your left and the golf course on your right. Park in the lot on your left across from the tennis courts. (*Note:* Clubhouse Road becomes Dewey's Mill Road, then Main Street, and finally River Road.)

TRIP OVERVIEW: Covered bridges are synonymous with Vermont, and so we have included this route that finishes at the much photographed Taftsville Covered Bridge, this tiny town's pride and joy. On the way there, you'll cruise along the breathtaking river valley with panoramic views of the energetic river and the layers of surrounding hills. We've

Take in lovely views of the waterfall and surrounding countryside from the Taftsville covered bridge.

classified it as an intermediate route, but high-end beginners with confidence on gradual descents should find it manageable. Pack good walking shoes and a picnic lunch so that you can hike to the bridge and relax there.

Leaving the area without visiting the Quechee Gorge would be like leaving Arizona without peeking into the Grand Canyon, so save enough time at the end of your skate to wander beside—and above—the gorge. You have melting glaciers to thank for this tremendous ravine, one of the state's most spectacular natural features.

The town of Quechee is an interesting mix: A contemporary resort community thrives within a historic New England village. Quechee's original settlers in the 1700s were deeded land to erect mills, and companies like Dewey's Mills flourished, eventually gaining recognition for making uniforms for the Boston Red Sox and New York Highlanders in the late 1800s. But by the 1950s, the mills began to close, and many of Quechee's homes and factories were abandoned. A decade later, investors searching for a location to build a four-season resort community chose Quechee, breathing life back into this town.

ROUTE DIRECTIONS:
0.0 From the parking lot, turn left onto River Road; skate past the golf course.
0.8 Roll over gentle hills.

2.0 Enjoy river views as you cruise along the northern bank.

2.5 Stop when you reach a sign to Sugar Bush Farm on your left, as Hillside Road joins on your right. ▼ CAUTION: Remove your skates to approach the Taftsville Covered Bridge and dam. Ahead is a steep descent known as Heartbreak Hill. We strongly advise that you do not attempt to skate down this hill to reach the bridge and picnic spot. Turn and skate back to your car.

63 •••• *Upper Valley*

LOCATION: Norwich and East Thetford, VT
RATING: Advanced
DISTANCE: 18.0 miles
TIMES TO AVOID: None
TERRAIN: Rolling hills on a rural road with a narrow shoulder
SURFACE: Coarse asphalt
AUTO TRAFFIC: Light
POINTS OF INTEREST: Montshire Museum of Science, Connecticut River, Dartmouth College, Hanover center, Woodstock village, Billings Farm and Museum, Vermont Raptor Center at the Vermont Institute of Natural Science

DRIVING DIRECTIONS:

TO NORWICH: Take I-91 to exit 13 (Hanover/NH 10A East). Turn right. Drive 0.3 mile and turn left onto (unmarked) Norwich State Highway. Park in the small municipal parking lot immediately on your left.

TO EAST THETFORD: Take I-91 to exit 14 (VT 113). Off the ramp, turn right onto VT 113. Drive 1.3 miles on VT 113. At a traffic light, turn left onto US 5 North. Immediately turn left into the parking lot of Wings Market and Deli. To begin, turn right out of the parking lot and head south on US 5, following the directions in reverse.

TRIP OVERVIEW: If you've already followed the River Road/Hanover trip (Tour 75) and it was a favorite, you'll enjoy this one, too. This trip is very similar, following along the Connecticut River in New England's Upper Valley region. Farmland reaches to the river, with steep hills rising over the water on either side. You'll be treated to lengthy sections of flatlands and challenged by tough hills. But you won't encounter many cars: Narrow US 5 runs beside I-91, which handles most of the through traffic. We've rated it an advanced route because of its length, but the downhill sections are not too tricky, and intermediate skaters might want to try the first 5 miles.

ROUTE DIRECTIONS (FROM NORWICH):

0.0 Leave the parking lot and turn left onto Norwich State Highway.

0.3 Glance across the river to see the Dartmouth College crew team's launch dock.

0.7 ▼ CAUTION: Stop and cross railroad tracks.

0.8 Merge with US 5 North.

1.2 Push up a gradual hill for 0.2 mile.

1.4 Drop down an easy descent with pleasant views.

1.8 Cruise by Kidder Farm on your left.

2.2 On an easy downhill, take in more views of the hills over the Connecticut River.

2.5 A church on your left marks the 2.5-mile mark and a possible turnaround point for anyone wishing to limit the trip to 5 miles.

4.8 ▼ CAUTION: Maneuver around choppy pavement for 0.2 mile.

5.2 Glide along level ground.

6.7 As you embark on a steady climb, take in views of the river snaking through the hills.

7.0 ▼ CAUTION: The road twists and turns.

8.5 ▼ CAUTION: Roll carefully over railroad tracks; enter the town of East Thetford.

9.0 At the intersection with VT 113 (with a gas station on your right), cross the street to Wings Market and Deli and grab a snack. Return to Norwich the way you came.

SKATING TIP: *When you are speed skating around corners, be sure your body stays at the same height as it is on the straights. Straightening up causes you to stroke behind your body, thus reducing your power.*

64 •••• State Capital

LOCATION: Montpelier, VT
RATING: Intermediate
DISTANCE: 3.6 miles
TIMES TO AVOID: None
TERRAIN: Limited rolling hills on a rural road with a wide shoulder
SURFACE: Coarse asphalt
AUTO TRAFFIC: Light
POINTS OF INTEREST: Downtown Montpelier, the Vermont Statehouse
    and State Complex, Hubbard Park and Tower (picnic sites, nature
    walks, stone tower with views), Supreme Court Building, Ver-
    mont Historical Society, Wood Art Gallery (affiliated with Ver-
    mont College), Northfield Falls and covered bridges, Barre Opera
    House, Norwich University's Military Museum, Rock of Ages (the
    world's largest granite quarries, in Barre)

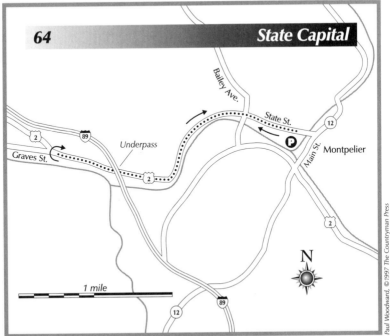

DRIVING DIRECTIONS: From I-89 in Montpelier, take exit 8 (Montpelier). As you exit, turn onto US 2 West. Drive on US 2 West for about 1 mile to the intersection with Main Street. Turn right onto Main Street and drive for about 0.5 mile to the intersection with State Street. Turn left onto State Street; in 0.2 mile, park in the public parking area on your left, just beyond the church.

TRIP OVERVIEW: If you traveled to the area with an advanced skater, let her tackle Mad River (Tour 65) while you roll along US 2, without the dramatic ups and downs. Begin in downtown Montpelier—the smallest state capital in the United States. Just a few miles from the center, government and commercial buildings are replaced by country stores and churches, farmland and dairy barns, cow pastures bordered by ancient stone walls, and sugar maples waiting to be tapped in early spring. Roll through the countryside along a relatively flat road (with a generous shoulder) following the bank of the Winooski River.

Work out early in the morning to avoid most of the traffic. Afterward, skate to one of Montpelier's unique restaurants for a hearty, well-deserved breakfast.

ROUTE DIRECTIONS:

0.0 From the parking lot, cross State Street and turn left, initially skating along the sidewalk.

0.1 Pass the Capitol Theatre and Vermont Museum on your right.

0.2 Roll by the Vermont Statehouse on your right.

0.4 ▼ CAUTION: Stop at a traffic light and cross Bailey Avenue.

0.5 Leave the business district and travel on the wide shoulder of US 2 (with a speed limit of 25 mph). Cruise along the bank of the Winooski River.

1.4 Duck under I-89.

1.5 Cruise along a narrower shoulder.

1.8 When Graves Street joins on your left, turn around and return to your car the way you came.

Note: You can continue for another 5 miles on US 2 to join the Mad River route (Tour 65). Be aware, though, that the road becomes hilly and the speed limit increases to 50 mph.

65 •••• *Mad River*

LOCATION: Moretown, VT
RATING: Advanced
DISTANCE: 7.4 miles (with the option to extend the trip)
TIMES TO AVOID: None
TERRAIN: Rolling hills on a rural road with a wide shoulder
SURFACE: Mostly smooth asphalt
AUTO TRAFFIC: Light
POINTS OF INTEREST: Sugarbush Resort, Vermont Icelandic Horse Farm, Joslin Round Barn, the Vermont Historical Society Museum, Northfield Falls and covered bridges, Barre Opera House, Morse Farm Sugar House & Museum, Rock of Ages (the world's largest granite quarries)

DRIVING DIRECTIONS: From I-89, take exit 9 (Middlesex/Moretown) to US 2 East. Follow US 2 East through the small village of Middlesex and turn right onto VT 100B South. Drive 3 miles and park along the shoulder.

TRIP OVERVIEW: This section of newly paved road offers a challenging workout for any advanced or expert skater. (Intermediates who are confident of their ability to tackle steep descents may be able to manage this route.) Rural VT 100B hugs the Mad River as it snakes through the narrow valley less than 10 miles from the state capital. Spectacular views make this an exhilarating trip for those willing to skate the streets (on a wide shoulder, of course).

The brisk Mad River winds through farmland and quaint New England villages between the Northfield and Green Mountain ranges. Covered bridges span it in places, charming reminders of its history. In the 1700s, settlers were drawn to the river because of its rich floodplain and milling power—some homes remain from this period. Now, of course, the area is known as a resort center, providing a wide range of recreational opportunities for the thousands of year-round visitors.

ROUTE DIRECTIONS:
  0.0 From the parking area, head southward on VT 100B with the Mad River on your left.
  2.3 Pump up a steep 0.2-mile hill.
  2.9 ▼ CAUTION: Negotiate a sharp descent (and glance up, if you're able, to appreciate the water, meadow, and mountain views).

3.7 The shoulder shrinks as you pass a large red (what else?) barn. Pause to enjoy the lovely rural sights before heading back along the road to your car.

Note: If you choose to continue, you will discover that the shoulder widens again at 4.8 miles; at 5.1 miles, you will reach the village of Moretown.

SKATING TIP: *When speed skating, lean forward from the waist, keeping your back straight and bending your knees. Be sure to keep your center of balance directly over your forward skate: Your leg power flows through this point.*

---

66 •••• *Waitsfield Covered Bridge*

LOCATION: Waitsfield, VT
RATING: Intermediate or advanced
DISTANCE: 2.2 miles (intermediate); 5.4 miles (advanced)
TIMES TO AVOID: None
TERRAIN: Rolling hills (some steep) on a country road with no shoulder
SURFACE: Coarse asphalt
AUTO TRAFFIC: Light
POINTS OF INTEREST: Sugarbush Resort, Vermont Icelandic Horse Farm, Bridge Street Marketplace, Joslin Round Barn, Vermont Historical Society Museum, Wood Art Gallery, Northfield Falls and covered bridges, Barre Opera House, Norwich University's Military Museum, Morse Farm Sugar House & Museum, Rock of Ages (world's largest granite quarries)

DRIVING DIRECTIONS: From I-89, take exit 9 (Middlesex/Moretown) to US 2 East. Follow US 2 East through the small village of Middlesex and turn right onto VT 100B South. After about 8 miles, at the intersection with VT 100, merge onto VT 100 South. Drive less than 5 miles into the town of Waitsfield. In the village, turn left onto Bridge Road (across from the Mobil station). Drive through the Great Eddy Covered Bridge to a small parking lot on your left. (*Note:* The road is now called East Warren Road.)

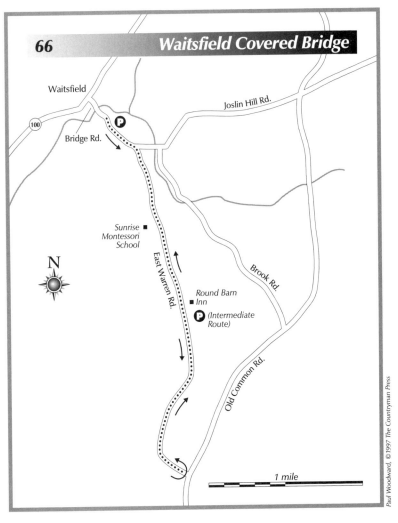

Paul Woodward, ©1997 The Countryman Press

TRIP OVERVIEW: If you've ever been tempted to join Athletes Anonymous (is there such a thing?), you've found the right route. Fitness addicts will be delighted with this challenging course that provides some of Vermont's most impressive scenery (and that's saying a lot for this state!). Pass farmhouses and country inns as you roll along this popular biking and jogging route, trending upward on the way out. As you crest near the 1.8-mile mark, you'll feel as if you can stretch out your arm and touch the Sugarbush summit. Intermediate skaters should drive up East Warren Road to the Round Barn Inn and start the trip from there. (Everyone else should *drive* the route just for the views!)

After your workout, stroll around the quaint village of Waitsfield, which is listed on the National Register of Historic Places. Many buildings remain from the 18th century, when this commercial center was just a mill town. The Joslin Round Barn is a town landmark—only a dozen or so Shaker-style round barns are still standing in the state. Waitsfield's Great Eddy Covered Bridge, spanning the Mad River, is also on the National Register, and is the state's second oldest covered bridge (dating from 1833). If you've brought a bathing suit, be brave and venture into the swimming hole just below the bridge, a popular spot with the locals.

ROUTE DIRECTIONS:

0.0 From the parking lot, turn left and head uphill on East Warren Road. (The speed limit here is 35 mph.)

0.3 Pass Joslin Hill Road on your left.

0.4 Push up a steep hill for 0.1 mile.

0.7 Roll by a red barn on your left.

0.9 Drop down a slight slope.

1.2 Cruise by the Sunrise Montessori School on your right.

1.4 ▼ CAUTION: Watch for sections of choppy pavement.

1.6 Approach the Round Barn Inn on your left.
Note: This is the starting point for the INTERMEDIATE route. Skaters should park here and follow the route directions below.

1.8 Enjoy views of the Sugarbush Ski Area and surrounding mountains.

2.0 The road levels and the pavement becomes smoother.

2.7 With Old Common Road on your left, turn around and retrace the route back to your car.
Note: You may continue to follow East Warren Road into Warren. The road is hilly, and eventually connects with VT 100.

---

67 •••• *Stowe Recreation Path*

LOCATION: Stowe, VT
RATING: Intermediate
DISTANCE: 10.6 miles
TIMES TO AVOID: None
TERRAIN: Gradual rolling hills on a paved path
SURFACE: Smooth asphalt
AUTO TRAFFIC: None

POINTS OF INTEREST: Stowe village, Stowe Skate Park (complete with hockey rink, slalom hill, and stunt equipment: half pipes, ramps, rails), Stowe's Gondola Skyride & Toll Road, Smugglers' Notch Ski Resort, Trapp Family Lodge, Ben & Jerry's factory tour, Cold Hollow Cider Mill, Mount Mansfield

DRIVING DIRECTIONS: From I-89, take exit 10 (Waterbury/Stowe) to VT 100 North. Drive 11 miles and enter the village of Stowe. Just beyond Mountain Road on your left, turn left into the parking lot of the Stowe Community Church. Public parking for the path is behind the church, down a hill.

TRIP OVERVIEW: This award-winning path is the pride of Stowe and the result of 25 years of community effort. The "walking path" concept was approved in 1964, but it wasn't until 1977—when a generous resident paid the Vermont Highway Department to design a route—that the idea gained momentum. It took another 12 years, 32 donated easements, hundreds of volunteer hours, dozens of permits and plans, and $680,000 for the 5.3-mile path to be completed. The Stowe Recreation Path has since earned many commendations, among them the Thousand Points of Light Award by President Bush, the Land and Water Conservation Fund Award, and the Take Pride in America Finalist Award.

It differs from other recreational paths because it curves along and crosses the West Branch River and rolls with the terrain. It is in harmony—rather than in conflict—with its surroundings. You'll cruise over the river on graceful bridges, rest on pathside benches, skate by pastures with grazing animals, and cut through wandering stone walls.

There are not a lot of signs screaming "Don't. . . !" but there are certain "user ethics" (as the brochure refers to them) that the community hopes all will follow. These include staying to the right and calling out in advance when you are approaching someone from behind. Locals *are* used to sharing the path with skaters: Nearby is Stowe Skate Park.

Stowe's population surges—as it has for 150 years—during the summer months and the winter ski season. If you visit off-season, you'll have more solitude along the path (and probably a better rate on a hotel room, too).

ROUTE DIRECTIONS:
0.0 Follow the path eastward from the parking lot.
0.3 The path leads over a bridge and curves to the right.

C. BRADLEY

You'll roll over a number of arched bridges along this popular path in Stowe.

0.5 Enjoy views of the Stowe Ski Area.
0.7 ▼ CAUTION: Grade crossing at Weeks Hill Road.
1.0 Cruise beside a brook.
1.2 Roll over an arched bridge.
1.3 Cross another wooden bridge.
1.4 Pass a row of condominiums.
1.5 ▼ CAUTION: Grade crossing.
1.6 ▼ CAUTION: Grade crossing.
1.9 Glide beside VT 100.
2.0 Cruise over a bridge.
2.1 ▼ CAUTION: Cross VT 100 and rejoin the path.
    (*Note:* Traffic is warned of the intersection with the path.)
2.5 Sidestep a commercial area of Stowe near Route 100 with the West Branch River on your left.
2.6 Cross a bridge.
2.7 Skirt a golf course.
3.0 Rest on a riverside bench.
3.2 Roll over a bridge.
4.3 Cross another bridge.
4.9 Cross a bridge.
5.3 The path ends at a parking lot off Brook Road; turn around and enjoy cruising along the path in the other direction.

68 ••••   *Moscow Road*

LOCATION: Stowe, VT
RATING: Intermediate
DISTANCE: 6.6 miles
TIMES TO AVOID: None
TERRAIN: Limited rolling hills on a country road with no shoulder
SURFACE: Coarse asphalt
AUTO TRAFFIC: Light
POINTS OF INTEREST: Stowe village, Stowe Ski Area, the Stowe Recreation Path (Tour 67), Stowe Skate Park, Stowe's Gondola Skyride & Toll Road, Trapp Family Lodge, Ben & Jerry's factory tour, Cabot Creamery Annex, Cold Hollow Cider Mill, Stowe Historical Society Museum

DRIVING DIRECTIONS: From I-89, take exit 10 (Waterbury/Stowe) and head north on VT 100. Drive about 7 miles and turn left onto Moscow Road. In another 0.5 mile, park on your left by the Getty Gas Station.

TRIP OVERVIEW: If you have more than a day to spend in Stowe, you'll need more than one in-line route! After an excursion along the Stowe Recreation Path, head to Moscow Road. Given the surrounding mountainous terrain, this lightly traveled country road is remarkably flat. (Any cars you do encounter should be moving relatively slowly: The speed limit is 35 mph.) Roll past charming country homes and farms so characteristic of Vermont you'll swear you've seen them on postcards. Intermediate skaters will not only get a good workout along this stretch, but they will also be distracted from any tired muscles by the scenery: The views of Mount Mansfield State Forest are super!

ROUTE DIRECTIONS:
0.0 From the Getty station parking lot, turn left onto River Road.
0.3 Roll by the Grace Bible Community Church on your right.
0.9 Pass Barrows Road on your right.
1.4 Trapp Hill Road (leading to the Trapp Family Lodge) intersects with Moscow Road on your right.
1.6 ▼ CAUTION: The road curls left and becomes Nebraska Valley Road.
2.0 Roll over a small bridge spanning Miller Brook.
2.9 Skate by cows grazing in their pasture on your left.
3.3 The paved road ends as Beech Hill Road joins on the left. Picnic near Miller Brook before heading back the way you came.

SKATING TIP: *When skating uphill, keep your eyes focused 5 feet in front of you, with your upper body over your knees and your knees bent. Strokes should be quick and short. Let your arms swing laterally across your body for extra power.*

69 •••• *South Burlington Bike Path*

LOCATION: South Burlington, VT
RATING: Beginner/intermediate
DISTANCE: Interconnecting paths totaling 6.0 miles or a 3.4-mile route
TIMES TO AVOID: None
TERRAIN: Flat, with some moderate hills on paved paths
SURFACE: Smooth asphalt
AUTO TRAFFIC: None
POINTS OF INTEREST: Dorset Street Park (playground, ball fields, picnic sites), Oakledge Park, Waterfront Park and Promenade, Perkins Pier, Leddy Park, Battery Park (summer amphitheater), Church Street Marketplace, Fleming Museum, Shelburne Museum, Vermont Teddy Bear Company tours, Ethan Allen Homestead

DRIVING DIRECTIONS: From I-89, take exit 13 to I-189 (Burlington and Shelburne). In less than 2 miles, I-189 ends at a traffic light at the junction with US 7. Turn left onto US 7 South. At the first light, turn left onto Swift Street. Follow Swift Street for 1.8 miles to the intersection with Dorset Street. Drive straight (through the traffic light) and turn left into the Dorset Street Park. Free parking is available there.

TRIP OVERVIEW: If you're looking to escape the congestion of the Burlington Bikeway, roll along the maze of bike paths in South Burlington. The paths—which connect the city's schools, parks, and neighborhoods—were intended to facilitate in-town commuting, but they are quite scenic as well, with views to the Green Mountains and across Lake Champlain to the Adirondacks. Radiating mainly from the Dorset Street Park, the paths roll and wind through many residential areas with indistinct start and finish points. If you're an adventuresome skater who enjoys not always knowing where you are, you'll get a kick out of cruising these paths without a plan. (If you like plans, refer to the route below or pick up a map of the entire "web" of paths at City Hall on Dorset Street.)

Better take this trip soon, though . . . there is talk of connecting these paths with the one in Burlington, which will bring on the crowds!

Burlington itself offers much in the way of dining and shopping. The Church Street Marketplace and Burlington Square Mall together contain more than 130 specialty shops, many of them offering unique merchandise produced locally. Combined, they make up the state's largest shopping center. Check out the entertainment schedule at the Church Street Marketplace—you wouldn't want to miss any special events or festivals while you're in town!

ROUTE DIRECTIONS: From the parking lot entrance, you have several options: You can turn left and skate into a residential neighborhood on smooth, level streets or you can cross Dorset Street and join the path that heads westward along Swift Street. Or you can use our recommended route described below.

0.0 From the parking lot, turn right onto the sidewalk/path that runs along Swift Street.

0.1 Turn left and cross Swift Street, now following the path that parallels Dorset Street.

0.5 Roll beside fields with great views of the distant Green Mountains.

1.1 Follow the path as it twists left, following the contour of Cross Fields Road.

1.3 Pump up a steep incline for 0.2 mile. Beginners should attempt to climb this hill because of the treat at the top: spectacular panoramic views of Lake Champlain, the Green Mountains, and Adirondacks in New York State. Recover from your effort on a trailside bench at the overlook.

1.4 Drop down a slight slope.

1.5 Roll behind a neighborhood.

1.7 The path ends at an exclusive residential area. (The pavement here is super, so you may want to cruise around the neighborhood before heading back along the path to your car.)

70 •••• *Burlington Bikeway*

LOCATION: Burlington, VT
RATING: Beginner
DISTANCE: 14.2 miles
TIMES TO AVOID: None
TERRAIN: Paved path and a brief section on a neighborhood street; flat with one small hill
SURFACE: Smooth asphalt
AUTO TRAFFIC: None on path; light on street
POINTS OF INTEREST: Oakledge Park, Waterfront Park and Promenade, Perkins Pier, North Beach, Leddy Park, Battery Park, Burlington downtown, University of Vermont, Church Street Marketplace, Fleming Museum, *Spirit of Ethan Allen II*, Shelburne Farms, Shelburne Museum, Ethan Allen Homestead

DRIVING DIRECTIONS: From I-89, take exit 13 to I-189 (Burlington and Shelburne). In less than 2 miles, I-189 ends at a traffic light at the junction with US 7. Turn right onto US 7 North and drive 0.5 mile. At a traffic light, turn left onto Flynn Avenue. Follow Flynn Avenue to the end and enter Oakledge Park. Leave your car in the area on your left. (Pay a moderate fee in-season.)

TRIP OVERVIEW: When the railroads were abandoned in the early 1960s, Burlington's once bustling port area deteriorated quickly. Within

172 •••• IN-LINE SKATE NEW ENGLAND

the decade, though, residents acted to convert the dock area into pleasing public space: The Waterfront Park and Promenade was created, and the railroad bed was paved for recreational use.

Their effort resulted in the creation of one of New England's best bike paths (and probably one of the top paths in the country). The 7.1-mile-long trail winds along the shoreline of Lake Champlain with spectacular views of the Adirondacks in New York and the islands that dot the lake. You'll pass seven public beaches and waterside parks on this route (some offer swimming) as well as a working train station and a strip of pathside shops that serve refreshments. Whether you're people-watching or soaking in the water views, you'll be delighted with what you see. The only drawbacks are strong wind gusts from the lake and crowds: If you're interested in a solitary weekend workout, skate early in the morning.

We'll issue a guarantee on this one: You *will* love it!

ROUTE DIRECTIONS:

0.0 From the parking lot, head toward the lake to join the path that runs along the water.
Note: A half-mile stretch of path that heads southward from the parking lot will eventually connect with the South Burlington Bike Path (Tour 69).

0.3 Pass diminutive Blanchard Beach.

0.5 ▼ CAUTION: Cross a wooden bridge and embark on a curving section of path. Control your speed.

0.6 Turn right onto Harrison Avenue. Follow the road for about two blocks, with the route clearly marked.

0.7 Turn left at the Vermont Railway. You're now skating along a sturdy fence by the tracks.

0.9 Roll over the bridge that spans Lakeside Avenue.

1.1 Briefly flirt with the water's edge.

1.3 Cruise by Roundhouse Point, Vermont Railway's headquarters.

1.8 Arrive at a marina known as Perkins Pier. As the path forks, turn left to skate around the docks. Rest on one of the benches, taking in great views of the lake.

2.0 ▼ CAUTION: Cross King Street.

2.1 Stop at one of the pathside shops for a drink or snack. Pass the working Union Railroad Station.

2.2 ▼ CAUTION: Head across the entrance road to the Waterfront Park and Promenade, a lively place that presents concerts and plays in the amphitheater and boasts an impressive kaleidoscope.

At the end of the Burlington Bikeway, skaters take a break and enjoy views of Lake Champlain.

2.8 ▼ CAUTION: Cross Depot Street, heading briefly uphill. Leave the urban area for a more rural setting.

3.3 Pass through a residential area.

3.8 Arrive at North Beach (with nearly 2000 feet of water frontage, lifeguards, picnic tables, and camping sites).

4.6 ▼ CAUTION: Cross Driftwood Lane.

4.8 ▼ CAUTION: Cross Leddy Park Road. (Popular Leddy Park has an indoor ice rink, hiking trails, a playground, and a large beach area.)

5.0 ▼ CAUTION: Cross Staniford Road.

5.4 ▼ CAUTION: Cross Starr Farm Road.

5.9 Cruise by some choice waterfront condominiums.

6.8 ▼ CAUTION: Cross North Road Extension.

7.1 The path ends at an overlook by the Winooski River. Return to your car the way you came.

71 •••• South Hero

LOCATION: South Hero, VT
RATING: Beginner
DISTANCE: 6.2 miles
TIMES TO AVOID: None

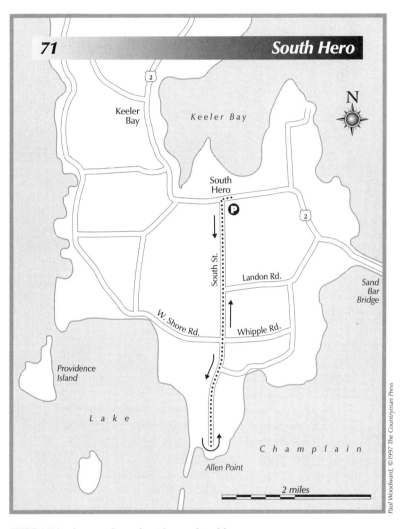

TERRAIN: Flat rural road with no shoulder
SURFACE: Smooth asphalt
AUTO TRAFFIC: Light
POINTS OF INTEREST: Hyde Log Cabin (built in 1783), Church Street Marketplace, Fleming Museum, *Spirit of Ethan Allen II* (boat excursions), Perkins Pier, Leddy Park, Battery Park, Shelburne Farms, Ethan Allen Homestead

DRIVING DIRECTIONS: From I-89 in Colchester, take exit 17 (Colchester). Upon exiting, follow signs for US 2 North. Drive approximately 5 miles on US 2 and cross the Sand Bar Bridge onto Grand Isle. In 2.3 miles, reach the small village of South Hero. Turn left into the parking lot of Seb's ice cream stand.

TRIP OVERVIEW: This is a "twofer" . . . you know, a two-for-one special. Enjoy the South Hero route today and the other Grand Isle trip, Adams Landing (Tour 72), tomorrow!

Grand Isle is north of Burlington, linked to the mainland by highway and a ferry route. South Hero is on Grand Isle's southern tip. In some ways, the area is typically Vermont: Cows graze in open pastures, apple orchards line the roads, historic homes—like the Hyde Log Cabin, one of the oldest in the country—have not been replaced with hotels or strip malls. And yet, very unlike the rest of the state, Grand Isle is surrounded by water!

The level terrain, smooth pavement, constant breeze, and superb views of the Green Mountains make this an easy qualifier for our *Best Routes* list. If you are visiting the Burlington area, Grand Isle is a "mustsee" spot. Follow the route described below, which takes you initially southward past several orchards, or explore the island on your own. If you head out early in the morning, you'll have the road to yourself.

ROUTE DIRECTIONS:
- 0.0 From the parking lot, turn left onto US 2, then immediately left onto South Street.
- 0.3 Glide by a cemetery on your right.
- 0.7 Pass one of the area's signature apple orchards on your right.
- 1.1 Continue straight as Landon Road intersects on your left.
- 1.4 Roll beside another orchard on your right.
- 1.8 ▼ CAUTION: Cross West Shore Road.
- 1.9 Stop and admire the spectacular views of Burlington and Lake Champlain.
- 3.1 When the road turns to gravel, turn around and cruise back to your car.

72 •••• *Adams Landing*

LOCATION: Grand Isle, VT
RATING: Beginner
DISTANCE: 4.0 miles
TIMES TO AVOID: None

TERRAIN: Flat rural road with no shoulder
SURFACE: Smooth asphalt
AUTO TRAFFIC: Light
POINTS OF INTEREST: Hyde Log Cabin (built in 1783), Isle La Motte, Burlington downtown, Fleming Museum, *Spirit of Ethan Allen II* (boat excursions), Leddy Park, Shelburne Farms, Shelburne Museum, Vermont Teddy Bear Company tours, Ethan Allen Homestead

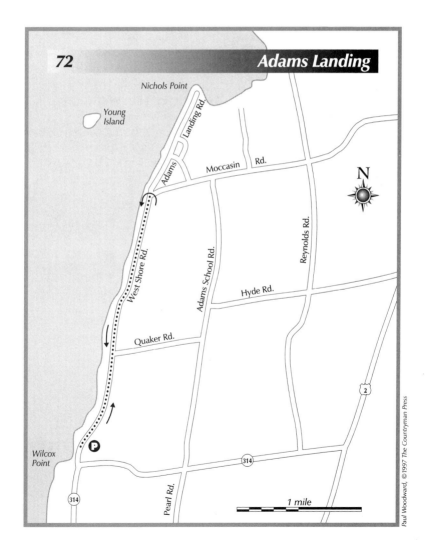

Paul Woodward, ©1997 The Countryman Press

DRIVING DIRECTIONS: From I-89 in Colchester, take exit 17 (Colchester). Upon exiting, follow signs to US 2 North. Drive about 5 miles and cross the Sand Bar Bridge onto Grand Isle. From the bridge, drive through South Hero to the intersection of VT 314 (just less than 4 miles) and turn left. Drive 2 miles to the ferry station, then 1 mile to the intersection with West Shore Road. Turn left onto West Shore Road and park on the shoulder.

TRIP OVERVIEW: If you've already followed the South Hero route (Tour 71), then you know that Grand Isle is a skater's paradise. Expansive views of the Adirondacks greatly enhance this trip on flat, lightly traveled roads. You'll roll by waterfront homes along the peaceful western shore of Lake Champlain.

Though it's a popular tourist destination, the region has managed to avoid commercialization and overdevelopment and preserve its ties to the past. The state's first settlement (at the northern end of Isle La Motte) was established by the French explorer Samuel de Champlain. And well before that, Native Americans came to hunt and fish on the islands, lured by the abundant wildlife.

ROUTE DIRECTIONS:
0.0 From the intersection of West Shore Road and VT 314, head north on West Shore Road.
0.8 Pass Quaker Road on your right.
1.2 Roll by a landing dock on your left.
2.0 At the intersection with Adams Landing Road (straight ahead) and Moccasin Avenue (on your right), turn around and head back to your car the way you came.
   Note: Adams Landing Road is a private road, but intermediate skaters may continue along Moccasin Avenue (with hilly terrain).

New Hampshire

1 Route number

N

40 miles

2

76

78
77 ● Conway

75

Lebanon ●

93

89

Concord
★

4

Portsmouth
●

73 74 9

Manchester ●

95

Paul Woodward, ©1997 The Countryman Press

Part Five

New Hampshire

73 •••• Connecticut River

LOCATION: Westmoreland, NH
RATING: Intermediate or advanced
DISTANCE: 6.0 miles (intermediate) and 13.8 miles (advanced)
TIMES TO AVOID: None
TERRAIN: Rolling hills on a country road with no shoulder
SURFACE: Coarse asphalt
AUTO TRAFFIC: Light
POINTS OF INTEREST: Stuart & John's Sugar House, Surry Mountain
    Recreation Area, Wheelock Park, Colony Mill Marketplace in
    Keene, Goose Pond, Monadnock Children's Museum, Mount
    Monadnock, Wyman Tavern, Horatio Colony House Museum,
    Fort No. 4

DRIVING DIRECTIONS: From I-91, take exit 3 (Brattleboro, Vermont,
and Keene, New Hampshire). Continue straight through the traffic
light, heading east on VT 9. Cross the bridge over the Connecticut River
and enter New Hampshire (now on NH 9). Drive about 13 miles to the
first traffic light and turn left onto the bypass for NH 12 North/NH 9

73 Connecticut River

N

Cheshire County Complex

Stuart & John's Sugar House

63

Connecticut River

VERMONT

River Rd.

Poocham Rd.

NEW HAMPSHIRE

1 mile

Paul Woodward, ©1997 The Countryman Press

East/NH 10 North. Drive 11 miles on NH 12 and turn left onto NH 63. Drive 0.2 mile and turn left into the parking lot for Stuart & John's Sugar House.

TRIP OVERVIEW: Views of the lofty Vermont hills rising over the Connecticut River dominate your surroundings along this stretch of road. In late September and early October, the colors are as spectacular as if they'd been spilled from an artist's palette. As you roll by green-shuttered farmhouses, dairy barns, and meadows dotted with grazing horses, it's not hard to imagine someone traveling this route a century ago and taking in the same sights. The route ends near the river, where you can relax and have a snack before heading back along the same country road.

Though Westmoreland center is not much more than a church and a town hall, nearby Keene has much to offer in the way of restaurants, specialty shops, and recreation areas. Take time to wander down Main Street, where much of the movie *Jumanji*, starring Robin Williams, was filmed.

ROUTE DIRECTIONS:
0.0 From the parking lot, turn left onto NH 63 South.
0.1 Roll by a red dairy barn on your right with charming country views of meadows and far-off hills.
0.5 Drop down a long, gradual hill, then work up a gentle incline.
1.0 Tackle a steep decline followed by a slight uphill.
2.1 Turn right onto River Road at the Cheshire County Complex.
2.3 ▼ CAUTION: The road curves sharply left.
2.5 ▼ CAUTION: Negotiate a steep descent.
2.8 Roll across a bridge that spans a lively branch of the Connecticut River.
2.9 Poocham Road joins from the left.
3.0 Push up a hill, and pause for a breather as you crest. Take in lovely views of the Connecticut River and the farms that spread across the valley below. INTERMEDIATE SKATERS should turn back here.
3.5 ADVANCED SKATERS: Drop easily down a hill and then cruise along level ground.
3.8 ▼ CAUTION: Head down a sharp decline.
4.9 ▼ CAUTION: Tackle another challenging descent.
5.5 Glide by a cemetery on your right with tranquil views of open fields. Enjoy flat terrain for the next mile.
6.9 As the road sweeps steeply uphill along the Connecticut River, turn to retrace the route back to your car. (You may want to enjoy a picnic lunch or a snack here before tackling the return leg.)

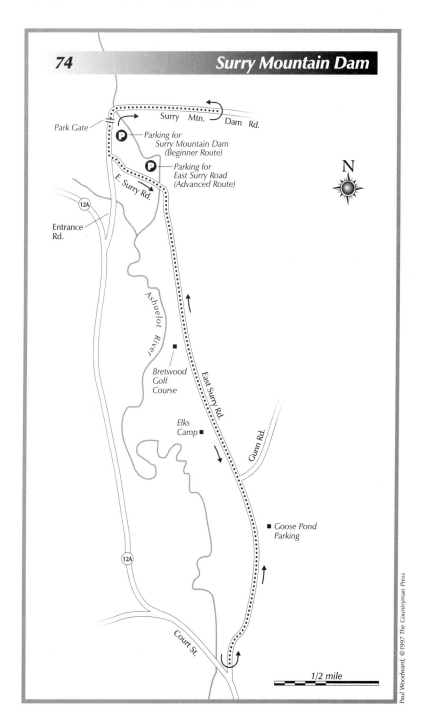

74   *Surry Mountain Dam*

Surry   Mtn.   Dam   Rd.

Park Gate

P — Parking for
Surry Mountain Dam
(Beginner Route)

P — Parking for
East Surry Road
(Advanced Route)

E. Surry Rd.

N

12A

Entrance
Rd.

Ashuelot River

■
Bretwood
Golf
Course

East Surry Rd.

Elks
Camp ■

Gunn Rd.

■ Goose Pond
Parking

12A

Court St.

1/2 mile

Paul Woodward, ©1997 The Countryman Press

74 ••••   *Surry Mountain Dam*

LOCATION: Surry, NH
RATING: Advanced or intermediate
DISTANCE: 6.0 miles (advanced); 1.0 mile (intermediate—dam route only)
TIMES TO AVOID: None
TERRAIN: Rolling hills on a country road with no shoulder
SURFACE: Coarse asphalt
AUTO TRAFFIC: Light
POINTS OF INTEREST: Surry Mountain Recreation Area, Otter Brook Recreation Area, Wheelock Park, Colony Mill Marketplace in Keene, Goose Pond, Monadnock Children's Museum, Mount Monadnock, Wyman Tavern, Horatio Colony House Museum

DRIVING DIRECTIONS: From I-91, take exit 3 (Brattleboro, Vermont, and Keene, New Hampshire). Continue straight through the traffic light, heading east on VT 9. Cross the bridge over the Connecticut River and enter New Hampshire (now on NH 9). Drive about 13 miles to the first traffic light and turn left onto the bypass for NH 12 North/NH 9 East/NH 10 North. In 2.5 miles, take the exit for Maple Avenue and NH 12A; turn right onto NH 12A. Drive 2.5 miles and bear right into the entrance for Surry Mountain Dam at a sign. In 0.3 mile, turn right onto East Surry Road. Park in 0.3 mile along the shoulder on the left side of the road.
Note: Parking is also available at nearby Surry Mountain Dam. However, we do not recommend this, as the pavement is choppy on the initial part of East Surry Road.

TRIP OVERVIEW: You may have heard of Keene, New Hampshire—after all, the city made the *Guinness Book of World Records* on October 29, 1994, when townspeople lit 10,540 jack-o'-lanterns at 8 PM in the town square! Or you may have heard of it because it is the center of activity in New Hampshire's southwest corner, nestled in a pretty valley near Mount Monadnock. But no matter how you first heard about Keene, from now on you'll remember it as a terrific place to take your skates.

On this route, you'll wind along East Surry Road with the Bretwood Golf Course on one side and charming country homes on the other. Then you follow an access road across a lofty dam with views over Surry Mountain Lake and the Ashuelot River.

Advanced skaters will be challenged by lengthy declines and

inclines, and intermediates can manage the Surry Mountain Dam portion. If you have any energy left after the skate, hike around pretty Goose Pond, or stop by the Surry Mountain Dam Recreation Area for a swim (and terrific views of high hills rimming the lake).

ROUTE DIRECTIONS:

0.0 From the parking area on East Surry Road, turn left and skate over a small bridge spanning the Ashuelot River. The trend on the way out is uphill.

0.5 Roll across smoother pavement.

0.9 Pass the entrance to the Bretwood Golf Course.

1.3 Cruise by Elks Camp on your right.

1.5 Continue straight as Gunn Road leaves on your left.

1.6 Pass the Goose Pond parking lot on your left.

2.5 At the intersection with Court Street, turn around and return to the parking area.

5.0 Skate past the parking area, and turn right onto dam access road. Head northward past the park gate, and embark on a moderate ascent. BEGINNER SKATERS can join here.

5.2 Curve right onto the massive dam.

5.5 Reverse direction across the dam and to your car.

75 •••• *River Road, Hanover*

LOCATION: Hanover, NH
RATING: Intermediate
DISTANCE: 4.0 miles
TIMES TO AVOID: None
TERRAIN: Rolling hills on a rural road with no shoulder
SURFACE: Smooth asphalt
AUTO TRAFFIC: Light
POINTS OF INTEREST: Hanover center, Hood Museum of Art, Hopkins Center, Orozco murals (Baker Library, Dartmouth), Montshire Museum of Science, Storrs Pond Recreation Area, Hanover Country Club, AVA Gallery (Lebanon), Billings Farm and Museum (Woodstock, Vermont), Appalachian Trail, the Museum at Lower Shaker Village (Enfield)

DRIVING DIRECTIONS: From I-95, take exit 13 (Hanover/NH 10A East). Follow 10A (West Wheelock Street) for 0.8 mile to the intersection with Main Street. Continue straight, passing the town common on your left and the Hanover Inn on your right. In 0.4 mile, turn left at a traffic light onto NH 10 North; drive 0.3 mile to a second traffic light. (Dartmouth Medical School is directly in front of you.) Turn right, still on NH 10 North. In 4.4 miles, turn left onto River Road; turn around to head southbound, and park on the wide shoulder.

TRIP OVERVIEW: For a road skate to be considered one of the best in New England, we look for smooth pavement, manageable terrain, a wide-enough shoulder, light traffic, and great scenery. The route on River Road, winding beside the Connecticut River along relatively flat ground, meets all these criteria. The superb views are even better—if you can believe it—in October, when autumn colors are splashed across the hills that rise over the river valley. As you pass farmhouses and riverfront homes along the way, you'll envy the view these folks wake to every day. Let your kids pack a picnic lunch and ride beside you on their bikes; you'll encounter very few cars on the road.

You'll want to explore the Hanover area after your skate. The town—sophisticated, yet rural—is crowded with delightful shops and restaurants, and strolling about the main street can easily occupy several hours. Teenagers may be interested in visiting Dartmouth; all kids will love the nearby Montshire Museum.

ROUTE DIRECTIONS:

0.0 ▼ CAUTION: Head north on River Road, initially braking on a steep 0.1-mile descent.

0.1 Roll slightly downhill for 0.4 mile, then work uphill.

0.7 Glide beside the Connecticut River.

0.8 Dip slightly, then push up an easy hill.

1.0 Cruise by riverfront homes.

1.4 Drop down a gentle slope.

1.8 Pass a lumberyard on the river's edge.

2.0 The route ends as the pavement turns to gravel. Take a break on the grassy spot by the river before heading back.

76 •••• *Franconia*

LOCATION: Franconia, NH
RATING: Intermediate or advanced
DISTANCE: 12.8 miles (intermediate); 22.8 miles (advanced)
TIMES TO AVOID: None
TERRAIN: Flat and gently rolling rural highway with one steep hill on the advanced route
SURFACE: Smooth asphalt
AUTO TRAFFIC: Light to moderate
POINTS OF INTEREST: Cannon Mountain aerial tramway, Echo Lake (swimming), Old Man of the Mountain, hiking trail to Bridal Veil Falls, Scotland Brook Wildlife Santuary, Sugar Hill Historic Museum, Lost River, Robert Frost Museum

DRIVING DIRECTIONS: From I-93 in Franconia, take exit 38 to NH 116 and NH 18. Turn right onto Main Street (NH 116 North); in 0.4 mile, park at the school.

TRIP OVERVIEW: You've probably been to the White Mountains, but you've probably never been on NH 116. Most tourists access the area via I-93 and NH 16, while NH 116 travels east of the national forest, threading through the Ham Branch River valley. It is a secondary road—wide, flat for the initial 6-plus miles, and composed of mostly

SKATING TIP: *When skating long distances, you'll feel more comfortable if you rest one or both of your arms on your lower back.*

S. HOOPER

The scenery along this route—here, with the mountains of Franconia Notch in the background—is breathtaking.

straight stretches, giving drivers good visibility. (There is no shoulder, but the traffic is relatively light.) Magnificent views of the Franconia Ridge surround you for the length of the route—it's like working out in a postcard!

Leave time to explore the popular Franconia area. You won't want to miss the many hiking trails, the Robert Frost Museum, and the Scotland Brook Wildlife Sanctuary.

ROUTE DIRECTIONS:

0.0 From the parking area, turn left onto NH 116 South (Main Street).

0.4 ● STOP. Turn right, still on NH 116 South (called Church Street in town).

0.6 As you lose the shoulder, the road remains wide. Impressive views extend to the Franconia Ridge.

1.2 Continue straight as a road to the Robert Frost Museum turns right.

2.4 Roll by the Franconia Inn and a small airport, with Kinsman Mountain dominating the eastern landscape.

3.1 Push over the route's first (easy) hill.

3.5 As you cruise along an extended straight stretch, look left to see the Cannon Mountain tramway.

4.4 Enter Easton as the straightaway ends.

5.4 After rolling up and over some gentle inclines, cross Judd Brook.

5.5 Pump up a brief, moderate ascent.

6.4 Reach the base of a pair of short, steep hills. INTERMEDIATE SKATERS should turn around here.

7.0 ADVANCED SKATERS: Push up an easier hill before leveling. With the Franconia Range behind you, it's clear to see how much distance you've covered.

7.4 Begin another mile-long straight stretch that trends slightly upward.

8.4 Cruise down a moderate descent.

9.0 Struggle up a long, difficult climb.

9.5 ▼ CAUTION: Brake—and stay right—on a fast, two-tiered drop that bends right. Continue to exercise caution along the next half-mile of twists and turns.

10.3 Embark on another flat, straight section of road.

11.4 ● STOP. At the intersection with NH 112, return to your car the way you came.

---

77 •••• *Albany Covered Bridge*

LOCATION: Albany, NH

RATING: Intermediate

DISTANCE: 14.0 miles

TIMES TO AVOID: Spring (when road surfaces will be sandy)

TERRAIN: Flat to gently rolling

SURFACE: Smooth, with limited sections of coarse asphalt

AUTO TRAFFIC: Very light

POINTS OF INTEREST: North Conway shopping, Conway Scenic Railroad, Story Land, swimming at Echo Lake (along the route), hiking and rock climbing in the White Mountains (the Boulder Loop Nature trailhead is along the route), wading in the Saco River

DRIVING DIRECTIONS: At the junction of NH 16 and NH 153 (Pleasant Street) in Conway, head north on Washington Street (from NH 16, Washington Street is directly across the street from NH 153). Park in a designated spot along Washington Street.

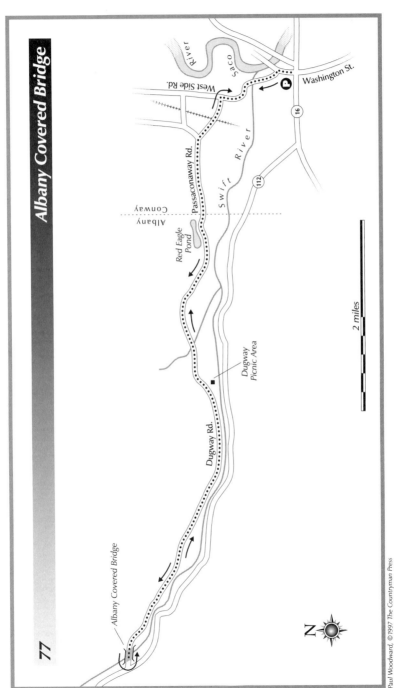

77

Albany Covered Bridge

Albany Covered Bridge

Dugway Rd.

Dugway Picnic Area

Red Eagle Pond

Albany
Conway

Passaconaway Rd.

Swift River

West Side Rd.

Saco River

Washington St.

16

112

2 miles

N

TRIP OVERVIEW: The mountains may tower over you and the roads that wind through them may pitch and heave, but deep in the valley, along the banks of the Swift River, the land is as level as a Kansas cornfield. And nearly as uncrowded, too—the section of Passaconaway Road we've included here runs along the northern side of the river and is not frequented by tourists. The road, ample at first, narrows as you proceed, but with so little traffic you need not be concerned. (The Kansas analogy may have been a slight exaggeration; after all, because you are following alongside a river, the road trends slightly upward on the way out.) The surroundings are, of course, spectacular—including the covered bridge at route's end—and there are a multitude of outdoor activities to enjoy after your skate: swimming or kayaking in the Swift River, picnicking, camping, hiking, and more.

ROUTE DIRECTIONS:

0.0 Begin by skating away from NH 16 on Washington Street.

0.1 Bear left onto Westside Road at a triangular common as Washington Street bears right.

0.3 Cross the Swift River, taking in mountain views to your left and right.

0.8 Turn left onto Passaconaway Road, heading toward the distant Moat Mountains.

1.0 Hop over a railroad crossing.

1.8 Roll up and over an easy hill just prior to crossing the Albany town line.

2.2 Pass Red Eagle Pond.

2.6 Push up a slight, two-tiered ascent.

3.3 Now on Dugway Road (renamed in Albany), cruise by Dugway Picnic Area on your left.

4.3 To your right, the ground plunges 30 feet to the river below.

4.6 Begin rolling over a series of hills.

5.3 Negotiate a moderate roller.

5.7 ▼ CAUTION: Brake on the initial drop of this two-step descent.

6.1 ▼ CAUTION: Brake on a downhill that drops you to river level.

6.8 Pass Covered Bridges camping and parking area.

7.0 Arrive at the Albany covered bridge (near the parking area for the Boulder Loop Trail). Turn around and return to your car.

78 •••• *Cathedral Ledge*

LOCATION: Conway, NH

RATING: Intermediate or advanced

DISTANCE: 14.4 miles (intermediate); 23.4 miles (advanced)

TIMES TO AVOID: Expect more traffic on weekends in summer and fall

TERRAIN: Flat to gently rolling, with tougher climbs on the second half of the route

SURFACE: Smooth asphalt

AUTO TRAFFIC: Light to moderate

POINTS OF INTEREST: North Conway shopping, Conway Scenic Railroad, Story Land, swimming at Echo Lake (along the route), hiking and rock climbing in the White Mountains, wading in the Saco River

DRIVING DIRECTIONS: At the junction of NH 16 and NH 153 (Pleasant Street) in Conway, head north on Washington Street (from NH 16, Washington Street is directly across the street from NH 153). Park in a designated spot along Washington Street.

TRIP OVERVIEW: A trip to the White Mountains region means struggling up steep mountain paths wearing heavy boots and carrying an even heavier pack, right? Not in this book! This skating route through the Conway area offers frequent views of the Presidential peaks as impressive as those you'd get from along the hiking trail—without the elevation gain.

You'll begin in Conway center, along roads with light in-town traffic. If road skating provokes anxiety, glance up at Cathedral Ledge (near the turnaround point for intermediates) and imagine yourself as one of the climbers clinging to the sheer face hundreds of feet above the ground. Suddenly, cruising beside recreational vehicles and station wagons seems quite manageable. As you roll along wide and straight Westside Road (the shortcut for those who can't endure the pace of tourist traffic on NH 16 through North Conway), expect to encounter a steady stream of cars (although if you're visiting off-season, you may have the road to yourself). The terrain changes noticeably at the 7.8-mile mark, where the level ground gives way to challenging hills. At this point, intermediates will have turned back, and advanced skaters may continue for an additional 4 grueling miles before returning the way they came.

ROUTE DIRECTIONS:

0.0 Skate north, away from NH 16, on Washington Street.

0.1 Bear left onto Westside Road at a triangular common as Washington Street bears right.

0.3 Leave the suburban Conway setting.

2.2 ▼ CAUTION: Roll across railroad tracks and enjoy a relaxing cruise along a brief section of bike lane on the road's shoulder.

3.2 Enjoy outstanding views for the next few miles as you roll along a flat, wide stretch of road.

5.7 Stay straight as roads to Echo Lake and White Horse Ledges turn left.

6.2 Bear left, still on Westside Road, as River Road heads right. Take in more impressive vistas: the Mount Cranmore Ski Area and the pyramid-shaped Kearsarge North.

On your side trip to Cathedral Ledge, look closely to see climbers clinging to the sheer rock walls.

6.7 Turn left at the junction with River Road, remaining on Westside Road. Immediately turn left again (following signs) for a side trip to the base of Cathedral Ledge.

7.2 Pause to admire the rock climbers. INTERMEDIATE SKATERS should reverse direction here.

7.7 ADVANCED SKATERS: Turn left onto Westside Road.

7.8 Cross into North Conway and power over some rollers.

8.5 Drop down a moderate descent.

9.6 Climb moderately on snaking terrain.

10.0 Attack a steep hill that curls right, then left.

10.7 Plunge down a moderate hill.

11.0 Pump up a brief but taxing ascent that bends to the left; pause to appreciate northerly views that encompass the Presidential Mountain Range.

11.2 Trend gradually upward.

11.7 Climb to the intersection with US 302; reverse direction and return to your car.

Route number

Maine

N

1

95

2

95

Bangor

Augusta ★

1

89
88   90
87 86   91   101
85
92 95 98
93 96 99
84   94 97 100

Routes on Mt. Desert Island

Portland
83
81
82
80
79

60 miles

Part Six

Maine

79 •••• *Goose Rocks Beach*

LOCATION: Goose Rocks Beach, ME
RATING: Intermediate
DISTANCE: 3.5 miles
TIMES TO AVOID: Expect increased traffic during summer and holiday
  weekends
TERRAIN: Flat
SURFACE: Smooth asphalt
AUTO TRAFFIC: Light to moderate
POINTS OF INTEREST: Goose Rocks Beach, Kennebunkport, Rachel
  Carson National Wildlife Refuge, Vaughns Preserve

DRIVING DIRECTIONS: Three miles north of the Kennebunk River on
ME 9 in Kennebunkport, turn onto New Biddeford Road. Park on the
shoulder at the road junction beyond the island.

TRIP OVERVIEW: You've heard of "surf and turf"? Here it is—although
served up a little different from what you're used to! First, the "turf":
Skate on wide, lightly traveled roads, passing enchanting Beaver Pond.
Just less than a mile into the route, roll into Goose Rocks Beach. Parking spaces are hard to come by here, and you'll be grateful that you
arrived on skates! Then—and here's the "surf" part—spread out your
towel and soak in some sun or enjoy lunch or a snack waterside. If you
thought to tuck a suit in your fanny pack, you can even take the
plunge. For a "turf" finish, cruise along flat, smooth roads, passing tidal
flats and Goose Rocks Creek on the way back to your car.
  One of Maine's most delightful skating routes!

ROUTE DIRECTIONS:
  0.0 Set out eastward on New Biddeford Road; bear left at the fork
    with Winter Harbor Road.
  0.6 New Biddeford Road ends at Goose Rocks Beach; turn right onto
    Town Road and skate beside the beach. Hop onto the sidewalk to
    avoid slow-moving traffic.
  1.0 Roll along level ground, with summer cottages separating you
    from the shore.
  1.3 Continue straight on Town Road, following it to its end, as Dyke
    Road heads right.
  2.0 Turn around, return to Dyke Road, and turn left.
  2.2 On a curve, cruise by Smith Brook (on your left) and Goose

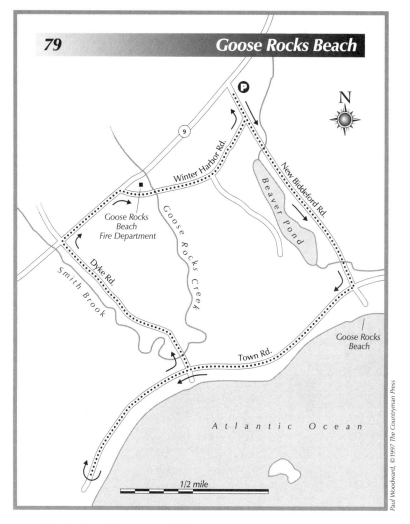

Rocks Creek (on your right).

2.5 Leave the marshes and ascend gradually.

2.7 ● STOP at the junction with ME 9. Turn right onto ME 9, skating on the ample (but rough) shoulder.

2.9 Turn right onto Winter Harbor Road and roll by the Goose Rocks Beach Fire Department.

3.5 ● STOP. Turn left onto New Biddeford Road and return to your car.

80 •••• Biddeford Pool

LOCATION: Biddeford, ME
RATING: Advanced
DISTANCE: 10.4 miles or 13.9 miles
TIMES TO AVOID: Expect increased traffic during summer and holiday
    weekends
TERRAIN: Flat with some rolling hills
SURFACE: Smooth and coarse asphalt
AUTO TRAFFIC: Moderate to heavy
POINTS OF INTEREST: Biddeford Pool, Hills Beach, East Point Wildlife
    Sanctuary, Fortunes Rocks Beach, Kennebunkport

DRIVING DIRECTIONS: From the junction of ME 9, ME 208, and ME
111 in Biddeford, follow ME 9 West/ME 208 South. In 2.6 miles, turn
left into the public boat access, which has an ample parking area.

TRIP OVERVIEW: If you'd rather eat from the buffet table than order
one main dish, you'll enjoy the variety of roadways and scenery on this

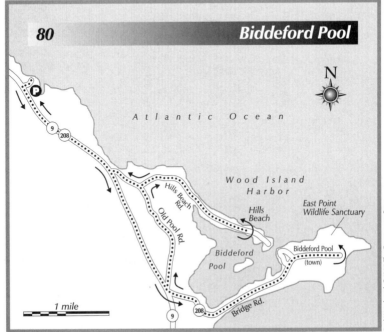

route. You'll cruise along the wide, smooth shoulder of busy ME 9 before venturing onto less crowded but tighter ME 208, which has more bends and curves. Next, roll along a straight stretch beside Biddeford Pool, then wind through a seaside village before arriving at the rugged coastline. You'll encounter fewer cars once you leave the main road, but because the roads are narrow and there is the potential for moderate traffic, the route earned an advanced rating.

Bring your sneakers and a picnic lunch so that you can take an extended seaside rest or investigate the wildlife and coastal habitat of East Point Wildlife Sanctuary. If you elect to return via the longer route, take the time to visit peaceful Hills Beach. Because of limited parking in the vicinity, the beach is rarely crowded—you may even have it all to yourself!

ROUTE DIRECTIONS:

0.0 Return to ME 9/ME 208 and turn left, skating on the wide shoulder.

1.0 Roll over easy hills, still on an ample shoulder.

1.4 Continue straight as Hills Beach Road turns left. (You have the option to return via Hills Beach Road.)

2.0 Skate beside guardrails with a water tower ahead.

2.8 Turn left onto wide 208 South (Bridge Road) with a minimal shoulder.

3.3 ▼ CAUTION: After a rolling hill, turn sharply left.

3.4 Bridge Road ends; turn left and skate between Biddeford Pool (on your left) and the Gulf of Maine.

4.5 Skate through the coastal village of Biddeford Pool on curves and hills.

4.6 Cruise along a wider, straighter stretch of road.

5.2 Reach the road's end and a spectacular section of rocky coastline. You'll want to remove your skates, scale the rocks, and relax or explore the tidal pools.
Note: The entrance to the East Point Wildlife Sanctuary is between two houses just prior to the end of this route.
Return the way you came, or add 3.5 miles to the tour by following this route:

7.4 Turn right onto narrow, winding Old Pool Road.

8.7 At a stop sign, turn right onto Hills Beach Road (as Old Pool Road ends).

9.2 Cruise along a straight tract.

9.8 Pass through a cluster of houses.

10.0 Roll between Biddeford Pool (on your right) and Wood Island Harbor.
10.5 With Hills Beach on your left, return to the Old Pool Road/Hills Beach Road junction.
12.2 Bear right, still on Hills Beach Road.
12.5 Glide by the University of New England's main campus and turn right, once again on ME 9/ME 208.
13.9 Turn right, heading down the access road to the boat ramp and your car.

81 •••• *Popham Beach*

LOCATION: Bath, ME
RATING: Advanced
DISTANCE: 14.0 miles
TIMES TO AVOID: Expect increased traffic during summer and holiday weekends
TERRAIN: Rolling, twisting road with two steep hills
SURFACE: Smooth asphalt
AUTO TRAFFIC: Light to moderate
POINTS OF INTEREST: The Bath Iron Works (shipbuilding concern; one of Maine's largest employers), Popham Beach State Park, Squirrel Point Light, Fort Baldwin, Fort Popham

DRIVING DIRECTIONS: From US 1 in Bath, follow signs to ME 209. Drive 6.8 miles on ME 209 South. At Parker Head Drive, park along the shoulder of the road.

TRIP OVERVIEW: Interested in a great workout? You'll feel the burn as you pump up two extended climbs on the way to Popham Beach. Follow a narrow country road that rolls and curves alongside the swiftly flowing Kennebec River (a popular destination for white-water rafters). Although traffic is light, stay far to the right as you round the many corners. After 7 miles of tough skating, you'll be grateful for the opportunity to pull off your skates and relax on the sandy beach by the water. Don't get too comfortable, though. You'll need to psych yourself up for the return trip, which is as challenging as the initial leg.

Here's a bit of trivia to share with your skating companions: The beach was named for George Popham, who established the first English settlement in New England. He landed in August 1607 on the west

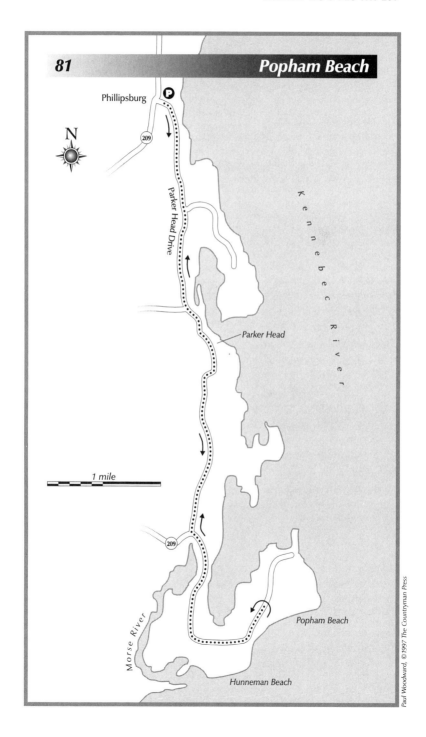

81 **Popham Beach**

Phillipsburg

N

209

Parker Head Drive

Kennebec River

Parker Head

1 mile

209

Morse River

Popham Beach

Hunneman Beach

bank of the Kennebec River (near today's Popham Beach). He was elected president of the colony he founded, but died the next year. The 120 or so colonists, disheartened by his death and by Maine's severe weather, abandoned Fort Popham and returned to England.

ROUTE DIRECTIONS:

0.0 Skate down Parker Head Drive, taking care to stay to the right of this narrow, winding country road.

0.25 Roll alongside the Kennebec River.

0.4 Dive into the woods on a tough ascent that persists for nearly half a mile.

1.0 ▼ CAUTION: Drop in stages, initially on a moderate descent that will require braking.

1.4 Descend past Morning Side Cemetery.

1.7 Skate past tidewaters of the Kennebec River and begin a steep climb.

2.2 Pass quarrylike rock formations on your left. Execute a snaking descent.

2.6 Pop up a short, steep hill.

2.8 Climb into a neighborhood and pass a second cemetery, now journeying away from the river.

3.4 Skate along the route's only straight tract.

4.0 Skirt a pond and resume the twists and turns.

4.5 As the coil of road loosens, descend gradually for 0.5 mile.

5.0 ● STOP. Turn left on 209 South with the Morse River on your right.

5.8 Follow the curves on a tame downhill.

6.3 Glide through tidal flats on a wider shoulder.

6.6 Lose the wide shoulder as sand dunes separate you from Popham Beach on your right.

7.0 At the end of the sandy beach, rest, relax, then return to your car the way you came.

SKATING TIP: *Don't get caught in the "striding rut." Incorporate different skating skills into your workout. Doing so not only improves your technique, but also increases the intensity of your workout.*

82 •••• *South Portland Greenway*

LOCATION: South Portland, ME
RATING: Beginner
DISTANCE: 4.6 miles
TIMES TO AVOID: None
TERRAIN: Flat path with road crossings
SURFACE: Smooth asphalt
AUTO TRAFFIC: None, except at frequent road intersections
POINTS OF INTEREST: Portland Harbor, Spring Point Museum and Lighthouse, Portland Museum of Art, Wadsworth-Longfellow House

DRIVING DIRECTIONS: From I-295, take exit 4 (US 1, South Main Street to South Portland). At the first traffic light, turn left onto Broadway, following signs to Cape Elizabeth. Follow Broadway for 3.5 miles to the end and turn left. Immediately make another left turn into a public parking lot at Cushing Point.

TRIP OVERVIEW: The urban bike path that skirts Portland Harbor (with views to downtown Portland) provides a safe place for the beginning skater to practice. It also offers advanced skaters the opportunity for a good interval workout: Skate hard between street crossings! The intersections are frequent and several are busy, but these have "walk" lights to facilitate crossing. After rolling through bustling urban neighborhoods and along the marshes of Portland Harbor, you'll reach the trail's end. (There are plans to extend the path, so you may find it directly accessible from the parking area at Cushing Point.) When you've retraced the route to your car, remove your skates and stroll along the path at Fort Preble and Fort Hill, or visit the Spring Point Museum and lighthouse and hunt for treasures along the adjacent beach.

ROUTE DIRECTIONS:
  0.0 Return to Broadway and turn right, skating along the wide shoulder of this busy road.
  0.4 Turn right onto Stanford Street. Look for the skating path that ducks behind houses on your left.
  0.5 ● STOP. Cross Crescent Avenue.
  0.6 Pass a baseball field on your right.
  0.7 ● STOP. Cross Roosevelt Street.
  0.8 ● STOP. Cross Harriet Street.

0.9 City views emerge as you approach Portland Harbor.

1.3 ● STOP. Cross busy Cottage Road.

1.5 ● STOP. Cross busier ME 77.

1.6 ● STOP. Cross Waterman Street, which has heavy traffic. Head diagonally to your left, obeying the traffic signal.

1.8 Skate over a wooden bridge.

2.0 ● STOP. Cross Buttonwood Street.

2.3 At the container storage port at the base of Turner Island, the trail ends: Return to your car the way you came.

83 •••• *Falmouth*

LOCATION: Falmouth, ME
RATING: Intermediate
DISTANCE: 5.5 miles
TIMES TO AVOID: None
TERRAIN: Wide country roads with long, gradual hills and one moderate hill
SURFACE: Smooth asphalt
AUTO TRAFFIC: Light for all but a 0.3-mile section of moderate
POINTS OF INTEREST: Portland, Freeport (outlet shopping, L.L. Bean), Gilsland Farm, Portland Museum of Art

DRIVING DIRECTIONS: From the Maine Turnpike (I-495), take exit 10 to ME 26 North and ME 100 North. In 0.3 mile, turn right onto Leighton Road. Drive another 0.5 mile to Falmouth Road and turn right. In 0.8 mile, turn left onto Woodville Road and 0.3 mile later turn left at Falmouth High School and park.

TRIP OVERVIEW: If you are traveling with a shopper who is begging for a few hours in Freeport, or if you are driving to the Bar Harbor area and need to stretch your legs, stop for a skate in Falmouth. Cars and neighbors are few and far between on this loop that follows wide roads, some with paved shoulders. You'll be able to work up speed on several long, flat sections, but will have to push hard to crest one moderate uphill. (On the moderate downhill that follows a half-mile later, cross railroad tracks with care.) You'll roll past working farms as well as farmland that now sprouts upscale homes instead of cornstalks. It's hard to imagine life as a Maine farmer—today or in years past. The state is carpeted with

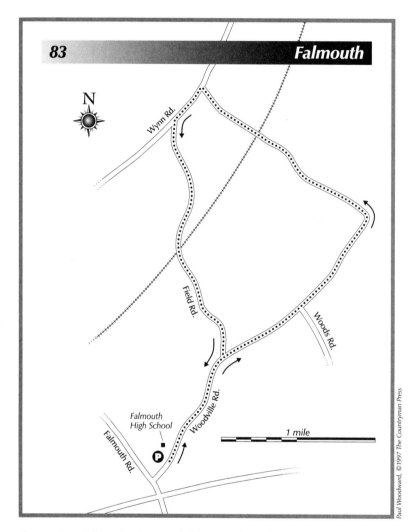

dense glacial deposits that are infertile and overly drained. The soil can
support pine trees and potatoes, but not much more. The loop returns
you to your car.

Feeling good? Try doing a few laps!

ROUTE DIRECTIONS:

0.0 Turn left onto the ample shoulder of wide Woodville Road.

0.5 Continue straight as Field Road goes left.

1.0 Roll gently downhill.

1.2 Stay straight as Woods Road leaves on the right.

1.8 The road bends left before bisecting broad fields.

2.4 Cruise by a tiny pond as the gradual descent bottoms out.

2.6 Now embark on a climb. Hop over railroad tracks (which see daily—but infrequent—use).

2.7 The ascent steepens, then planes after 0.2 mile.

3.1 ● STOP. Turn left onto busier Wynn Road—sufficiently wide, but lacking a shoulder. Pass a number of executive homes.

3.4 ▼ CAUTION: Cross Wynn Road, turn left onto Field Road, and head gently downhill.

3.7 After passing a tired farm, drop down a moderate, two-tiered descent.

4.2 ▼ CAUTION: As the pitch levels, brake and cross the railroad tracks again.

4.5 Climb on a gradual slope for 0.5 mile back up to Woodville Road.

5.0 Turn right onto Woodville Road and return to your car. (Still fresh? Take another lap!)

84 •••• *Christina's World*

LOCATION: Cushing, ME
RATING: Advanced or intermediate
DISTANCE: 16.7 miles or 12.9 miles
TIMES TO AVOID: None
TERRAIN: Long, gradual hills
SURFACE: Smooth asphalt
AUTO TRAFFIC: Light to very light
POINTS OF INTEREST: Olson Homestead, Fort Saint Georges, Owls Head, Marshall Point Lighthouse

DRIVING DIRECTIONS: At the junction of US 1 and ME 97 in South Warren, head south on ME 97. In 1.1 miles, turn left on Spearmill Road. Drive another 0.8 mile and bear right, merging with Cushing Road. In 3.7 miles, arrive in Cushing and park downtown along Broad Cove.

TRIP OVERVIEW: Enter *Christina's World*. Follow quiet country roads running along one of the few undeveloped peninsulas jutting into the Atlantic Ocean. At the tip of Hawthorne Point, you can stand where Andrew Wyeth did to create his famous painting of the polio-stricken Christina Olson as she lay in the field below the old farmhouse.

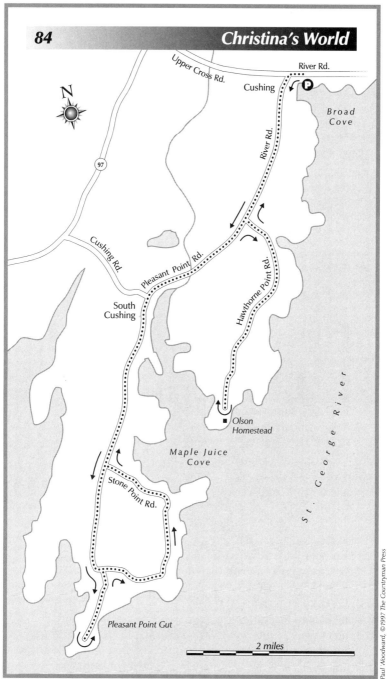

84 **Christina's World**

Upper Cross Rd.

River Rd.

Cushing

P

Broad Cove

River Rd.

97

Cushing Rd.

Pleasant Point Rd.

South Cushing

Hawthorne Point Rd.

St. George River

■ Olson Homestead

Maple Juice Cove

Stone Point Rd.

Pleasant Point Gut

2 miles

Paul Woodward, ©1997 The Countryman Press

208 •••• *IN-LINE SKATE NEW ENGLAND*

It's not just the destination that makes this trip worthwhile. Cruise by ponds, beside farms, and through woods before winding along the St. George River and numerous inlets. Pleasant Point marks the halfway point: The smooth road narrows, darting in and out of woods as it follows the shoreline. Three-quarters of the way along the route you visit the Olson residence on Hawthorne Point. Unmarked and unpretentious, the house sits atop a bluff and probably goes unnoticed by all who are not aware of its history.

ROUTE DIRECTIONS:

0.0 Continue east on River Road and almost immediately turn left, still on River Road, as Upper Cross Road heads straight. Pump up a moderate ascent.

1.5 Stay straight as Hawthorne Point Road leaves on the left.

1.6 Brake on a long, moderate descent.

2.8 As you enter South Cushing, continue straight on Pleasant Point Road (as Cushing Road splits right), rolling beside Maple Juice Cove.

4.1 Climb to a junction in heavy evergreen woods. Pleasant Point Road heads straight and Stone Point Road heads left—you continue straight.

5.3 Bear right at an intersection after an easy descent for a 1.3-mile out-and-back on this dead-end stretch.

6.6 Back at the intersection, turn right onto Stone Point Road and cruise along this smooth, narrow road that seems more like a path.

7.1 Pass close to the water called Pleasant Point Gut.

7.5 Roll beside the St. George River on your right.

8.1 Curve left along Maple Juice Cove.

8.4 Climb up and over a moderate hill.

8.8 After a gradual ascent, turn right at an intersection, now reversing direction on Pleasant Point Road.
INTERMEDIATE SKATERS: Skate 4.1 miles to your car for a total 12.9-mile skate (without a visit to the Olson Homestead). ADVANCED SKATERS (for a total skate of 16.7 miles): Continue 2.6 miles to the intersection with Hawthorne Point Road.

11.4 Turn right onto Hawthorne Point Road.

11.6 Suffer up a tough hill in a country, neighborhood setting.

12.2 Brake on a steep descent.

13.3 Reach the Olson Homestead and *Christina's World.* Pause, reflect, then turn around and return to Cushing Road.

15.2 Turn right onto Cushing Road.

16.7 Arrive at your car.

85 •••• *Owls Head*

LOCATION: Rockland, ME
RATING: Advanced or intermediate
DISTANCE: 14.6 miles (advanced); 9.6 miles (intermediate)
TIMES TO AVOID: None
TERRAIN: Mostly flat, with two moderate hills on the advanced route
SURFACE: Smooth asphalt
AUTO TRAFFIC: Moderate
POINTS OF INTEREST: Rockport, Harbor Park, Rockport Park, Maine
    Sport Outfitters, Maine Coast Artists Gallery, Beauchamp Point,
    Children's Chapel, Aldemere Farm, Laite Park, Megunticook Lake

DRIVING DIRECTIONS: At the junction of US 1 and ME 73 (Main Street) in Rockland, turn south onto ME 73, following a sign to Owls Head. In 1.8 miles, turn left onto North Shore Drive (guided by a sign to Owls Head State Park Light). Drive 0.2 mile and park on the shoulder near the intersection of Ash Point Drive and North Shore Drive.

TRIP OVERVIEW: If you want *just* a workout, turn the page. But if you want to combine skating with sight-seeing, read on. Along this route, you will have the opportunity to visit historic Owls Head Light, Birch Point Beach, and the quaint harbor town of Owls Head. At the lighthouse, spread out lunch at the picnic area (with rest rooms,) and then wave-watch from the pebbly beach. Beautiful Birch Point Beach (at the 8-mile mark), which has limited parking and therefore is more easily accessed on skates, will entice you to take a swim (and also offers visitors portable rest rooms). Allow yourself several hours for this "skate-seeing" route—you'll be disappointed if you don't have time to linger—and carry a backpack with a comfortable pair of walking shoes, a bathing suit, lunch, and plenty to drink.

In addition to this lighthouse, you'll encounter two sandy beaches on this trip.

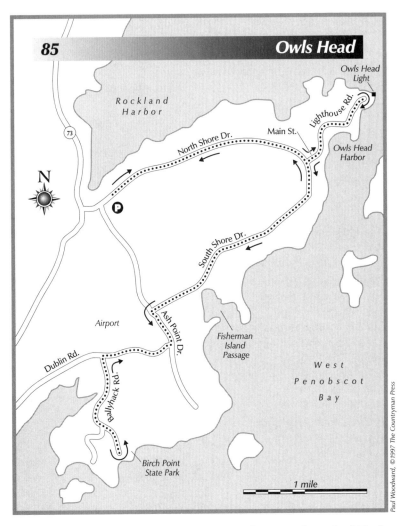

85   *Owls Head*

Rockland Harbor

Owls Head Light

Lighthouse Rd.

North Shore Dr.

Main St.

Owls Head Harbor

73

N

P

South Shore Dr.

Airport

Ash Point Dr.

Dublin Rd.

Ballyhack Rd.

Fisherman Island Passage

W e s t
P e n o b s c o t
B a y

Birch Point State Park

1 mile

Paul Woodward, ©1997 The Countryman Press

To shorten the loop to 9.6 miles and eliminate the only difficult hills, park at the Owls Head Light parking area and begin the skate there.

ROUTE DIRECTIONS:

0.0 ADVANCED SKATERS: Head eastward on smooth North Shore Drive through a suburban area with views of the Camden Hills to your left across Rockland Harbor.

0.7 Push over a brief but tough climb, now rolling through woods.

1.3 Feel the burn as you continue to ascend.

1.7 Brake on a moderate descent, taking in distant views of West Penobscot Bay.

2.5 ▼ CAUTION: Stop mid-descent at the intersection with Main Street. Turn left onto Main Street, following a sign to Owls Head Light. The descent continues to require braking as you near Owls Head Harbor.

2.7 Turn left onto Lighthouse Road.

3.2 ● STOP. Lighthouse Road turns to dirt. (You'll reach the Owls Head Light picnic and parking area in 0.1 mile and the lighthouse in 0.2 mile.) INTERMEDIATE SKATERS: Begin here.

3.9 Return to North Shore Drive and turn left. (North Shore Drive now becomes South Shore Drive.)

5.1 After a series of easy hills, descend moderately.

5.7 Cross a wooden bridge overlooking Fisherman Island Passage.

6.3 ● STOP. Turn left onto Ash Point Drive.

6.6 Turn right onto Dublin Road. Roll through open surroundings, passing a small airport and a marsh.

7.4 Turn left onto gently rolling Ballyhack Road.

8.0 The pavement ends. Exchange skates for shoes and shortly, at a fork, bear left following the sign to Birch Point State Park; arrive at the beach in 0.5 mile. Return to your car the way you came. ADVANCED SKATERS: Skip the side trip to Owls Head Light for a total skate of 14.6 miles.

86 •••• *Chickawaukie Pond*

LOCATION: Rockport, ME
RATING: Intermediate
DISTANCE: 12.8 miles
TIMES TO AVOID: None
TERRAIN: Long, gradual hills on scenic roads with wide shoulders
SURFACE: Smooth asphalt
AUTO TRAFFIC: Moderate
POINTS OF INTEREST: Camden, Rockport, Rockport Park, Maine Sport Outfitters, Harbor Park, Maine Coast Artists Gallery, Beauchamp Point, Children's Chapel, Aldemere Farm, Laite Park, Megunticook Lake

DRIVING DIRECTIONS: At the junction of US 1 and ME 90 in Rockport, turn west onto ME 90. Park at an appropriate spot on the shoulder of the road.

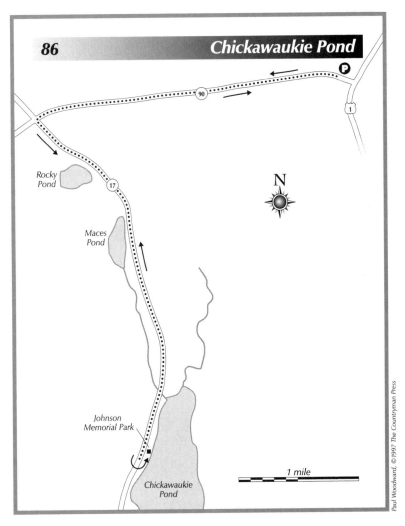

86   *Chickawaukie Pond*

Rocky
Pond

Maces
Pond

Johnson
Memorial Park

Chickawaukie
Pond

N

1 mile

Paul Woodward, ©1997 The Countryman Press

TRIP OVERVIEW: You won't find wider shoulders on a football team—and you certainly won't find them on many roads in Maine. That's why these smooth Rockport roads are popular with skaters, cyclists, and runners, despite the fact that they're well traveled. If you have the stamina for long, gradual hills and the skill to manage the descents that follow, you'll enjoy this high-speed skate. You'll cruise by scenic ponds before reaching the shores of Chickawaukie Pond. Head back to your car the way you came, initially tackling an extended, though gradual, hill on ME 17.

When you're done, trade your skates for walking shoes and explore the seaside villages of Rockport and Camden. Spread out a picnic lunch at Rockport Park, a delightful spot overlooking the harbor. And don't miss the in-line hockey rink at Maine Sport Outfitters (a terrific place to rent bikes, canoes, kayaks, and camping equipment), located north of Rockport on US 1.

ROUTE DIRECTIONS:

0.0 Head west on ME 90, skating along the wide shoulder.

0.3 Commence the first lengthy climb with views across farmland to the Camden Hills.

0.7 Reach the end of the hill's steepest pitch.

1.6 Crest and rest.

2.7 ▼ CAUTION: Stop. Turn left at this busy intersection with ME 17 and head southward.

3.2 Pass Rocky Pond on your right.

3.8 Cruise by Maces Pond. (For a taste of Holland, look at the hillside on the right side of the road: See the windmill?)

4.0 Skate up an easy ascent, passing a cemetery on your left as you crest.

4.8 Embark on an extended descent to Chickawaukie Pond.

5.4 Conclude your descent at the edge of the pond.

6.4 Finish up at Rockland's Johnson Memorial Park and Recreation Facility. Reverse direction to return to your car.

87 •••• *Camden*

LOCATION: Camden, ME
RATING: Intermediate
DISTANCE: 6.4 miles
TIMES TO AVOID: Summer weekends expect significant slow-moving traffic
TERRAIN: Flat, with a pair of easy hills
SURFACE: Smooth asphalt
AUTO TRAFFIC: Light, with the exception of summer weekends
POINTS OF INTEREST: Camden Hills State Park (hiking trails, camping), Camden, Penobscot Bay, Rockport, Rockport Park, Harbor Park, Maine Coast Artists Gallery, Beauchamp Point, Children's Chapel, Aldemere Farm, Laite Park, Megunticook Lake

DRIVING DIRECTIONS: At the junction of US 1 and Bayview Street in Camden (just north of the junction of US 1 and ME 105), turn east onto Bayview Street. Drive until you find an empty metered parking spot along the street.

TRIP OVERVIEW: If you're a believer in love at first sight, visit Camden. You'll fall hard for this coastal town, its streets lined with upscale shops and its cozy harbor rimmed by the Camden Hills. In fact, you'll find yourself examining all of the ways you might change your life so that you can move to the Maine coast. Perhaps you could run a bed & breakfast or write the great American novel or sell paintings of the windjammers that dot the harbor . . . the possibilities are endless!

Take a self-guided tour of this seaside village—on skates, that is. Begin your sight-seeing trip in an active neighborhood (near a playground—drop the kids and a big person there). Soon you'll leave the village behind as you roll through lush woods. Cruise beside the clipped lawns of a golf course, gazing at the majestic Camden Hills rising over a petite pond. Reverse your direction and—with the addition of a roll down a quiet peninsula—return to Bayview Street the way you came.

But don't leave Camden yet! Stop by Megunticook Lake, 3 miles from Camden village, where you can swim and picnic at Barrett's Cove. Or relax at an oceanside beach area—Laite Park, nestled beside Camden Harbor—and watch the windjammers and luxury boats slip in and out of the harbor. We bet this won't be your last trip to Camden!

ROUTE DIRECTIONS:

0.0 Continue south down Bayview Street and pump up a demanding, but brief, ascent.

0.4 Glide past the park and playground. (Look for tiny Curtis Island in the harbor.)

0.7 Press up another short hill and depart the congested neighborhood as the road narrows.

1.1 Tackle a pair of sharp right turns on a slight decline; fly by a cemetery.

1.5 ● STOP. Turn left onto wider Chestnut Street.

2.0 To your right, view the Camden Hills across farmland and Lilly Pond.

2.2 As Candlewood Road turns left, continue straight (though you'll return by way of Candlewood).

2.5 ● STOP. Turn left onto Mechanic Street and roll around the perimeter of Deadman Point (a peninsula), with Rockport Harbor on your right.

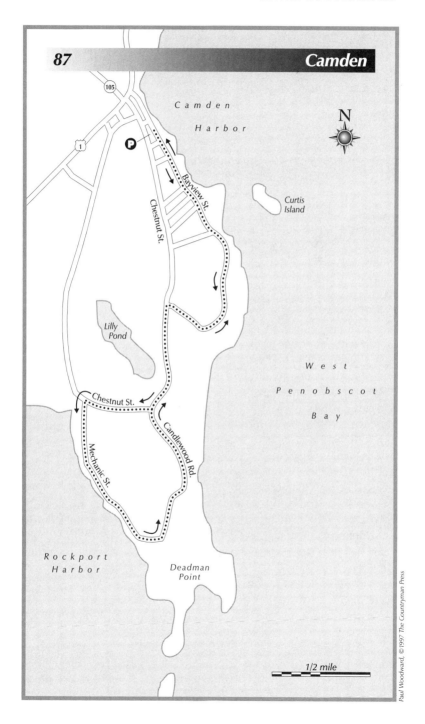

87

Camden

105

1

P

Camden
Harbor

N

Bayview St.

Chestnut St.

Curtis
Island

Lilly
Pond

Chestnut St.

West

Penobscot

Bay

Candlewood Rd.

Mechanic St.

Rockport
Harbor

Deadman
Point

1/2 mile

3.4 Turn left onto Candlewood Road.

4.2 ● STOP. Turn right onto Chestnut Street, now back on the original outbound route.

4.9 Turn right onto Bayview Street and continue for 1.5 miles to return to your car.

88 •••• *Youngstown Road*

LOCATION: Lincolnville, ME
RATING: Advanced
DISTANCE: 5.6 miles
TIMES TO AVOID: None
TERRAIN: Wide, rolling rural road
SURFACE: Smooth asphalt
AUTO TRAFFIC: Light
POINTS OF INTEREST: Camden Hills State Park (hiking trails, camping), Camden, Penobscot Bay, Children's Chapel, Laite Park, Maine Sport Outfitters, Rockport Park, Harbor Park, Maine Coast Artists Gallery, Beauchamp Point, Aldemere Farm, Megunticook Lake

DRIVING DIRECTIONS: From US 1 in Lincolnville, head west on ME 173. In 2.2 miles, turn left onto Youngstown Road and park in the Camden Hills State Park turnout on your left.

TRIP OVERVIEW: Thankfully, this is not a complicated route, because you're going to be too busy gawking at the delightful scenery to pay a lot of attention to intersections, stop signs, and right and left turns. Youngstown Road is a wide rural road that travels through scenic backcountry adjacent to the Maine coast. Start at one of the many parking areas for the Camden Hills hiking trails: Let your hiking buddies go their way as you go yours. The Camden Hills, looming over Penobscot Bay's northern shore, rival the peaks of Mount Desert Island for the title of "Finest Coastal Hiking Area in the Northeast." Or, if you have loads of energy (as well as your hiking gear in the car), blast the skating route, then chase your friends to the top of Bald Rock Mountain for sensational views over West Penobscot Bay.

If time allows, stop by the Children's Chapel, a lovely open-air chapel overlooking Penobscot Bay. A stroll through the rock, flower, and herb gardens provides a relaxing follow-up to your intensive workout!

ROUTE DIRECTIONS:
0.0 From the parking area, turn left onto Youngstown Road.
0.2 Begin to climb; soon, push hard up a tough, two-tiered hill.
0.9 Embark on a series of rollers. Enjoy sweeping views over the valley to your right.
2.2 Climb a moderate hill with Cameron Mountain on your left.
2.8 ▼ CAUTION: Stop at the junction of ME 52. Turn, and reverse the route to reach your car.

SKATING TIP: *To achieve maximum power on each speed-skating stroke, start from as deep a bend as possible. This will increase the length of your stroke.*

---

89 •••• *Saturday Cove*

LOCATION: Northport, ME
RATING: Advanced
DISTANCE: 9.6 miles
TIMES TO AVOID: Spring (the road's surface may be sandy)
TERRAIN: Gently rolling with a few short, steep hills
SURFACE: Smooth asphalt with some broken pavement
AUTO TRAFFIC: Very light
POINTS OF INTEREST: Durham State Forest, Camden Hills State Park, Camden, Penobscot Bay
DRIVING DIRECTIONS: From the junction of US 1 and ME 52 in Camden, drive north on US 1 for 11 miles. Park on the shoulder at the junction of US 1 and Shore Road, just south of the village of Northport.

An alternative (if parking is not available at the junction) is to follow the skating route directions to the school (4.4 miles away) and do the route in reverse.

TRIP OVERVIEW: Saturday Cove—doesn't the very name entice you, like a whiff of warm brownies? Take a delightful excursion along the edge of West Penobscot Bay, with rolling hills adding appeal and an occasional challenge. Congested villages bracket this route, and parking spots are hard to come by in Northport. You may need to drive to the end and skate the route in reverse (refer to the driving directions).

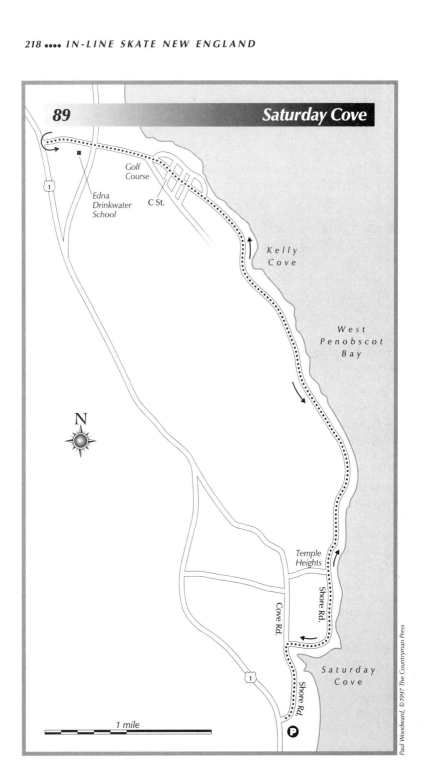

89

Saturday Cove

Golf Course

C St.

Edna Drinkwater School

Kelly Cove

West Penobscot Bay

N

Temple Heights

Shore Rd.

Cove Rd.

Saturday Cove

Shore Rd.

1 mile

Paul Woodward, ©1997 The Countryman Press

Although the road's surface is in very good condition for most of the way, short sections of deteriorating pavement (as well as narrow back roads) earned the trip an advanced rating.

ROUTE DIRECTIONS:
0.0 Skate northeast on Shore Road, heading away from US 1.

0.2 Beyond a cluster of homes, bear right as Cove Road splits left. Brake as you drop down a moderate descent.

0.5 Pass by quaint Saturday Cove and begin a short, steep ascent.

1.0 Braking may be required as you roll down a moderate descent. Skirt the upper stretches of West Penobscot Bay and Hutchins Island and arrive at the village of Temple Heights.

1.7 Brake on a moderate downhill that brings you to the edge of West Penobscot Bay, now on rougher pavement.

2.0 A quick rise leads to grand views across Belfast Bay and up the Penobscot River.

2.7 Pass a rocky stretch of seashore along Kelly Cove, descending gently.

3.1 After a roller, you'll dodge another rockbound section of the bay.

3.5 Travel through the congested neighborhoods of Bayside and scoot over a roller.

3.8 Continue past C Street.

4.0 As you leave the residential area, the road widens.

4.2 Glide past a golf course on your left.

4.4 Pass the Edna Drinkwater School.

4.8 Stop at the junction with US 1 and return to your car.

90 •••• *Verona Island*

LOCATION: Bucksport, ME
RATING: Intermediate
DISTANCE: 9.1 miles or 17.2 miles
TIMES TO AVOID: None
TERRAIN: Gently rolling with a limited number of longer, moderate hills
SURFACE: Smooth asphalt
AUTO TRAFFIC: Very light
POINTS OF INTEREST: Fort Knox State Park, Penobscot River, Bucksport, Bangor

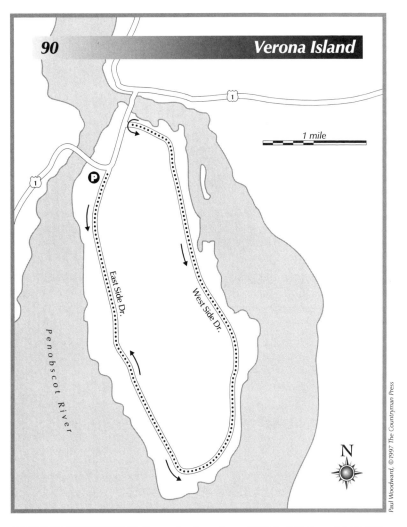

90   *Verona Island*

1 mile

East Side Dr.

West Side Dr.

Penobscot River

N

Paul Woodward, ©1997 The Countryman Press

DRIVING DIRECTIONS: From the junction of US 1, ME 3, and ME 174 in Bucksport, head north on US 1 across the Penobscot River. In 0.25 mile, park at the picnic area on your right.

TRIP OVERVIEW: Smooth pavement? Check. Light traffic? Check. Easy to find? Check again. Add pleasant scenery to the list, and you have the ingredients for a great skate—especially if you're en route to Bar Harbor. Park the car, trade sneakers for skates, and work out the kinks! From the picnic area, skate over gentle hills for 8.5 miles, with farmland and river views as you roll along the Eastern Channel at about the

4-mile mark. The more you enjoy solitude, the happier you'll become toward route's end, as the island becomes more sparsely populated the farther you go. Upon completion of the horseshoe that is East Side and West Side Drives, reverse direction and return to your car. (Interested in a shortcut? If you can endure a brief stint on US 1—along an ample shoulder—you'll reach your car in about 0.5 mile.)

ROUTE DIRECTIONS:
0.0 Head south, away from US 1, on East Side Drive.
0.5 Skate through a lightly populated residential area on gently rolling terrain.
1.0 Enjoy a flat tract.
2.0 Speed down a pair of short hills.
2.5 Negotiate a moderate downhill. (Experienced skaters will not need to brake.)
3.0 To your right, glimpse the Penobscot River.
3.2 Drop down another moderate descent as the road narrows slightly.
3.8 As the road bends sharply left on a moderate descent, dart through thick deciduous woods.
4.5 Rolling over easy hills, look right to the Eastern Channel. (This side of the loop, called East Side Drive, is very sparsely populated.)
5.0 Pass a cemetery on your right and head up and over a moderate hill.
6.0 Skate over more gentle rollers through mile 8.5.
8.6 ▼ CAUTION: Stop as you approach the intersection with US 1. Here, reverse direction and return to your car. Or turn left and head uphill, skating with care on the ample shoulder of US 1. In about 0.5 mile, you'll be back at your car.

91 •••• *Newbury Neck*

LOCATION: Surry, ME
RATING: Advanced or intermediate
DISTANCE: 16.6 miles (advanced); 7.2 miles (intermediate)
TIMES TO AVOID: None
TERRAIN: One challenging hill (advanced); gently rolling (intermediate)
SURFACE: Smooth asphalt
AUTO TRAFFIC: Light to very light

POINTS OF INTEREST: Surry village, East Blue Hill, Patten Bay and Union River Bay, swimming beach, Acadia National Park

DRIVING DIRECTIONS: From the junction of US 1, ME 3, and ME 172 in Ellsworth, take ME 172 South. Drive 6.3 miles to Surry and turn left onto ME 176, following a sign to East Blue Hill. Almost immediately, bear left onto Newbury Neck Road. Park on the shoulder down from the junction with ME 176.

For the intermediate route, drive an additional 4.7 miles on Newbury Neck Road to a parking turnout on your right, across from a beach area.

TRIP OVERVIEW: Most people love Maine for the same reason: the varied and breathtaking scenery with—*and this is the important part*—very few other people enjoying it alongside you. This trip won't disappoint any fans of the great Pine Tree State. First, it is uncomplicated, like Maine itself. Skate down Newbury Neck Road and back. That's it. Advanced skaters will face one tough hill early on, but cruise along the remainder. Next, there are no crowds! The route follows a virtually untraveled section of the Maine coast. And finally, the surroundings are lovely, as you are embraced by water along nearly the entire route. At the halfway point, you'll glide by a local swimming spot on Union River Bay. Truly one of the great Maine skates!

ROUTE DIRECTIONS:
0.0 After taking in the panorama across Patten Bay to the village of Surry, skate down Newbury Neck Road, heading south.
0.5 Rise and fall with easy hills, continuing to enjoy views of the bay.
0.7 Take on a 0.3-mile series of moderately difficult uphill stages.
1.0 Crest and rest on a long descent that affords broad views to Union River Bay. As the road curls to the right and steepens, be prepared to lean back for extra braking power.
1.5 Roll along level terrain with diminished views.
2.0 As harbor views return, look ahead to see radio towers.
2.5 Continue along flat terrain in a rural residential setting.
3.0 Pass the broadcast towers as you flirt with the bay.
3.5 Pass Cross Street (which joins from the right) on slightly rolling ground. Expect to encounter even fewer cars now as you travel on a dead-end road.
4.5 After working around a gentle curve, you'll be treated to dazzling views of Union River Bay.

4.7 With a beach area on your left and the parking turnout on your right, the road narrows. INTERMEDIATE SKATERS: Begin the skate here.

5.7 Duck away from the harbor area.

6.5 Glide past wide fields that stretch to the bay and Haskell Point.

7.6 Hop over an easy roller.

8.3 ● STOP as the road turns to dirt. Reverse direction to return to your car.

92 •••• Bass Harbor Point, Mount Desert Island

LOCATION: Bass Harbor, ME, on Mount Desert Island
RATING: Intermediate
DISTANCE: 8.0 miles
TIMES TO AVOID: None
TERRAIN: Flat and gently rolling, with one moderate hill
SURFACE: Predominantly smooth asphalt
AUTO TRAFFIC: Very light with a section of moderate
POINTS OF INTEREST: Bass Harbor, Bass Harbor Head Lighthouse, Acadia National Park

DRIVING DIRECTIONS: From ME 102 South in Bernard on Mount Desert Island, turn right onto Bernard Road, following a sign to Bernard. In 0.4 mile, turn right onto Lopaus Point Road. Drive another 0.4 mile and park in the gravel turnout on your left.

TRIP OVERVIEW: Your skate to the Bass Harbor Head Lighthouse begins on a road that feels more like a bike path. Roll through the fishing village that rims Bass Harbor before ascending through evergreen forest and finally arriving at the lighthouse that overlooks the rugged coastline. The beacon was built in 1858 to warn sailors about the bar across the bay's eastern entrance. The French explorer Samuel de Champlain, who named Maine's largest island Mount Desert Island because of its bare top, ran aground in this area in 1604. Automated in 1974, the light is now operated by the Coast Guard, and the residence and surrounding property are private. But a short hike through the woods and a rocky scramble to the harbor's edge bring you to the lighthouse overlook. So pack sturdy walking shoes and a picnic and plan on taking a lunch break at this delightful spot before retracing the route to your car.

ROUTE DIRECTIONS:

0.0   Begin the trip by returning the way you came by car to ME 102, skating past Mitchell Cove on your left and Bass Harbor on your right.

0.4   Turn left onto Bernard Road.

0.6   Skate through Bernard village on a gradual descent.

0.8   ▼ CAUTION: Stop and turn right onto ME 102. Stay right and be aware of traffic.

1.0   Bass Harbor comes into view on your right.

1.4   As Anns Point Road goes right, continue straight on ME 102.

1.7   Cross a bridge with Bass Harbor on your right and Bass Harbor Marsh on your left.

1.8   Turn right onto Flat Iron Road, directed by a sign: TO 102A.

2.1   Bear right onto ME 102A.

2.4   Glide by a cemetery on your left and Bass Harbor on your right.

2.7   Continue straight, following a sign for Bass Harbor Head Light.

2.9   Begin a moderate, 0.2-mile ascent.

3.5   Bear right onto Lighthouse Road, toward the U.S. Coast Guard Bass Harbor Head Lighthouse.

3.8   The pavement becomes coarse.

4.0   Arrive at the parking area for the lighthouse. Relax at the overlook before returning to your car.

Ending your workout at Bass Harbor Point by cartwheeling along the beach is optional!

93 •••• *Pretty Marsh, Mount Desert Island*

LOCATION: Pretty Marsh, ME
RATING: Advanced
DISTANCE: 13.2 miles
TIMES TO AVOID: None
TERRAIN: Wide, hilly rural road
SURFACE: Smooth asphalt
AUTO TRAFFIC: Light
POINTS OF INTEREST: Indian Point Nature Conservancy, boating, Acadia National Park (including hiking on nearby Beech, Mansell, and Bernard Mountains), swimming at Echo Lake

DRIVING DIRECTIONS: At the junction of ME 3, ME 102, and ME 198 (just after crossing onto Mount Desert Island), bear right onto ME 102 and ME 198 South. In 2 miles, turn right onto Indian Point Road just north of the village of Town Hill. Drive 6 miles to Pretty Marsh and turn right onto Bartletts Landing Road. Continue to the end of the road and park at the boat-ramp parking area. (You have just driven the route you will now skate!)

TRIP OVERVIEW: Because Mount Desert Island is known for its rocky coast and bald, windswept peaks, the route we've described here is somewhat of an anomaly. Indian Point Road, a wide road with plenty of hills and curves, is fringed with dense evergreen forest. The scent will make you think Christmas, even on the hottest summer day! Initially you will skate along the water: first at Bartlett Narrows, then along Pretty Marsh Harbor. If you have grown tired of towns that cater to tourists with overpriced boutiques and swanky restaurants, you'll enjoy touring Pretty Marsh. Because of its location on the far western edge of Mount Desert Island, it has remained unspoiled.

ROUTE DIRECTIONS:
0.0 Reversing the driving directions, embark on a short, steep ascent.
0.3 ▼ CAUTION: Crest, then brake on the back side of this moderate hill.
1.0 ▼ CAUTION: Stop on a downhill section after crossing over Pretty Marsh Harbor. Turn left onto Indian Point Road.
2.1 Look left through the woods for a view of Goose Marsh Pond.
2.6 Roll over a series of gentle hills.
3.0 ▼ CAUTION: Brake on a moderate descent, then tackle a demanding uphill section.

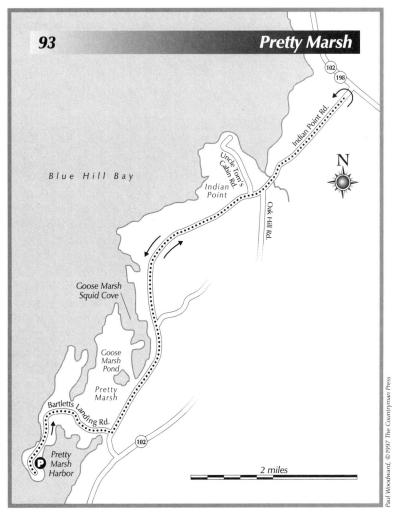

93 *Pretty Marsh*

Blue Hill Bay

Indian Point Rd.

Uncle Tom's Cabin Rd.

Indian Point

Oak Hill Rd.

N

Goose Marsh Squid Cove

Goose Marsh Pond

Pretty Marsh

Bartletts Landing Rd.

Pretty Marsh Harbor

2 miles

Paul Woodward, ©1997 The Countryman Press

3.4 Pump up a moderate hill, then brake on the descent.

4.4 At Indian Point, continue straight as Uncle Tom's Cabin Road goes left.

4.7 Drop down a two-tiered descent. Brake on the second tier as Oak Hill Road heads right.

5.3 Take on a moderate, two-tiered ascent, climbing through thick woods.

6.4 Descend easily, now in a rural neighborhood.

6.6 The route ends at the intersection with the combined ME 102 and ME 198. Head back to your car the way you came.

94 •••• *Seal Cove, Mount Desert Island*

LOCATION: Seal Cove, ME
RATING: Intermediate
DISTANCE: 9.4 miles
TIMES TO AVOID: Expect increased traffic during summer and holiday weekends
TERRAIN: Gently rolling with a couple of moderate hills
SURFACE: Smooth asphalt
AUTO TRAFFIC: Light to moderate
POINTS OF INTEREST: Seal Cove, Acadia National Park

DRIVING DIRECTIONS: Follow ME 102 South to Mount Desert Island. In Somesville, turn right onto ME 102, following a sign to Beech Mountain. In about 7 miles, turn right onto Cape Road and drive 1 mile to where the pavement ends and the surface turns to gravel. Park on the shoulder.

TRIP OVERVIEW: This is an unexpected gem on a remote part of Mount Desert Island. At first you'll roll by Blue Hill Bay, inspiration for any Maine writer, with lobster trap buoys scattered about, seagulls crying overhead, and lobster boats bobbing just off the rockbound coast. From 1.4 to 3.3 miles, head inland on ideal skating turf through evergreen forest. Finally, enjoy skating along a lightly traveled road through a harborside village hugging Goose Cove. Enjoy!

ROUTE DIRECTIONS:
- 0.0 Head back the way you came on Cape Road to ME 102, with Seal Cove on your right. Watch for broken pavement and patches of sand.
- 0.5 Take on a moderate ascent as you head away from the bay.
- 0.6 Descend—moderately at times—a lengthy hill.
- 0.9 ▼ CAUTION: Still heading downhill, stop at the intersection with ME 102. Turn right onto ME 102 and endure a short section on this moderately traveled road with no shoulder.
- 1.4 Turn left onto Kelleytown Road, a smooth road with fewer cars.
- 1.7 Begin a gradual ascent.
- 2.0 Crest and look left for a glimpse of Bernard Mountain.
- 2.5 Ascend gradually through wetlands dotted with hemlocks.
- 3.3 ▼ CAUTION: Stop at the intersection with ME 102, then proceed straight across onto Clark Point Road.
- 3.4 Descend moderately to the tip of Nutter Point on Goose Cove.

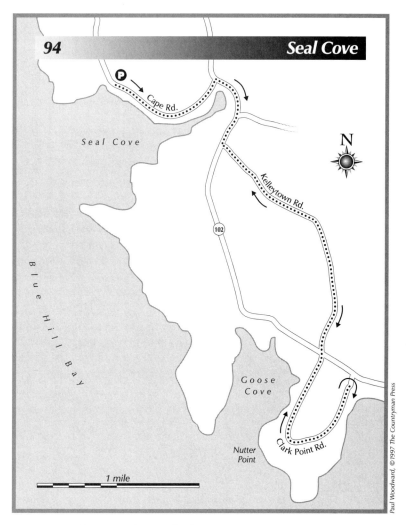

Paul Woodward, ©1997 The Countryman Press

4.0 Leave the cove on a gradual ascent.

4.7 ● STOP. After a trek through a marshy area, reach a stop sign at the intersection with ME 102. Turn around, and return to your car the way you came.

95 •••• *Southwest Harbor, Mount Desert Island*

LOCATION: Manset, ME
RATING: Intermediate
DISTANCE: 4.4 miles
TIMES TO AVOID: Summer weekends (parking is scarce)
TERRAIN: Flat and gently rolling
SURFACE: Smooth asphalt
AUTO TRAFFIC: Light to moderate
POINTS OF INTEREST: Southwest Harbor, Acadia National Park (Seawall, Wonderland, Ship Harbor Nature Trail)

DRIVING DIRECTIONS: From the junction of ME 102 and ME 102A in Manset on Mount Desert Island, take ME 102A South. In 2.7 miles, park on the wide shoulder of the road just before the entrance to Acadia National Park (Seawall). Alternative parking is at the end of the route.

TRIP OVERVIEW: Southwest Harbor doesn't cater to tourists; it's a true coastal village. The buildings contain canneries and lobster pounds, not bed & breakfasts and trendy restaurants. And the folks who live here depend on the sea to survive: They fish, lobster, build boats, or guard the coast.

As you begin your skate on a wide section of ME 102A, you'll encounter moderate traffic. The road is straight enough, however, to provide drivers with good visibility. After exiting ME 102A, you'll pass briefly through a commercial fishing area, and then travel beyond Southwest Harbor on a quiet side road lined with courtly seaside homes before returning to Seawall on ME 102A.

ROUTE DIRECTIONS:
0.0 Reverse your auto route, heading north on ME 102A.
0.5 Enter a residential area.
1.0 Climb to the top of a modest bluff with views to the Atlantic Ocean.
1.8 Turn right onto Mansell Avenue and descend gradually into a commercial area.
2.0 ● STOP. Turn right onto Shore Road and drink in views across Southwest Harbor to eastern Mount Desert Island.
2.3 Turn right onto Kings Lane.
2.6 ● STOP. Turn left, now on ME 102A.
4.4 Return to your car.

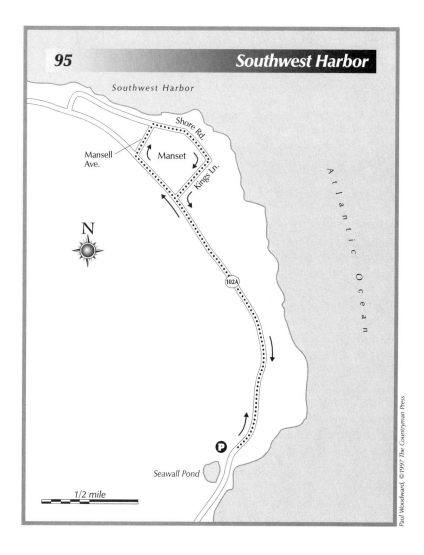

95

Southwest Harbor

Southwest Harbor

Shore Rd.

Mansell
Ave.

Manset

Kings Ln.

N

102A

Atlantic Ocean

Seawall Pond

1/2 mile

Paul Woodward, © 1997 The Countryman Press

96 •••• *Fernald Cove, Mount Desert Island*

LOCATION: Southwest Harbor and Somesville, ME
RATING: Advanced
DISTANCE: 10.2 miles
TIMES TO AVOID: None
TERRAIN: Hilly
SURFACE: Smooth asphalt with occasional coarse sections
AUTO TRAFFIC: Light to moderate
POINTS OF INTEREST: Echo Lake, Valley Cove, Fernald Point, Acadia
National Park hiking trails

DRIVING DIRECTIONS: Follow ME 102 South to Mount Desert Island.
In Somesville, stay straight on ME 102 (avoid the leg splitting right). At
the Echo Lake turnoff, continue straight, and in 3 miles turn left onto
Fernald Point Road. Drive 0.8 mile to the Valley Cove parking area.

TRIP OVERVIEW: Fernald Cove, near the start of the route, offers some
choice picnic spots with views across the cove to the narrows of Somes
Sound and Northeast and Southwest Harbors.
    After a brief warm-up on quiet Fernald Point Road, you'll be con-
fronted with the challenging terrain of ME 102. Set a steady tempo as
you cruise along the road's adequate shoulder, attacking uphill and
coasting on the way down. Before beginning the return trip to your car,
hop off ME 102 and catch 2 miles of a scenic—but equally demanding—loop that winds through the village of Hall Quarry. (Be aware that
the back roads may have sandy sections in spring.)

ROUTE DIRECTIONS:
 0.0 Return to ME 102 along Fernald Point Road (the way you drove
      in).
 0.1 Pass the head of Fernald Cove, taking in the grand panoramas of
      Somes Sound. Begin a gradual ascent.
 0.4 Climb briefly up a steep pitch that interrupts the more gradual,
      continuous climb from the cove.
 0.5 Welcome smoother pavement.
 0.7 Pass a golf course's manicured lawns.
 0.8 ● STOP at the bottom of a short hill; turn right onto ME 102.
 1.1 Begin a moderate 0.4-mile ascent on the ample shoulder of ME
      102.
 1.9 Embark on another intermediate ascent, cresting in 0.3 mile at

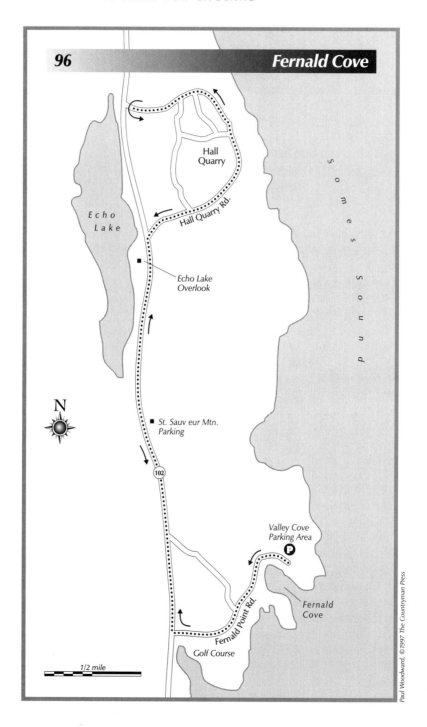

96   *Fernald Cove*

Hall Quarry

Echo Lake

Hall Quarry Rd.

Echo Lake Overlook

S o m e s   S o u n d

N

St. Sauv eur Mtn. Parking

102

Valley Cove Parking Area

Fernald Point Rd.

Fernald Cove

Golf Course

1/2 mile

Paul Woodward, ©1997 The Countryman Press

the St. Sauveur Mountain parking area.

2.2 Reenergize on an extended descent followed by a pair of rolling hills.

3.0 Pass an Echo Lake overlook on your left.

3.3 Slow down on a descent, and turn right onto Hall Quarry Road. Labor up a short hill as you begin the loop.

3.8 ▼ CAUTION: After descending gradually, you'll pick up speed on an abrupt, steep decline.

4.0 ▼ CAUTION: Brake as you descend into Hall Quarry with inspiring views across Somes Sound to Parkman and Sargent Mountains.

4.3 Pass through Hall Quarry village. After curving left, climb briefly up a steep, tiered ascent.

5.1 Stop before dropping down to meet ME 102. Reverse direction and return to your car.
    ▼ CAUTION: Stay alert on the descents into Hall Quarry, as well as at the intersection of ME 102 and Hall Quarry Road and on the trip along ME 102 to Fernald Point Road.

97 •••• Beech Mountain, Mount Desert Island

LOCATION: Somesville, ME
RATING: Expert
DISTANCE: 5.8 miles
TIMES TO AVOID: Spring (because of sand on the road)
TERRAIN: Hilly
SURFACE: Smooth and coarse asphalt
AUTO TRAFFIC: Very light
POINTS OF INTEREST: Echo Lake, Beech Mountain and Cliffs, fire tower overlook of Mount Desert Island

DRIVING DIRECTIONS: Follow ME 102 South to Mount Desert Island. In Somesville, turn right onto ME 102 (as another part of the ME 102 loop goes straight), following a sign for Beech Mountain. In 0.2 mile, turn left onto Beech Hill Road guided by a sign to Beech Mountain and Cliffs. In 0.2 mile, park on the side of the road at the base of a hill.

TRIP OVERVIEW: There's no rest for the weary on this route! An immediate, stiff climb foreshadows the challenges ahead as you initiate your attack on Beech Mountain. That's right—you'll climb the mountain on your skates, starting at 80 feet above sea level and finishing at nearly 500 feet! It's a grueling trip to be sure, and even the flatter section provides no relief because it's open and the winds are strong. As you near the end, you will be confronted with a final stiff ascent on smooth pavement. Bring along sturdy shoes so that you'll be able to climb to the nearby summit of Beech Mountain (at 839 feet). From the fire tower, you can relish the spectacular views of Mount Desert Island, and from Beech Cliffs, you will survey Echo Lake below. (If your schedule allows, explore more of Mount Desert Island: Its low peaks are easily accessed along well-marked trails and carriage roads.) Tough? You bet. Rewarding? Indeed.

ROUTE DIRECTIONS:

0.0 Skate up a moderate incline on Beech Hill Road.

0.7 Descend, passing the Beech Hill Cross Road intersection on your left.

0.9 Push uphill past an intersection where Ripple Road joins from the right.

1.2 Climb gradually through open farmland. Look for Sargent Mountain on your left.

1.5 Notice the fire tower atop Beech Mountain.

2.2 Drop back into the woods and brake on the only descent on the way out.

2.4 Ascending in mixed woods, pass through a gate into Acadia National Park.

2.7 Pump hard up the final steep climb.

2.9 Arrive at the parking lot for Beech Mountain and Cliffs. When you're ready, turn around and return to your car.

▼ CAUTION: On the return trip, use your brakes on the first 0.3 mile of the descent and on the final descent before reaching your car.

SKATING TIP: For a speed-skating stroke, push from the center of your skate, not the toe. In other words, push straight out to the side of your body, not behind you.

98 •••• *Northeast Harbor, Mount Desert Island*

LOCATION: Northeast Harbor, ME
RATING: Intermediate
DISTANCE: 6.6 miles
TIMES TO AVOID: None
TERRAIN: Flat, with some gently rolling hills
SURFACE: Smooth and coarse asphalt
AUTO TRAFFIC: Light
POINTS OF INTEREST: The Robert Abbe Museum of Stone Age Antiquities, Somes Sound, Northeast Harbor, Acadia National Park hiking trails

DRIVING DIRECTIONS: From the junction of ME 3 West, ME 102, and ME 198 South in Somesville, Maine, take the combined ME 3 and ME 198 to Northeast Harbor. Turn right in Northeast Harbor onto ME 198 as ME 3 continues straight. In 0.65 mile, turn left off ME 198 (also called Harborside Road) onto Harbor Drive following signs to CHAMBER OF COMMERCE and MARINA. Drive 0.3 mile to the boat-launch parking area.

TRIP OVERVIEW: Each of the villages that borders Acadia National Park offers a different perspective of life on Mount Desert Island. Northeast Harbor, where you'll begin this trip, is neither a traditional coastal town nor a glitzy tourist spot. Rather, it is a peaceful retreat for summer residents, with a bay that offers shelter to sailboats at rest. From the boat launch and marina, you will tour the peninsula, rolling past steepled churches, farmhouses with red barns and vegetable gardens, and harborside mansions. Finally, enjoy an easy skate beside Somes Sound to an overlook (and the entrance to Acadia National Park). After you've skated back to your car, enjoy a picnic lunch on the marina's expansive lawn.

ROUTE DIRECTIONS:
0.0 Continue south on Harbor Drive.
0.1 Merge with Huntington Road, which angles in from the right.
0.3 Turn right onto South Shore Road.
0.8 Skate pass a quaint harbor on your left.
1.0 Turn right onto Manchester Road.
1.2 After passing Summit Road on your right, gently descend a twisting hill and skate through an area of majestic oceanfront homes.

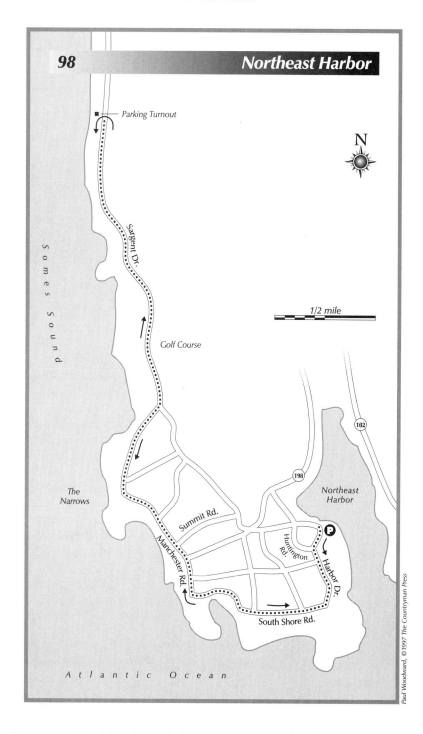

98 Northeast Harbor

Parking Turnout

N

Somes Sound

Sargent Dr.

1/2 mile

Golf Course

102

198

The
Narrows

Northeast
Harbor

Summit Rd.

Huntington
Rd.

P

Manchester Rd.

Harbor Dr.

South Shore Rd.

Atlantic Ocean

Paul Woodward, ©1997 The Countryman Press

1.8 On your left, pass the Narrows of Somes Sound as the parade of mansions marches on.

2.1 Leave Manchester Road and turn left onto Sargent Drive.

2.5 Skate by a golf course on your right and roll over several tame hills.

3.1 Begin a moderate descent.

3.3 Arrive at a parking turnout for Somes Sound and an entrance to Acadia National Park. Reverse your direction to your car.

99 •••• Ingraham Point, Mount Desert Island

LOCATION: Seal Harbor, ME
RATING: Advanced
DISTANCE: 4.0 miles
TIMES TO AVOID: Spring (as sections will be sandy)
TERRAIN: Gently rolling, with one steep hill
SURFACE: Smooth and coarse asphalt
AUTO TRAFFIC: Very light
POINTS OF INTEREST: Hunters Head, Seal Harbor, Day Mountain, Thunder Hole, Park Loop Road, Sand Beach, Otter Cliffs, the Bubbles, hiking and cycling trails

DRIVING DIRECTIONS: Eight miles south of Bar Harbor on ME 3, turn left onto Cooksie Drive (just beyond the Park Loop Road overpass). Park along the shoulder of Cooksie Drive.

TRIP OVERVIEW: From the start, you'll take in views of the vast Atlantic Ocean from the cliffs of Ingraham Point. As you roll along tight and twisting Cooksie Drive, the ocean views are punctuated by estates that stretch along the bluff. After a tricky descent, skate along Seal Harbor (seals do congregate along the Maine coast!) before heading back along Ingraham Point to your car.

Before you begin, assess the traffic along these narrow oceanside roads. If it is heavy, choose another route: Southwest Harbor (Tour 95), Fernald Cove (Tour 96), and Northeast Harbor (Tour 98) are nearby and relatively unaffected by auto traffic.

This route is central to many popular spots in Acadia National Park—allow plenty of time to explore on foot or by bicycle before you leave the area.

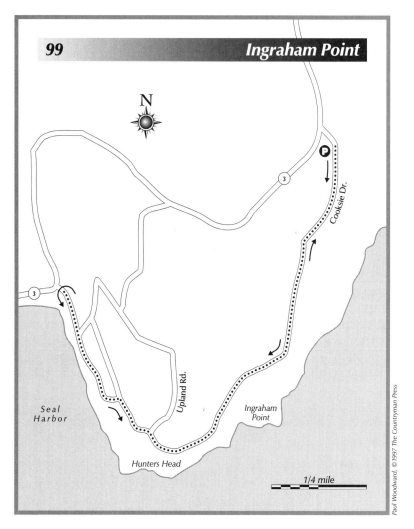

99   *Ingraham Point*

N

Cooksie Dr.

Upland Rd.

Seal
Harbor

Ingraham
Point

Hunters Head

1/4 mile

Paul Woodward, ©1997 The Countryman Press

ROUTE DIRECTIONS:

0.0   Skate along Cooksie Drive, initially on a gradual descent through thick evergreen woods.

0.3   Heads up through twists and turns!

0.5   Relish a short, straight section as you approach an elegant seaside neighborhood.

0.9   Pass a small parking turnout perched high above the water with easterly views to Hunters Head.

1.2   ▼ CAUTION: A massive stone wall intrudes on this narrow sec-

tion of road, further limiting your skating space.
1.4 After a gradual climb, bear left at an intersection with Upland Road. (Less confident skaters should turn around here.)
1.6 ▼ CAUTION: Begin a challenging, left-bending descent on potentially sandy pavement.
1.8 Level off by Seal Harbor.
2.0 Stop at the junction with ME 3 and reverse direction to return to your car.

100 •••• Schooner Head, Mount Desert Island

LOCATION: Bar Harbor, ME
RATING: Intermediate
DISTANCE: 5.0 miles
TIMES TO AVOID: None
TERRAIN: Flat and gently rolling
SURFACE: Smooth asphalt
AUTO TRAFFIC: Light
POINTS OF INTEREST: Acadia Park Loop Road, Bar Harbor, Champlain Mountain, Great Head, Sand Beach, Bar Island (you can walk from Bar Harbor at low tide)

DRIVING DIRECTIONS: From Bar Harbor and the junction of ME 3 and ME 233, drive 1.5 miles on ME 3 East. Turn left onto Schooner Head Road and park on the wide shoulder 0.1 mile from the intersection with ME 3.

TRIP OVERVIEW: Much of the New England coastline is privately owned, with seaside mansions lined up one after the other, vying for ocean views and water frontage. That's what makes Acadia National Park so special. In the park (which occupies about one-half of Mount Desert Island), the natural beauty of the coastal mountains, the islands, and the rockbound coast has been preserved for 3 million annual visitors to enjoy. Although in-line skating is not permitted on the park's 120 miles of trails and gravel carriage roads, you can explore the park on foot or by bicycle after your skate. And for tamer, swankier fun, check out the shops and restaurants of popular Bar Harbor.

But first, skate on smooth, wide Schooner Head Road, catching an occasional glimpse of Frenchman Bay. Before reaching your destination—the magnificent Schooner Head overlook—take in the sight of Champlain Mountain's dramatic cliffs. And remember: The views are courtesy of folks like John D. Rockefeller, who donated more than 11,000 acres to prevent development of this unique area.

ROUTE DIRECTIONS:

0.0 Cruise along Schooner Head Road, passing through a sparsely populated residential area.

0.2 Pass an access road to Jackson Laboratories on your right; gradually descend for 1 mile through mixed woods.

0.6 Stay straight as Seely Road goes left, now on grainier pavement.

1.1 Sneak a peak between private residences to Frenchman Bay.

1.2 Gaze beyond the marsh (to your right) at the impressive sheer face of Champlain Mountain.

2.1 After temporarily losing sight of Champlain Mountain, enjoy a second look.

2.3 Power up a brief climb to a stop sign; turn left.

2.5 Arrive at Schooner Head overlook and relax. Reverse direction to return to your car.

SKATING TIP: *To increase the intensity of a workout, keep both skates on the ground by pumping. This will increase the use of the large muscle groups in the lower body and raise your heart rate. Hint: Swizzles or scooters work great!*

---

101 •••• *Lamoine Beach*

LOCATION: Lamoine, ME
RATING: Intermediate
DISTANCE: 10.4 miles
TIMES TO AVOID: None
TERRAIN: One long, gradual climb, then gently rolling
SURFACE: Smooth asphalt
AUTO TRAFFIC: Very light
POINTS OF INTEREST: Lamoine Beach and picnic area, Lamoine State Park (beach and play area), Marlboro Beach

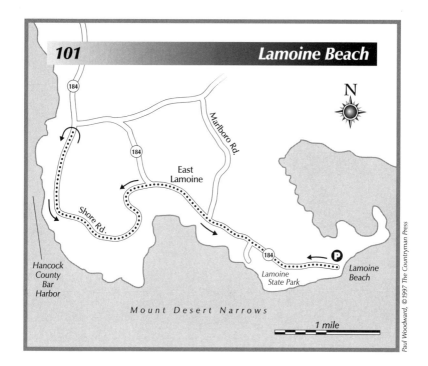

101   *Lamoine Beach*

Hancock
County
Bar
Harbor

Mount Desert Narrows

1 mile

Paul Woodward, ©1997 The Countryman Press

DRIVING DIRECTIONS: From the junction of ME 3 and ME 204, south of Ellsworth, take ME 204. In 1.7 miles, turn right onto ME 184 South. Drive another 3 miles to Lamoine Beach and the parking area.

TRIP OVERVIEW: This route serves up a delicious combination plate for the group with diverse interests. Skaters leave from the tip of Meadow Point peninsula at Lamoine Beach, which offers choice picnic spots and a sandy beach—a rarity in Maine. Climb a long, gradual hill on ME 184 before cruising by Lamoine State Park, another swimming and picnicking area. Finish the outbound route on skater-friendly Shore Road—wide, quiet, and smooth. Once you've completed the return leg, enjoy the calm waters of the bay with the lofty outline of Mount Desert Island on the horizon.

ROUTE DIRECTIONS:
  0.0 Head east on ME 184, retracing the route you drove. Warm up on a gradual climb, enjoying views across Eastern Bay to Mount Desert Island.
  0.8 Pass the entrance to Lamoine State Park on your left.

1.1 Descend a gentle hill with occasional views to Mount Desert Narrows.

1.6 Continue straight as Marlboro Road splits right.

2.2 Travel through sleepy East Lamoine village.

2.4 Turn left onto (potentially unmarked) Shore Road and roll through a sparsely populated neighborhood.

4.1 Glimpse Hancock County Bar Harbor.

4.5 Roll through an open area with more dramatic water views.

5.2 ● STOP: Arrive at the intersection with ME 184. Reverse direction to return to your car.

Resources

BOOKS

Della Penna, Craig P. *Great Rail-Trails of the Northeast.* Amherst, Mass.: New England Cartographics, 1995.

Holmes, Robert. *Passport's Illustrated Travel Guide to Boston & New England.* Lincolnwood, Ill.: Passport Books, 1994.

Howells, Bob. *Backroads of New England: Colorful Drives and Historic Routes.* Houston: Gulf Publishing Company, 1995.

Lewis, Cynthia C. and Thomas J. Lewis. *Best Hikes with Children in Connecticut, Massachusetts, and Rhode Island.* Seattle: The Mountaineers, 1991.

Lewis, Cynthia C. and Thomas J. Lewis. *Best Hikes with Children in Vermont, New Hampshire, and Maine.* Seattle: The Mountaineers, 1991.

Muse, Vance. *The Smithsonian Guide to Historic America: Northern New England.* New York: Stewart, Tabori & Chang, 1989.

Powell, Mark and John Svensson. *In-Line Skating.* Champaign, Ill.: Human Kinetics Publishers, 1993.

Sternfield, Jonathan. *The Berkshire Book: A Complete Guide.* Great Barrington, Mass.: Berkshire House, Publishers, 1986.

Tougias, Mike. *Country Roads of Massachusetts.* Castine, Maine: Country Roads Press, 1995.

Wiencek, Henry. *The Smithsonian Guide to Historic America: Southern New England.* New York: Stewart, Tabori & Chang, 1989.

Williams, Wendy. *The Best Bike Paths of New England.* New York: Simon & Schuster, 1996.

ASSOCIATIONS, CLUBS, PROGRAMS

International In-line Skating Association (IISA)
3720 Farragut Avenue
Suite 400
Kensington, MD 20895
301-942-9770
iisahq@erols.com

The IISA Gear Up! Campaign
(for free information about safe skating and lessons in your area)
1-800-56-SKATE

Instructor Certification Program (ICP)
201 North Front Street
Suite 306
Wilmington, NC 28401
910-762-7004

In-Line Club of Boston
Kendall Square
PO Box 1195
Cambridge, MA 02142
Contact: Damon Poole
617-932-5457

ALL ABOUT US

CYNTHIA COPELAND LEWIS has written eight books, including a hiking series with her husband, Tom: *Best Hikes with Children . . .* in various part of New England (published by The Mountaineers). Her most popular book, *Really Important Stuff My Kids Have Taught Me* (Workman, 1994), has sold nearly a quarter of a million copies. She interpreted Carolyn's and Tom's field notes to write this manuscript and also took a number of the photographs. She stays busy teaching Sunday school, organizing community and school events, and being a stay-at-home mom for her three terrific kids: Anya, 10; Alexandra, 7; and Aaron, 3.

CAROLYN BRADLEY wrote and starred in the highly acclaimed in-line fitness video *SkateFit: The Complete In-Line Workout.* She is a former member of Team Rollerblade and has traveled all over the world promoting the sport. Carolyn produced and directed Camp Rollerblade for several years. She is currently the fitness editor of *On the Edge,* an in-line skating magazine (when she is not chasing after her two energetic—but completely adorable—daughters: Christina, 3, and Julianna, 1½). She is married to a very patient and supportive husband, Brian.

For our book, Carolyn used her many industry contacts to pinpoint the top spots to skate. To conduct her research, she journeyed through Vermont, Rhode Island, the Connecticut shore, the Northampton area, and the Berkshires.

THOMAS J. LEWIS developed the concept of a regional in-line skate guide during the fall of 1995 upon realizing how little information existed on the subject. He has been in-line skating since 1984 and has twice won the 22k skate race up Pack Monadnock. He is also an avid cyclist (earning the title of New England's top master cyclist in 1996). Tom coauthored (with wife Cindy) the *Best Hikes with Children . . .* series. With a Ph.D. from MIT, Tom has written many scientific publications and currently works for Markem Corporation as a health and environmental chemist.

Despite his hectic work and athletic schedule, Tom spends a great deal of time with his three children. When he traveled to Maine to skate routes in Acadia, along the coast, and in southern parts of the state, 10-year-old daughter Anya accompanied him. For his Cape Cod field work, he brought the entire family along. And 7-year-old daughter Alex helped him research the White Mountains skating treks. Taking notes in northwestern Connecticut and the Boston area was also a family affair. Many of the photographs in the book are Tom's.

BOOKS FROM THE COUNTRYMAN PRESS

Thank you for buying *In-Line Skate New England.* We offer many more books on outdoor recreation—guides to hiking, biking, fly fishing, and canoeing—as well as general travel guides to New England and books on gardening, history, and nature.

Books for the Active Traveler

Cape Cod: An Explorer's Guide Second Edition
Connecticut: An Explorer's Guide Second Edition
Maine: An Explorer's Guide Eighth Edition
Massachusetts: An Explorer's Guide
New Hampshire: An Explorer's Guide Third Edition
Rhode Island: An Explorer's Guide
Vermont: An Explorer's Guide Seventh Edition
The Hudson Valley and Catskill Mountains: An Explorer's Guide Second
    Edition
Fifty Hikes in Massachusetts Second Edition
25 Mountain Bike Tours in Massachusetts
25 Bicycle Tours in Maine
30 Bicycle Tours in New Hampshire
50 Hikes in Vermont Fifth Edition
Walks & Rambles on Cape Cod and the Islands
Walks & Rambles in Rhode Island
Fishing Vermont's Streams and Lakes
Good Fishing in the Adirondacks

Country Books, City Books . . .

Reading the Forested Landscape: A Natural History of New England
Living with Herbs: A Treasury of Useful Plants for the Home and Garden
The Other Islands of New York City
The Architecture of the Shakers
The King Arthur Flour 200th Anniversary Cookbook

Our books are available at bookstores and outdoor stores everywhere. For more information or a free catalog, please call 1-800-245-4151 or write to us at The Countryman Press, PO Box 748, Woodstock, Vermont 05091. You can find us on the Internet at www.wwnorton.com.